A. D. Jameson

I FIND YOUR LACK OF FAITH DISTURBING

SARAH JOYCE

A. D. Jameson is the author of four previous books, including *Cinemaps: An Atlas of 35 Great Movies*, a collaboration with the artist Andrew DeGraff. A former blogger for *HTMLGIANT*, he has also published his fiction in *Conjunctions*, *Denver Quarterly*, *Unstuck*, and other publications.

T0057979

I FIND YOUR LACK OF FAITH DISTURBING

I FIND YOUR
DISTU

STAR WARS
AND THE TRIUMPH OF
GEEK
CULTURE

A. D. JAMESON

FARRAR, STRAUS AND GIROUX · NEW YORK

Farrar, Straus and Giroux
175 Varick Street, New York 10014

Published in 2018 by Farrar, Straus and Giroux
First paperback edition, 2019

The Library of Congress has cataloged the hardcover edition as follows:
    Names: Jameson, A. D., 1976– author.
    Title: I find your lack of faith disturbing : Star Wars and the
        triumph of geek culture / A. D. Jameson.
    Description: First edition. | New York : Farrar, Straus and
        Giroux, 2018. | Includes bibliographical references and
        index.
    Identifiers: LCCN 2017038357 | ISBN 9780374537364
        (cloth) | ISBN 9780374717070 (e-book)
    Subjects: LCSH: Star Wars films—History and criticism. |
        Fans (Persons)
    Classification: LCC PN1995.9.S695 J35 2018 |
        DDC 791.43/75—dc23
    LC record available at https://lccn.loc.gov/2017038357

Paperback ISBN: 978-0-374-53843-9

Designed by Richard Oriolo

Our books may be purchased in bulk for promotional,
educational, or business use. Please contact your local
bookseller or the Macmillan Corporate and Premium Sales
Department at 1-800-221-7945, extension 5442, or by
e-mail at MacmillanSpecialMarkets@macmillan.com.

www.fsgbooks.com
www.twitter.com/fsgbooks • www.facebook.com/fsgbooks

For Elf, from your comrade, Paladin

"Fascinating trade," said the old man, and a wistful look came into his eyes, "doing the coastlines was always my favorite. Used to have endless fun doing the little bits in fjords . . ."

—Douglas Adams,
The Hitchhiker's Guide to the Galaxy

"But do you really mean, Sir," said Peter, "that there could be other worlds—all over the place, just round the corner—like that?"

"Nothing is more probable," said the Professor, taking off his spectacles and beginning to polish them, while he muttered to himself, "I wonder what they *do* teach them at these schools."

—C. S. Lewis,
The Lion, the Witch and the Wardrobe

CONTENTS

I FIND YOUR LACK OF FAITH DISTURBING

INTRODUCTION

The Golden Age of Geekdom

've always been a geek. And what's more, I'm old enough
to remember when it wasn't cool to be one.

When I was in school, back in the 1980s and '90s, I
spent each week looking forward to Friday night—not
because I had dates or plans to meet up with my friends,
but because that was when my local PBS station aired three

episodes of *Star Trek* commercial-free: two episodes of *The Original Series*, plus one of *The Next Generation*. I tuned in religiously, regardless of whether or not I'd already seen them, taking notes on the plots and the names of the writers and directors. This was before the World Wide Web, before I even had a computer. If that wasn't nerdy enough, I savored the fact that, due to the lack of commercials, I was seeing each episode of *The Original Series* as it had originally aired, without any of its scenes missing. (The shows got trimmed down in syndication, to allow for extra advertising.)

The rest of the time I spent reading. I was especially fond of comic books like *The Uncanny X-Men*, a tale of misunderstood mutant outcasts. I took them with me wherever I went, concealing them from the other kids, afraid my hobby would lead to teasing and bullying—although I really don't know why I bothered, since I was teased and bullied anyway. I redrew my favorite panels, and spent what money I had on back issues, all the while wondering whether puberty might reveal me to be a mutant. I routinely longed for the X-Men's leader, Professor X, to come rolling up in his wheelchair and whisk me away to his boarding school, a private institute "for gifted children" where the freaks and the outcasts ruled.

In some ways, that fantasy came true—it was just a little bit behind schedule. When I turned seventeen, I headed to college, where I finally met other people like me. At Penn State, I moved into the honors dorm, Atherton Hall, where, despite my social awkwardness, I quickly made friends with dozens of other students who couldn't care less about football or the Greek system. Instead, they spent their free time obsessing over *The Princess Bride*, *The Hitchhiker's Guide to the Galaxy*, and *Mystery Science Theater 3000*. That was 1994, and Atherton Hall was "the Geek Dorm."

The next four years passed blissfully. I was living in a fantasy world, my mutant paradise, where the coolest kids were the ones who sewed their own *Star Trek* uniforms, and could recite huge swaths of *Star Wars* from memory. We commandeered the big-screen TV lounge to watch the *Evil Dead* trilogy, camped out in the lobby to conduct *Dungeons & Dragons* campaigns, and whiled away weekends playing the then-new fantasy-trading-card game *Magic: The Gathering*, all while debating the finer points of *The Lord of the Rings*.

I also started using the Internet, and sending and receiving e-mails, including lengthy chain letters analyzing unintended sexual innuendo in *Star Wars*, as well as lists of every episode of *Star Trek*. Those, plus the burgeoning Internet Movie Database, rapidly rendered my old *Trek* notebooks obsolete. I stumbled into chat rooms where people were arguing endlessly about science fiction, fantasy, and superhero comics, and having tremendously long conversations dissecting things like last week's episodes of *Babylon 5* and *The X-Files*. I realized with no small amount of surprise that, as obsessed as I was, others were yet more obsessed.

That realization made me back away from geek life. I was less nerdy than my youth had led me to believe. I had other interests: creative writing, punk rock, experimental films. And I was increasingly aware of the fact that, outside the Geek Dorm's ivied walls, the rest of the world was patiently waiting. So it was that, at the end of my senior year, I convinced myself I needed to grow up. I sold my comics and my *Magic* cards, bought a car, got a job, and prepared to enter adulthood.

I needn't have bothered. It was 1998, and geeks were about to inherit the earth.

HAD I BEEN paying closer attention while in college, I might have noticed that the real world was quietly changing. In early 1997, George Lucas rereleased the original *Star Wars* trilogy to theaters, in the form of the *Special Editions*. I was of course tremendously excited, and went to see the films with my friends, but failed to observe how the movies played with others. As far as I knew, we nerds were the only ones buying tickets—but if so, then how did the theaters sell out? Unbeknownst to me, geek was going mainstream.

Two years later is arguably when geek "broke." On March 31, 1999, Americans woke up to find *The Matrix* playing at their local multiplexes. The film proved a smash hit, the must-see movie of the summer, and deeply influential for years to come. Other geek milestones followed in rapid succession. *Star Wars: Episode I—The Phantom Menace* was released to tremendous fanfare on May 19, and while reactions were conflicted (to say the least), it still wound up becoming the highest-grossing movie of the year. *The Iron Giant* arrived in theaters on August 6, and while it didn't fare well commercially, it heralded a new, adult-oriented approach to animation, and enabled its director, Brad Bird, to later make the better-known Pixar hit *The Incredibles*. Finally, the *Star Trek* parody *Galaxy Quest* came out on Christmas Day, doing surprisingly well by appealing to general viewers as well as Trekkers.

To understand the change that was under way, it's important to remember what else was popular at that time. *Seinfeld* had just gone off the air, ceding its kingdom to the likes of *Frasier*, *Friends*, *E.R.*, and *Sex and the City*. The box office, meanwhile, was dominated by films like *Saving Private Ryan*, *There's Something About Mary*, *Rush Hour*, and *Patch Adams*, none of which scream "geek." Three other top films at the time—*Armageddon*, *Deep Impact*, and *Godzilla*—are nominally science fiction, but in reality they're disaster films. Hollywood was still trying to make another *Independence Day*, which had lit up screens in 1996. In 1997, the king of the box office and the Academy Awards was *Titanic*, followed by *The Lost World: Jurassic Park*, *Liar Liar*, *As Good as It Gets*, and *Good Will Hunting*. With the exceptions of *Men in Black* and the *Star Wars Special Editions*, geeks were mostly underground, delighting in TV shows like *Deep Space 9*, *Babylon 5*, and *Mystery Science Theater 3000*, as well as movies like *Star Trek: First Contact*, *The Fifth Element*, and *Starship Troopers*.

After 1999, however, things really started to change. July 14, 2000, saw the release of Bryan Singer's *X-Men*, the first blockbuster film starring Marvel characters, which would mark the beginning of a new wave of superhero movies. The following year, the two highest-grossing films were *Harry Potter and the Sorcerer's Stone*—based of course on the first *Harry Potter* book, which had been published in 1997—and *The Lord of the Rings: The Fellowship of the Ring*. Both not only proved to be crossover hits, but launched franchises that inspired dozens of imitators, promising plenty more fantasy to come. In 2002, the top four films were Sam Raimi's *Spider-Man*, which became the first movie to earn $100 million in its opening weekend, then *The Two Towers*, *Attack of the Clones*, and *Harry Potter and the Chamber of Secrets*. The geek renaissance was under way.

For my own part, I initially kept my distance, distraught over how Hollywood was mishandling my beloved childhood heroes. The *X-Men* movie, for instance, disappointed me because of the liberties that Singer and company took with the material. Wolverine and his fellow mutants wore black leather outfits and knew wire-fu, just like in *The Matrix*. Looking back now, I can see that my fragile, newfound sense of adulthood required that I dismiss movies like *X-Men* and *Spider-Man* in favor of artworks that I considered more sophisticated: the foreign films of the French New Wave, the underground experimental cinema that I could find in New York City, and the independent films being released to art-house screens by companies like Miramax and Sony Pictures Classics. Secretly, though, I still saw all the superhero and science fiction films, even while I kept waiting for the geek fad to die out.

But a funny thing happened. The geek renaissance didn't end. Flash-forward to 2010, when the box office top ten looked like this:

1. *Toy Story 3*
2. *Alice in Wonderland*
3. *Iron Man 2*
4. *The Twilight Saga: Eclipse*
5. *Harry Potter and the Deathly Hallows Part 1*
6. *Inception*
7. *Despicable Me*
8. *Shrek Forever After*
9. *How to Train Your Dragon*
10. *Tangled*

Gone were the likes of *Saving Private Ryan*, *Titanic*, and *There's Something About Mary*—war films, relationship dramas, and gross-out romantic comedies. All that remained was computer animation, fantasy, science fiction, and fairy tales. This reversal of fortune hasn't been short-lived. Since 2010, Marvel's ongoing superhero adventures, *The Hunger Games* series, *Frozen*, *Jurassic World*, and *Star Wars: The Force Awakens* have ranked among the highest-grossing movies of all time. The song remains the same as we continue down the list. Everywhere we find giant robots, witches and wizards, dystopian futures, superheroes, dragons, and talking apes. And while television took longer to catch up, the premieres of *Battlestar Galactica* and *Lost* in 2004 brought the geek renaissance into everyone's living rooms. Since then, TV's most popular programs have included *The Big Bang Theory*, *The Walking Dead*, *Game of Thrones*, and *Stranger Things*.

Nor is there any sign that this phenomenon's slowing

down. The Marvel Cinematic Universe already consists of nineteen films, *Iron Man* through *Avengers: Infinity War*, with another half dozen announced, and who knows how many more in the works. In a recent article in *Bloomberg Businessweek*, Marvel Studios head Kevin Feige claimed that Marvel is planning films through at least 2028. Meanwhile, DC Comics has been struggling to create its own superhero universe, centered on Batman, Superman, and Wonder Woman. At the same time, Fox has released ten *X-Men* movies, with another five in development. And all three companies have expanded to TV, via shows like *Daredevil*, *Jessica Jones*, *Arrow*, *Supergirl*, and *Legion*—and that's just to mention the superheroes.

Given all of this, it's unsurprising that being labeled a geek has shifted from a stigma to an outright badge of honor, so much so that in the mid-2000s, "geek chic" became a fashion trend, as celebrities like Justin Timberlake and David Beckham began sporting horn-rimmed glasses and suspenders. Since then, black-rim glasses have remained perennial favorites with fashionistas ranging from hipsters to tween girls. October 2015 saw Party City selling a Teen Girls Hello Kitty Nerd Accessory Kit, which included oversize glasses, an adjustable necktie, and "a geek chic standard pocket protector featuring Hello Kitty's face." The accompanying paragraph at the Party City website proclaimed: "Nerds have never been so adorable!" It's also become acceptable, even cool, for adults to display their love of artworks previously fit only for kids and social outcasts. Alicia Keys won praise and admiration by singing a playfully soulful rendition of the *Gummi Bears* theme song during a 2012 appearance on *Late Night with Jimmy Fallon*, and popular comedians like Jon Stewart and Stephen Colbert revel in their extensive knowledge of *Star Wars*, *Star Trek*, and *The Lord of the Rings*. Colbert even made a cameo appearance in *The Hobbit: The Desolation of Smaug*. In the year 2018, geek is not only mainstream, it's entrenched, much more than a fad. Comic books, superhero movies, and complex fantasy TV series have become familiar, even beloved objects in the cultural landscape, no longer worthy only of derision. Incoming college freshmen have grown up watching Hugh Jackman play Wolverine, and the kids who read *Harry Potter* are starting to have kids of their own. Even older geeks like me, initially skeptical of geek culture going mainstream, have long since returned to the fantasy fold, making peace with the fact that *X-Men* is no longer a little-known comic but a blockbuster movie franchise. Like most people, I now find myself eagerly anticipating the latest superhero movies, and enjoying the fact that I can read graphic novels on the subway without attracting snickers or stares. Put another way: the geeks won.

OF COURSE, not everyone has been happy to see the geeks conquer the culture. Some have been doing their best to ignore geek art, which they find unserious and inartistic and wish would simply disappear, slinking back underground. Others are more alarmed by the boom in escapist fantasy, being convinced that the United States is amusing itself to death, its younger generations trapped as lifelong infants careening toward disaster.

Let's start with the less hysterical reactions. While the movies and the TV shows and the comics that geeks like have been massively successful financially, they haven't been as critically acclaimed. The Academy Awards are hardly a perfect yardstick, but look at how few Oscars have gone to the movies that geeks embrace. The nominations and major awards remain reserved for the same sort of films that have won them for decades: "prestige" pictures like *Moonlight*, *Spotlight*, *Birdman*, and *12 Years a Slave*. Heath Ledger may have posthumously won an Oscar for his turn as the Joker in *The Dark Knight*, but the movie itself wasn't nominated for Best Picture. That omission caused something of an uproar, and played a factor in the category's expansion from five to upwards of ten films, but despite that change, geek movies haven't been receiving the extra nominations. A campaign to get *Deadpool* nominated for Best Picture wound up mostly being a stunt, and movies like *Captain America: Civil War* and *Iron Man 3* were put up only for technical awards. And the geekier movies that do get nominated, such as *Her*, *Gravity*, and *The Martian*, tend to downplay their science fiction and fantasy angles; indeed, *Her* and *Gravity* inspired debate as to whether they even *are* science fiction films. Meanwhile, animation is shunted off into its own category, creating the impression that films like Disney's *Frozen* and *Zootopia* and Hayao Miyazaki's *The Wind Rises* aren't fit to compete with live-action pictures.

The same holds true for artistic credibility. Steven Spielberg may have made his name and fortune directing *Raiders of the Lost Ark* and *Jurassic Park*, but he's taken seriously as a filmmaker more for having made movies like *Schindler's List* and *Saving Private Ryan*. His colleague George Lucas is routinely criticized for having let the evil empire of *Star Wars* consume him and all his filmmaking ambition. While making *Return of the Jedi* in the early 1980s, Lucas spoke openly about his desire to quit *Star Wars* in order to make experimental films, abstract "nonlinear" works that would lack both story and characters. Those avant-garde works never materialized, and in 1994 Lucas sat down to write the screenplay for *The Phantom Menace*. (And if you suggest that the *Star Wars* films are in any way experimental, you'll meet with laughter and ridicule.) The only real exception is Peter Jackson's *Lord of the Rings* trilogy, which won multiple nominations and awards, including Best Picture and Best Director in 2003, for *Return of the King*.

Actors face a similar stigma. Andy Serkis has risen to fame thanks to his performance as Gollum in *The Lord of the Rings* and *The Hobbit: An Unexpected Journey*, as the chimpanzee Caesar in the new *Planet of the Apes* series, and as Supreme Leader Snoke in the new *Star Wars* films. But those performances have largely been overlooked by awards committees. And while actors like Jennifer Lawrence, Amy Adams, and James Franco appear in superhero movies, they win their Oscars for films like (in Lawrence's case) *Silver Linings Playbook*. The conventional wisdom here is that actors suffer through larger franchise films in order to gain the financial freedom and critical prestige needed to take roles in smaller independent productions. Jeremy Irons said as much when he accepted the part of Alfred in Zack Snyder's *Batman v Superman: Dawn of Justice*—that he did so because "it'll be a big movie, and do me no harm, and help me when I want to do smaller films, which are maybe more interesting for me." And when renowned actors like Sir Patrick Stewart and Sir Ian McKellan appear in flicks like *X-Men*, *Star Trek*, and *The Lord of the Rings*, they're the ones bringing prestige to the picture, not the other way around.

A similar anti-geek attitude persists among movie reviewers, where, if anything, the prejudices are even fiercer. Many mainstream critics apparently consider it their duty to warn viewers away from big-budget slop, shepherding them instead toward smaller, more independent fare. Par for the course is Drew Hunt's *Chicago Reader* dismissal of *Thor: The Dark World*. He begins by describing it as "a bloated sequel to Kenneth Branagh's half-assed Shakespearean space opera *Thor*" (which the same paper's head critic, J. R. Jones, summed up as "eminently missable"), then criticizes the story for being "ridiculously complicated." The plots of geek movies are commonly dismissed as nonexistent or too difficult to follow—and sometimes both at once. But they are never, like Goldilocks's preferred bowl of porridge, just right. Fellow *Chicago Reader* critic Ben Sachs called *The Avengers* Marvel Studios' "costliest special-effects demo to date." Like Hunt, he found the plot impossible to follow, writing, "somewhere beneath the nonstop digital explosions"—the explosions aren't even real, folks!—"lies a story about superheroes fighting an evil demigod from space." Later on, he summarized the whole affair as "overlong, monotonous, violent, and simple-minded." Just as we saw with the Academy Awards, these films may occasionally exhibit nifty technical advances, but they aren't worth taking seriously as art.

This is the prestige attitude toward geek culture, rooted in a longstanding belief that works produced in the more commercial genres are neither sophisticated nor "literary." Writing in *The New Yorker*, the critic Anthony Lane labels *Iron Man 3* a "whiny and logorrheic mess," and a juvenile entertainment at best. Referring to the film's three main characters—Tony Stark, the Mandarin, and Aldrich Killian— Lane writes, "Take away the toys, in all three cases, and what are you left with? Boys." The implication is clear: anyone who takes the film seriously is just a boy as well. Even a widely celebrated film like *Gravity* comes in for criticism because, as David Denby declares, it isn't "a film of ideas, like Kubrick's techno-mystic *2001*." Labeling it instead an adventure film, Denby compares it to a "fairground ride," albeit a "wild" one, which is a roundabout way of saying that the movie's a roller coaster. Throughout the critical press, there persists a snobbish sense that these movies are little more than visual excess. In 2010, once again in the pages of *The New Yorker*, Anthony Lane damned *Scott Pilgrim vs. the World* as being "no more than a skit . . . padded out with visual fluff," while the core itself remained "hollow." In his capsule review, Lane adds that despite the film's "restless graphic wit," its downside is "an emotional paucity, likely to leave an audience bewitched but unbothered."

And these are the more charitable responses to some of the *better* recent geek movies! In the meantime, just about anybody will tell you that the multiplexes are filled to the rafters with nothing but big dumb action blockbusters. As this familiar story goes, today's cinemagoers exist in a fallen state, inundated by a constant stream of lowbrow generic crap: superhero adaptations, high fantasy, science fiction. Movies based on comic books and video games. Franchises, endless sequels, remakes, and reboots.

This story has been told many times, to the point where it's now taken as the gospel truth. Even its villains have come to believe it. As George Lucas candidly put it, "Popcorn pictures have always ruled. Why do people go see these popcorn pictures when they're not good? Why is the public so stupid? That's not my fault." More recently, Simon Pegg, long a patron saint of geekdom, surprised his fans during a *Radio Times* interview in which he called geek culture "childish," a morass of unchallenging, infantilizing genre films that "[take] our focus away from real-world issues" (as opposed to "gritty, amoral art movies" like "*The Godfather, Taxi Driver, Bonnie and Clyde* and *The French Connection*"). He's not alone: many other self-professed fanboys are happy to parrot the argument that modern Hollywood has become creatively bankrupt, completely dominated by drivel. In 2009, the nerdy Milwaukee native Mike Stoklasa made a splash with his "Mr. Plinkett" reviews, in which he humorously critiqued later *Star Trek* movies and the *Star Wars* prequel trilogy from the perspective of an outrageously cranky old man. Stoklasa parlayed his newfound fame into creating a genuine Web film review series, *Half in the Bag*, where he and his cohost, Jay Bauman, routinely complain that they can no longer withstand the current onslaught of superhero movies and fantasy franchise sequels. But the duo protest too much, and their fans know that Mike and Jay will gladly keep the faith, watching and reviewing all the new geeky movies, which they obviously love.

But many critics really do believe the anti-geek gospel, and that the rise of the geeks is rending the fabric of society itself. Alejandro G. Iñárritu, director of the Oscar-winning *Birdman*, called superhero movies "poison," "cultural genocide," "very right wing," and a sign of stunted growth: "I think there's nothing wrong with being fixated on superheroes when you are seven years old, but I think there's a disease in not growing up." Many agree. Since at least 2008, there's been growing concern over the well-being of young people in their twenties and thirties, so-called millennials, who seem lost or broken in regard to previous generations. In particular, young men have come under attack in books like Gary Cross's *Men to Boys: The Making of Modern Immaturity*, Kay S. Hymowitz's *Manning Up: How the Rise of Women Has Turned Men into Boys*, and Hanna Rosin's *The End of Men and the Rise of Women*. All of those authors find fault with guys like me—and there are a lot of guys like me—who despite having come of age around the turn of the millennium still haven't bothered with "adulting," being far too interested instead in "kiddy" things like *X-Men* and *Teenage Mutant Ninja Turtles*. Kay Hymowitz opens her book with a lament, "Where Have the Good Men Gone?," in which she describes a postapocalyptic dating scene where unmarried young women wring their hands in despair over guys who would rather watch *Star Wars* than propose.

Gary Cross, a professor at my alma mater, Penn State, makes even more extreme versions of these arguments in his book, where he paints a picture of a culture well along the path to extinction. Ever since World War II, he writes, men have been under decreasing pressure to mature, which for Cross means giving up the fantastical, simplistic thrills of youth "for cultivated and complex pleasures." This echoes Anthony Lane's complaint about *Scott Pilgrim*: dazzling, but ultimately "hollow." Cross believes that "the refusal of today's young men to abandon their childhood toys marks a dramatic break from traditional means of maturation in personal culture and pleasure." (Here I look up to fondly gaze at my NECA Teenage Mutant Ninja Turtle figures, which I purchased in 2007 for fifty dollars.) Cross primarily singles out video games as the culprit, the reason why grown men today won't quit playing with what Cross considers toys, but he also takes passing swipes at animation, fantasy movies, and roller coasters (so he presumably wouldn't like *Gravity*). In Cross's view, because these toys and pastimes are now being marketed to young adults, and not just preadolescents, boys are no longer abandoning childhood action fantasies the way they used to, and are thereby refusing "to enter a real world of male power and action." This causes adult men to remain adrift in their love of youthful fantasies, spending their time and money on toys and games instead of forming "relationships with women and family." Such men, hopelessly lonely and endlessly chasing nostalgic thrills, also lose touch with history, tradition, and the past, focused solely on the present. (My Turtle figures whisper to me, "Don't worry. We still love you.") In his book's introduction, "Where Have All the Men Gone?," Cross anticipates Kay Hymowitz's complaint about the dating scene in more than just his title. He describes a contemptible modern figure, the "boy-man," who would rather live at home and watch action movies than get a job or get hitched. By remaining unmarried into their late twenties ("twenty-seven on average"), these piteous creatures "have a long time to nurture the boy-man's life and to develop habits of thought and practice that few 'good women' can break even when it becomes time to 'settle down.'" Apparently if you can't pry the Turtle figures out of a fella's hands by the time he's graduated college, he's doomed to slobbish bachelorhood for life. In what I'm sure is yet another sign of my own hopeless immaturity, Cross's diatribe makes me think of Bill Murray's famous line in *Ghostbusters*: "Human sacrifice, dogs and cats living together . . . mass hysteria!"

But why, precisely, are geeky interests such as fantasy, cartoons, science fiction, and video games automatically considered juvenile, not to mention emotionally empty and puerile? What makes them bad, and appropriate only for children? Are superhero movies just dumb summer blockbusters and escapist entertainment? Can they ever be more than "special effects demos"? Can they be profound and moving films about serious issues, let alone serious art?

In the coming pages, I will address all of those questions

and more, as well as defend the geeks from their detractors. The rise of geek culture hardly signals the end of serious art or Western culture. Nor is there necessarily anything wrong with twenty- and thirtysomethings, not to mention even older adults, who revel in fantasy fare. I will also argue that the widespread critical narrative that great U.S. cinema ended in the 1970s is nothing more than a myth. If anything, geek culture has *preserved* many of the artistic advances made in the 1970s, even if our current Golden Age of Geekdom now presents unique problems for art and the culture as a whole.

Obviously we have a great deal to discuss. But before we can tackle all of it, we need to first reexamine the film that brought geek culture into the mainstream and has been the obsession of geeks, even their religion, ever since. So let's slip on our glasses and pocket protectors, and take a closer look at the movie that started it all: *Star Wars*.

THE STORY SO FAR

PART I

one.

"OH, I'M BACK OUT IN SPACE AGAIN"

The Realism of *Star Wars*

Star Wars has achieved such a legendary status in our culture and warped the entertainment industry to such an extent that it's difficult today to see it as a product of its time. Instead, critics then and now have tended to emphasize how George Lucas broke with—some would even say betrayed—American cinema of the 1970s, making something totally unlike the movie that won the Best Picture Oscar that year, Woody Allen's *Annie Hall*. Whereas Allen crafted one of the most sophisticated and adult romantic comedies ever made—one that trusts its audience to recognize Marshall McLuhan and references to Marcel Ophüls's *The Sorrow and the Pity*—Lucas served up a shiny retread of *Buck Rogers* and *Flash Gordon*, in which Luke and Han vie to kiss Princess Leia. And while Lucas didn't win Best Picture or Best Director, his film set the agenda for the next forty years, during which time studios have repeatedly struggled to re-create its success, leaving pictures like *Annie Hall* in the dust.

At least, that's the account offered by Peter Biskind in his 1998 volume *Easy Riders, Raging Bulls*, which documents in gossipy detail how the fifteen years between 1967 and 1982, the so-called New Hollywood, became the last great period for American cinema. According to Biskind, as the classic Hollywood studio system broke down in the mid- to late 1960s, rebels like Warren Beatty, Dennis Hopper, Jack Nicholson, Francis Ford Coppola, and Martin Scorsese fought their way out from under both censorship and the factory-like production methods of the big studios to produce classics like *Bonnie and Clyde*, *Easy Rider*, *The Godfather*, *Chinatown*, *Taxi Driver*, and *Apocalypse Now*. With those canonical films and others, the artists of the New Hollywood reinvigorated a stale U.S. film scene with techniques and concepts drawn from European cinema and the counterculture (not to mention drug use). The result, Biskind repeatedly asserts, was a torrent of gritty and psychologically complex movies, "character- or theme-driven," transcendent of genre, and (above all else) astonishingly adult, challenging viewers with "fractured narratives riven by flashbacks and psychedelic dream sequences," as well as downbeat endings.

As the story goes, the New Hollywood didn't last long. Instead, these serious, intelligent, sophisticated adult films were displaced by the one-two punch of *Jaws* and *Star Wars*, which ushered in the modern Hollywood era of epic blockbusters designed to sell toys to little children. Biskind opens his chapter on *Star Wars*, "Star Bucks," with a quote from Paul Schrader: "*Star Wars* was the film that ate the heart and soul of Hollywood. It created the big budget comic book mentality." With *Star Wars*, supposedly, George Lucas turned his back on his peers, creating what Biskind calls "the mirror opposite of the New Hollywood films": a simple, straightforward tale with "accessible two-dimensional characters whose adventures ended happily." Whereas the New Hollywood directors drew on recent advances in European cinema and experimental documentary filmmaking, Lucas dumbed it all down again, "infantilizing" viewers in a return to "the pre-'60s Golden Age of movies," an era that Lucas apparently longed for, having paid tribute to it in his 1973 film, *American Graffiti*. As it happens, Lucas set *American Graffiti* in September 1962 (right as the Vietnam War was escalating), but Biskind's point is clearly that Lucas was keen on rolling back the artistic and political advances of the counterculture, serving up with *Star Wars* a simplistic "good vs. evil" type morality play in lieu of sex, drugs, and rock and roll. The result, Biskind argues, is that filmgoers today "are the children of Lucas, not Coppola," crass consumers with ADHD, just looking to be entertained, rather than self-conscious, self-critical connoisseurs of moody European art. Later, Biskind writes that "the success of *Star Wars*, coupled with the failure of *New York, New York*"—Martin Scorsese's costly flop, released one month after *Star Wars*—"meant that the kind of movies Scorsese made were replaced with the kind of movies Lucas (and Spielberg) made." Spectacular junk crowded out more enriching cinema. As evidence, Biskind quotes Robert Altman's complaint that by 1997, American multiplexes had become "one big amusement park" (roller coasters again!), devoid of worthwhile movies, a condition that Altman calls nothing less than "the death of film." Still not content, Biskind scores a coup by giving the last word of the chapter to the editor of *Star Wars*—George Lucas's ex-wife—Marcia Lucas: "I'm disgusted by the American film industry. There are so few good films, and part of me thinks *Star Wars* is partly responsible for the direction the industry has gone in, and I feel badly about that." *A New Hope*? More like, "Abandon hope all ye who enter here."

But while Lucas's science fiction epic differs in many ways from the works of Scorsese and Coppola, it's hardly the "mirror opposite" that Peter Biskind claims. *Star Wars* wasn't a simplistic return to earlier Hollywood films; nor did it reject cutting-edge techniques derived from foreign cinema and documentaries. Indeed, insisting on those points misses how *Star Wars* was very much a product of the New Hollywood, and why it was so successful.

THE NEW HOLLYWOOD did indeed emerge, as Biskind writes, in the midst of the Classic Hollywood's breakdown, springing up amidst the ruins of a tried-and-true production model that endured from roughly 1927 to 1967. As the baby boomers entered their teens and twenties in the mid-1960s, big Hollywood movies like *Cleopatra* and *Doctor Doolittle* started flopping, failing to find any purchase with a burgeoning youth culture that was more interested in rock and roll and drugs, civil rights and sexual liberation. Studio executives were forced to rely on emerging filmmakers like Warren Beatty and Mike Nichols, who alone seemed to possess the secret of how to appeal to their peers, many of whom were turning on, tuning in, and dropping out. Those artists and others used the opportunity to pursue creative freedom, refusing to sign long-term studio contracts, and pushing against the limits of Hollywood's new ratings system, established in 1968 to replace the outdated censorship of the Hays Code, which had been the law of the land since 1934. Indeed, movies like *Bonnie and Clyde* and *The Graduate* reveled in the elimination of the code, which had prohibited profanity, the glamorization of crime and criminals, and realistic depictions of adult relationships to the point where even married couples couldn't be depicted as sleeping in the same bed, or kissing lustfully.

But in other ways, nothing really changed. Hollywood

remained an industry, adjusting its product to suit changing tastes, going where the money was. And even the most aesthetically ambitious works of the New Hollywood were still genre pictures. *Easy Rider* was trippy, and included a five-minute-long LSD sequence set in a New Orleans graveyard, but it was also a biker movie, produced to cash in on the success of other, more underground biker films, such as *The Wild Angels*, which had starred Peter Fonda. Fonda had also appeared in *The Trip*, a movie about LSD written by his *Easy Rider* costar Jack Nicholson, who was at that time still laboring in obscurity. After *Easy Rider* struck a nerve with college students, other New Hollywood movies—*The Rain People, Five Easy Pieces, Two-Lane Blacktop, American Graffiti*— similarly hit the road, capitalizing on the youthful allure of feeding one's head via the open highway system. Meanwhile, *Taxi Driver* was an urban vigilante film, a follow-up to hits like *Dirty Harry*, *Magnum Force*, and *Death Wish*, as well as blaxploitation films. Scratch the surface of any New Hollywood classic, and you'll find a genre film made to placate audience demand. *The French Connection*, *Mean Streets*, and *The Godfather*, parts one and two, are crime/gangster pictures, long a Hollywood staple; *Annie Hall* and *Alice Doesn't Live Here Anymore* are romantic comedies. But while these films are all genre pictures, none of them are *generic*. The reason audiences responded so strongly to those films, and why we think them classics today, is because the people who made them did more than strictly adhere to formulas, going above and beyond traditional genre requirements.

Biskind certainly gets this. Throughout *Easy Riders, Rag-*

ing Bulls, he routinely calls attention to how the artists of the New Hollywood "transcended" and "deconstructed" formulaic genres, making their pictures look less contrived by, say, casting unconventional-looking actors, and shooting on actual locations. But Biskind goes further in his appraisal of the New Hollywood, presenting it as a body of work that appealed to "a new generation . . . that seemed to want movies about real people in real situations." Although Biskind never explicitly says so, it's clear he thinks that art progresses by better capturing life itself, meaning that the more a given artwork looks like real life, the better it is. That's why he heaps so much praise upon Martin Scorsese's *Mean Streets*, which he calls "one of a kind, a bravura directorial performance. Nothing quite like it had ever been seen before." Scorsese succeeded, Biskind claims, because he listened to his professor at NYU, Haig Manoogian, who encouraged his students "to make films about their own lives, what they knew," thereby avoiding typical Hollywood clichés. According to Biskind, *Mean Streets* is "a gangster film, a genre film . . . in name only," overcoming "artificial formulas with little claim on our attention" thanks to Scorsese's ability to document "life as he knew it." By Biskind's logic, *Star Wars* is the "polar opposite" of *Mean Streets* because it looks nothing at all like real life. If only Lucas had been a classmate of Scorsese's, studying at the feet of Professor Manoogian, then he would have stuck with making pictures like *American Graffiti*, documenting his teenage years in Modesto, California!

Easy Riders, Raging Bulls is a gripping read, catching the reader up in the dizzying reversals of fortune that are, I presume, commonplace in Hollywood. One day William Friedkin is on top of the world for having made *The Exorcist*, the next he's losing millions on an arty film like *Sorcerer*, which isn't about a sorcerer, and which had the misfortune of opening one month after *Star Wars*. But although Biskind routinely praises the New Hollywood for its realism, he never offers a coherent or compelling account of what realism *is*. Rather, he perpetuates a common mistake by presenting realism as a kind of content or subject matter: cops, Peoria, ulcers, kitchen sinks. For Biskind, realism means better capturing reality itself, which is why he writes that the New Hollywood was "art imitating life imitating art," the two blending together in a heady whirlwind until the one could no longer be distinguished from the other. And that's why Biskind takes pains to portray both Steven Spielberg and George Lucas as utter squares, nebbish nerds unhip to the times. Being dweebs, they had no real lives to document.

But while many people certainly use "realism" as a synonym for "the everyday," and "fantasy" as a synonym for "outlandish," that's too simplistic, and doesn't capture how realism and fantasy actually work. An artwork is more than just its subject matter, and realism is more than just a kind of content—realism isn't cops with ulcers living in Peoria, with dirty dishes filling the sink. An artist can make a TV show about cops that bears no similarity to real life— such as *Twin Peaks*, whose police officers and FBI agents are archetypes, personifying idealized concepts. Meanwhile, another artist can create a fantasy novel in which

30   I FIND YOUR LACK OF FAITH DISTURBING

supernatural elements are designed to seem as mundane as anything else in the world. That's because realism refers to *how* the artist portrays his or her subject matter, whether that happens to be cops or something else, such as aliens (who may or may not have ulcers). Put another way, realism is a *mode* or way of making art, regardless of subject matter, regardless of content.

Here's a simple way to think about it. All art is artifice, all artworks being equally artificial—equally fake, equally unreal. A painting of a bowl of fruit *isn't* a bowl of fruit, no matter how much it may happen to look like one. (If you're ever in any doubt, just try licking a still life the next time you're in a museum; you'll find that a painting, regardless of its appearance, is always paint on a canvas.) But obviously not all artworks *look* equally artificial. A painter can make a painting of a bowl of fruit look abstract—she can make it look more like paint than it looks like fruit—but she can also make it look more like actual fruit than it does like paint, and thereby make you hungry, and want to lick it. (Please don't lick paintings.) Realism is that latter case— when the artwork looks more like the thing being represented (its subject, fruit) than it does like the thing that's doing the representing (paint).

Put another way, realism is the use of artifice to conceal any sign of artifice. It's using makeup, say, to make a black eye look like a real black eye, not like makeup. It's using makeup to conceal the fact that it's *makeup*. In the final scene in *Star Trek Beyond*, Chris Pine's Captain Kirk sports a black eye, a leftover from his fight with the villainous Krall, who was portrayed by Idris Elba. Supposedly, Elba really punched Pine on set (accidentally), meaning Kirk's black eye was genuine—or at least, that's what Elba claimed at the film's premiere at Comic-Con. But for those of us on this side of the screen, it's impossible to tell whether Elba was telling the truth, or simply telling a good story. Kirk's shiner might be real, or it might be fake, or it might be a combination of the two, an authentic injury augmented with makeup. The point of realism is to make the real *indistinguishable* from the fake. And in this way, realism is the opposite of other modes of making art, in which the artifice is left openly on display as artifice, modes such as symbolism, allegory, expressionism, pantomime, and camp—all of which tend to represent ideals, and as such are unconcerned with appearing true to life.

Realist techniques can be applied in any artistic medium, and to any type of artwork, regardless of subject matter or genre. Peter Biskind recounts how in 1973 Ellen Burstyn, having become a star for her work on *The Exorcist*, selected Martin Scorsese to direct *Alice Doesn't Live Here Anymore*. The original screenplay for *Alice* struck Burstyn as corny, reminding her of "a Rock Hudson–Doris Day movie," but watching Scorsese's movie *Mean Streets* had led her to think that he could give it "the opposite of a polish," a "roughing up." In other words, Burstyn thought that Scorsese could take the corn out of the screenplay, and make it realist. By minimizing the film's most formulaic aspects, Scorsese concealed the contrivances demanded by the genre, making the characters seem less like stock types being played by Ellen Burstyn and Kris Kristofferson, and more like the spirited single mom Alice and her rancher boyfriend David.

Lucas may have set *Star Wars* a long time ago in a galaxy far, far away, but he gave that place and its inhabitants the same roughing up that Scorsese gave *Alice.* This was hardly accidental. As soon as he had started directing feature-length films, Lucas had begun entertaining the possibility of making a big-screen adaptation of *Flash Gordon,* having fallen in love with the serials as a kid, when they aired on TV. But he didn't want to simply re-create those movies. As he recounted it in 1979, he'd realized as an adult how "crude and badly done" those serials were—how hokey they were, hokier even than a Rock Hudson–Doris Day romance. Lucas, who still loved the serials despite their being "so awful," started wondering "what would happen if they were done really well." By "done really well," he means "realist"—transforming schlock into a film where the sets didn't wobble when actors bumped them, and where the spaceships weren't plastic models suspended on strings, with sizzling fireworks attached.

As it turned out, Lucas couldn't secure the rights to adapt *Flash Gordon,* so he decided to make his own version. And like Ellen Burstyn and Martin Scorsese, he went on to make something much greater than a simple genre exercise: he made a realist New Hollywood film par excellence, even if the result differed from contemporary works by exploring a different genre. *Star Wars* proved revolutionary by looking nothing at all like the *Flash Gordon* serials, or like any previous pulp, the same way *Alice Doesn't Live Here Anymore* looked different from previous romantic comedies.

INDEED, MUCH OF *Star Wars'* success is due to its realism, which immediately and thoroughly convinces viewers that they are watching humans and aliens skip from planet to planet in a vast, crowded other galaxy with its own detailed history. As Michael Kaminski puts it at his site *The Secret History of Star Wars*, "Lucas has created an impressive world that is not always explained but simply taken for granted." The film's immersive quality owes much to its consistently matter-of-fact tone, which renders the remarkable mundane. While the Wookies and droids and X-Wings are all new to us, the viewers, they are entirely unremarkable to Luke, Han, and Leia. We may marvel at Tatooine's twin suns, but when Luke stares at them, he is yearning to escape the planet he considers farthest away from "a bright center to the universe." Later, when he meets R2-D2 and C-3PO, he barely takes any notice of the duo. To him, they're just more chores, and he doesn't express any interest in the pair until he learns that they recently belonged to the Rebel Alliance. (Even then, he's disappointed, as C-3PO is unable to say much about the matter.)

The film shares Luke's attitude. In the first shot of the droids, aboard Princess Leia's blockade-runner, another robot, similar to C-3PO but lighter-colored, staggers about in the background, reeling as the Rebel ship shakes from the

Empire's laser blasts. That droid is unnamed and uncommented on; the film is entirely uninterested in it. Similarly, the *Millennium Falcon* fails to impress Luke, who calls it "a piece of junk." He's not alone: Han Solo must repeatedly convince others that the ship's "got it where it counts." Unlike in previous science fiction films, no one makes a fuss about the miraculous technology surrounding them. Compare *Star Wars* with *Forbidden Planet*, a clear influence on Lucas, where Dr. Morbius exposits at great length to Commander John J. Adams and his crew about the marvels of Robby the Robot, as well as the Krell and their vast infrastructure.

Forbidden Planet also makes spaceflight look dangerous and complex, the province of highly specialized crews (which helped inspire *Star Trek*'s Starfleet). The opening scene of the film depicts the crew "squaring away" as their ship decelerates to below the speed of light, after which they emerge from their energy chambers groaning and rubbing their necks. But in *Star Wars*, spaceflight is familiar, everyday. The producer Gary Kurtz has recounted how he struggled at first to understand why Lucas wanted to make a science fiction film that took its starships for granted. Finally, he grasped that Lucas wanted "spaceships that were operated like cars . . . People turned them on, drove them somewhere, and didn't talk about what an unusual thing they were doing." The characters don't pay them any mind, the same way that you and I filter out the sight and sound of the traffic that fills our streets. One need not be an engineer in order to drive a car or to make repairs, and Han and

Chewie resemble nothing so much as gearheads as they struggle to fix the *Millennium Falcon*. Even though their conversation rarely extends beyond lines like "*This* one goes there, *that* one goes there!" they're so engrossed in their repair work that we believe they know what they're doing. They simply feel no obligation to describe the *Millennium Falcon* to each other, or to Luke—or to the viewer. We know that their spaceship has a hyperdrive, and that Chewie can "punch it," but beyond that, not much is said, or needs to be said. And while some consider *Star Wars*' dialogue risible—Harrison Ford famously complained to Lucas, "You can type this shit, George, but you sure can't say it"—Lucas instructed his actors to deliver the purplish prose straight, never winking at the camera. In the end, Harrison Ford *did* find a way to say it, and what's more, to make it sound natural and relaxed. The performances aren't self-conscious, and there is never a hint that anyone on-screen knows that he, she, or it is a character in a movie. Nor are there any visitors from outside their galaxy. The world of *Star Wars* is hermetic, closed off, a place unto itself, unaware that anyone else (namely us) is watching.

Lucas also broke with previous science fiction films by making his movie look not shiny and sleek, but scuffed and dirty. Lucas had a distinct vision as to how the ships should look: as though they really worked. When Industrial Light & Magic designed rockets that were "sleek and NASA-like," Lucas objected, opting instead for "a romantic, quasi-military feel." The *Millennium Falcon* is dented, nicked, and carbon-scored (which is precisely what prompts Luke to exclaim, upon first seeing it, "What a piece of junk!"). It's a machine that looks like an actual machine, a product of industry. Just like the droids, it's clearly been through a hell of a lot. To make the setting even more convincing, Lucas had maritime engineers build a life-size model of the ship, which measured 250 by 122 by 45 feet. The other starships, while smaller models, were also excessively detailed, with pinups done to scale and remote-control laser cannons that could really swivel around.

Lucas's realist vision also led him to scuff up all of John Barry's sets, and all of the droids. Poor Artoo "was rolled in the dirt, kicked, and nicked with a saw." Lucas wanted a robot that looked as though it had been around for decades, passed from one owner to another, and not always coming out the best for wear. (Few masters have been as kind as young Luke, who indulges his possessions with oil baths.) This aesthetic prevails throughout *Star Wars* and its two sequels, whose worlds and things look lived-in and worn. Even the Imperial Stormtroopers have scuffs and nicks in their armor.

Complementing this realist effect was Lucas's approach to the film's sound design. He resisted the impulse to score his movie with the otherworldly sounds that were then the norm for science fiction films; think of the spooky, warbling tones of the theremin or ondes Martenot, or the tape-based "electronic tonalities" that Louis and Bebe Barron created for *Forbidden Planet*. To be sure, many of the iconic sounds of *Star Wars*—the voice of R2-D2 and the noises made by the blasters and lightsabers—were completely manufactured.

But they have a gritty, "organic" quality, thanks to the work of the sound designer Ben Burtt, who incorporated real-world elements like blenders and jets and dry ice. As he put it, "The sounds of the real world are complicated and kind of dirty [and] simply cannot be reproduced on a synthesizer." Lucas and Burtt took care to pair those sounds with the imagery. Burtt recorded a trained bear, Cinnamon, for Chewbacca's voice, going so far as to match where the sound was in Cinnamon's throat to specific movements in the actor Peter Mayhew's posture, and to movements in the Wookie mask.

ANOTHER WAY in which the rebels of the New Hollywood revolutionized filmmaking was their use of location shooting, which was motivated by several factors. The invention of faster film stock, lighter-weight cameras, and more portable sound recording equipment enabled young directors to get out of L.A., away from not only soundstages and back lots but meddling studio executives and their accountants. Heading to unfamiliar environs was also a means of making fresher, more realist movies. Steven Spielberg told Peter Biskind that he "was hell bent on shooting on the open sea" when making *Jaws*, knowing that if he hadn't done so, the audience would never have believed that the mechanical shark was real. Biskind agrees, crediting Spielberg's "New Hollywood approach" to location shooting as the primary reason why *Jaws* avoided being a formulaic monster movie. Along the same lines, William Friedkin traveled to Iraq to shoot the opening sequence of *The Exorcist*, then later refused to shoot *Sorcerer* anywhere other than Israel, France, and the Dominican Republic.

But realism doesn't demand the use of actual locations, since a skilled artist can make a soundstage or back lot look not like a fake set but like a real place. Nor does realism demand that real locations play themselves, so to speak. *Apocalypse Now* was shot in the Philippines, not Vietnam. But realism *does* demand the impression that the setting extends, spatially and temporally, beyond the limits of the artwork. We must believe that more of the place exists outside the edges of the film frame, as well as that the place was there before the artwork began, and will still be there after it ends. Furthermore, realism demands that settings and the objects those settings contain appear subject to the passage of time, to entropy. That's why "gritty" is so often used as a synonym for realism. ("Grit" just means "dirt," after all.) Hence, location shooting can be extremely helpful when making realist motion pictures, since real locations tend not to look brand-new but exhibit wear and tear, as well as extraneous, "unnecessary" details that contribute to the impression that the setting wasn't constructed exclusively for the artwork.

You can see this effect at work if you compare the appearance of New York City in *Breakfast at Tiffany's* with its appearance in *Taxi Driver*. In *Breakfast*, when Audrey Hepburn and George Peppard wind up kissing in an alley in the rain, it's clearly a fake alley and fake rain—it's the Paramount Pictures studio lot, not an actual NYC side street.

But when Martin Scorsese shot *Taxi Driver*, he did so entirely on location in the city of his birth, in actual apartment buildings and diners, and during an actual summer heat wave. Having lighter equipment and faster film stocks meant that Scorsese could also shoot inside taxicabs, using streetlights at night. The end result is a more convincing portrait of New York, streaked with grit and grime, and crammed with extras going about their business, seemingly unaware that they're on-screen.

While Lucas would change his tune when making the *Star Wars* prequels, in his youth he wanted the otherworldly planets in *Star Wars* to look and feel real, which is why he took his production to far-flung places like Tunisia, whose deserts stood in for Luke's home planet Tatooine, and Tikal National Park in Guatemala, which provided the Rebel Alliance base on the fourth moon of Yavin. The president of 20th Century Fox, Alan Ladd, Jr., tried to convince Lucas to shoot closer to L.A., but the director insisted on Guatemala. Just like Spielberg, just like Scorsese, Lucas wanted something more than the deserts and forests of California and Arizona, made so familiar to viewers by so many other movies. Later, in *The Empire Strikes Back*, the production set up shop in Finse, Norway, staging the Empire's assault on the Rebel's Hoth base on the Hardangerjøkulen Glacier. And while a great deal of production was done on soundstages, environments like the Death Star and Dagobah are meant to blend seamlessly with the scenes shot on actual locations, and come across as actual places. Throughout, the films give the impression that were the camera to pan left or right, or glide backward or forward, it would discover not the limits of the set but more of the world. One comes away with the feeling that in addition to all the marvels on display, even more lie out of sight, beyond the edges of the frame.

ADMITTEDLY, ONE PLACE where Lucas departed from his New Hollywood peers was with the casting of his film. For Biskind, one of the accomplishments of the New Hollywood was how it "banished the vanilla features" of the studio system, bringing with it "a gritty new realism and ethnicity." The man is being slightly coy: he means that the New Hollywood opened the doors for actors from different ethnic backgrounds—Jews, Italians, blacks—thereby making Hollywood less Waspy. Movie-star good looks—think Cary Grant and Grace Kelly—gave way to actors like Gene Hackman, Elliott Gould, Shelley Duvall, and Diane Keaton, actors who didn't look like the previous generation of actors, who in comparison looked impossibly handsome, formulaic, and fake.

While Carrie Fisher and Harrison Ford are both of Jewish ancestry, Lucas himself is white-bread and square, and *Star Wars* is not remembered for its ethnic diversity. Indeed, Lucas cast Billy Dee Williams in *The Empire Strikes Back* after many criticized *Star Wars* for being so lily-white. But the director did understand the value in casting unfamiliar faces, which made it easier for audience members to suspend their disbelief, and imagine that they were seeing

Luke, Leia, and Han—the characters being represented—rather than the actors who were doing the representing. Biskind acknowledges this, observing how though "*Star Wars* was about as far as you can get from a realistic drama, Lucas, like his peers, did not want to cast stars." Smaller roles, such as Uncle Owen and Aunt Beru, went to actors like Phil Brown and Shelagh Fraser, who looked like ordinary people. Lucas also understood the power of hiring dozens of extras, human and otherwise, filling Mos Eisley and its cantina with myriad life-forms. The cantina scene was one of the last ones that Lucas shot—in fact, he reshot it, after requesting an additional $20,000 from Fox. He knew the film's success depended on it.

Star Wars debuted on May 25, 1977, and the end result speaks for itself. As the ILM visual effects artist Richard Edlund put it: "The illusion was there. We didn't have to build a spaceship, we didn't have to send a guy out in space, and we gave the audience the impression that, 'Oh, I'm back out in space again.'" Watching the film today, one still gets the sense that the galaxy far, far away is vastly larger than what we see on-screen. It is, simply put, another world.

two

THE CHILDREN OF SPIELBERG AND LUCAS

Star Wars, to put it mildly, turned out to be a hit. In the United States alone, it ran for more than a year, well into July 1978, selling nearly a hundred million tickets, enough for it to be seen by nearly half the population at the time—though of course many fans bought multiple tickets. Just about everyone caught the fever, and for a while *Star Wars* was everywhere, a pop culture sensation. Mark Hamill went on *The Muppet Show* and pretended that Miss Piggy was Princess Leia. People roller-skated to disco remixes of John Williams's bombastic score. William Shatner covered "Rocket Man." Things got nuts.

For most people, *Star Wars* came wholly out of left field, unprecedented in a culture busy grooving to Stevie Wonder and Fleetwood Mac, watching *Happy Days* and *The Jeffersons*, and making hits of movies like *Rocky* and *A Star Is Born*. Even George Lucas was taken aback by his film's success. In the days leading up to its release, he'd gloomily resigned himself to the notion that it might bomb, or at best recoup its costs.

But *Star Wars* hardly sprang into being out of nothing, the product of a virgin birth, like Anakin Skywalker in the saga's prequel trilogy. As with other watershed films, such as *Birth of a Nation*, *Citizen Kane*, and *Breathless*, there was precedent for what George Lucas was doing, provided you knew where to look. Well before Artoo and Threepio wandered into view, and well before Luke used the Force, other films, such as *Rosemary's Baby* and *The Exorcist*, had delivered a more realist take on the supernatural. Indeed, the film critic Roger Ebert found *The Exorcist* so "raw and painful"—so realist—that he wondered in his review whether anyone could enjoy the finished product: "Are people so numb they need movies of this intensity in order to feel anything at all?" He concluded that the movie just barely remained "cinematic escapism and not a confrontation with real life," which might sound extreme today, but reminds us how audiences at the time were shocked by how skillfully the director William Friedkin surpassed familiar horror film conventions, what Ebert calls "the delicious chills of a Vincent Price thriller." Friedkin played the genre straight, cutting out and diminishing any signs of self-consciousness. And a decade prior to *Star Wars*, Stanley Kubrick's *2001: A Space Odyssey* applied realism to science fiction, representing spaceships and moon bases as practical, plausible constructions. Its astronauts had to deal with zero gravity toilets and packaged synthetic foods, sandwiches of uncertain origin, even as the vast distance between Earth and Jupiter necessitated cryogenic sleep and lengthy delays in radio transmissions.

Lucas admired *2001*, in particular the work of the special effects artist Douglas Trumbull, whom he asked to supervise the effects for *Star Wars*. (Trumbull declined, and Lucas wound up working with John Dykstra, Trumbull's assistant on the science fiction film *Silent Running*.) But Lucas's masterpiece differed from *2001*, as well as from *Rosemary's Baby* and *The Exorcist*, in an essential way, a crucial difference that would go on to have profound consequences for the geeks.

BUT BEFORE WE get to that, we should first clarify what geeks are, and what they want from fantasy art. As we shall see, not all fantasy is geeky, and not everybody who likes fantasy is a geek. What's more, one geek can be geekier than another. This is because "geek" describes a mind-set, a way of looking at the world, and as such it also describes a particular approach to making and consuming fantasy art. (The geekier a person is, the more they're looking for that approach—the more they want the artwork to conform to a geeky logic.)

The English language has known geeks since at least the 1870s. The word *geek* first appeared in print as a northern U.S. slang term for an offensively foolish person, possibly derived from the earlier word *geck*, which shows up in Shakespeare's plays *Twelfth Night* and *Cymbeline*. Its meaning transformed throughout the 1900s: by 1919, it referred to sensationalist circus performers who did things like bite the heads off chickens. Only after World War II did *geek* begin acquiring its more modern meaning of a social outcast obsessively dedicated to some pursuit—for instance, Jack Kerouac used it in 1957 to complain about overeager students at Brooklyn College. And while in theory one can "geek out" over anything—cars, wines, ham radios, making cupcakes—in the 1980s, the word started referring primarily to maladjusted weirdos who obsessed over computers and related technologies, becoming more or less synonymous with *nerd*—people like Leonard and Sheldon and their friends on *The Big Bang Theory*, who nasally debate the minutiae of astrophysics and neuroscience as if they were matters of life and death.

Geek has also come to describe someone obsessed with science fiction, fantasy, and superheroes, three otherwise disparate genres united by their fundamental commitment to the unreal or the imagined—to fantasy in its most basic sense. That word, *fantasy* (spelled various ways), entered Middle English from Old French between the late thirteenth and early fourteenth centuries, referring to the imagined as opposed to the real, having been derived from the Latin *phantasia* and the Greek *phantasía*, which literally meant making the imagined visible. Today, that's precisely what geek culture is obsessed with. Whether it's spaceships, aliens, zombies, vampires, werewolves, kaiju, magical rings, people with superpowers, gods, wizards, giants, fairies, elves, goblins, sentient robots, or talking toys and animals, the artworks that geeks chiefly favor fundamentally deal with portraying supernatural beings and items that have never really existed. At its heart, geek art is the art of the unreal.

We can see this distinction more clearly if we examine the genres that typically *aren't* considered geeky. Routinely missing from discussions and posts at geek blogs and websites like *io9*, *Den of Geek*, and *ICv2* (which specializes in "The Business of Geek Culture") are movies and books and TV shows unconcerned with the supernatural: genres like true crime, period drama, romance, sports, war, and Westerns. When these genres do catch the attention of the geeks, it's usually because they've been infused with some measure of fantasy: *RoboCop*, *Warm Bodies*, *Westworld*. The rest of the time, geeks are happy to ignore or downplay movies like *La La Land*, *Moonlight*, *The Revenant*, *12 Years a Slave*. *Empire* magazine's "Geek Queen" Helen O'Hara more than once insisted that Amy Adams should receive praise and awards for her performance in the science fiction film *Arrival*, not Tom Ford's psychological thriller *Nocturnal Animals*. One year earlier, legions of geeks lined up to declare *The Revenant* overrated, and *Mad Max: Fury Road* by far the greatest film of 2015. On their online movie review program *Half in the Bag*, Mike Stoklasa and Jay Bauman begrudgingly admitted that Alejandro G. Iñárritu is a technically proficient filmmaker, but dismissed the film's "all natural lighting" conceit and harsh shooting conditions as gimmicky and ultimately unaffecting, Bauman declaring it "a technical marvel [without] much else going on." One year before that, the duo derided *Boyhood* as similarly gimmicky, vastly preferring the supernatural horror films *Krampus* and *It Follows*.

Time and again, geeks demonstrate their preference for fantasy. When the finale of *Breaking Bad* aired in September 2013, the geek blog *Topless Robot* posted a thread where folks could discuss the show, but the site editor Luke Y. Thompson semi-apologized for the action, owing to the fact that "[we] never really came to a consensus on whether this was nerdy or not-nerdy." The question wasn't whether *chemistry* is nerdy; instead, the debate arose from the fact that *Breaking Bad* didn't concern anything *supernatural*. One year earlier, the site's founder and original editor, Rob Bricken, similarly semi-apologized for posting a link to the trailer for *The Lone Ranger* despite not knowing whether it was "a nerdy movie or not."

Recognizing geek culture's commitment to the supernatural clarifies its antagonism with the great movies of the New Hollywood. From *Easy Rider* to *Raging Bull*, from *Bonnie and Clyde* to *Heaven's Gate*, the movies made between 1967 and 1982 that critics like Peter Biskind champion were rooted in the genres geeks tend to avoid. With few exceptions, the movies of the New Hollywood were devoid of supernatural elements, not being set on alien planets or featuring vampires, zombies, or wizards. This strong anti-fantasy bias persists today. The current filmmakers most lauded by critics, and therefore most associated with serious, adult moviemaking, are people like Oliver Stone, Spike Lee, the Coen Brothers, Kathryn Bigelow, and Paul Thomas Anderson, who work in the same genres that the New Hollywood popularized. Their colleague Wes Anderson, whose *Royal Tennenbaums* and *Grand Budapest Hotel* are certainly offbeat, similarly avoids making movies that feature ghosts and monsters. (His *Fantastic Mr. Fox* is the exception that proves the rule.) And while Quentin Tarantino admittedly draws from a different pool of influences than most prestigious filmmakers when he makes pictures like *Pulp Fiction* and *Kill Bill*, even his preferred genres of choice—exploitation films and martial arts films—hail from the 1960s and '70s, and are mostly not fantastical.

The most critically lauded Hollywood director of the past thirty years whose films deal with the supernatural is undoubtedly David Lynch. *Blue Velvet*, *Twin Peaks*, *Mulholland Drive*—none of those films would ever be confused with the prestige pictures of the New Hollywood. But neither would they be confused with *Star Trek* or *Pacific Rim*. Lynch proves something of a special case, an inheritor of an altogether different legacy: surrealism and experimental cinema. While Lynch is clearly fascinated by the mysterious and the absurd, he is willing to leave them as such—as irrational and unexplained and inexplicable, akin to nightmares and daydreams.

In this regard, Lynch's work is less like *Star Wars*, and more like *2001*, *Rosemary's Baby*, and *The Exorcist*, all of which revolve around what you might call mystical forces. In the case of *Rosemary's Baby* and *The Exorcist*, those forces are divine. We learn very little about the satanic powers tormenting Rosemary and Regan, respectively; we just know they're Christian demons. *Rosemary's Baby* is chiefly concerned with subjectively conveying Rosemary's experience as she falls prey to a conspiracy, not with representing Satan as something practical and real. In the case of *The Exorcist*, our point of view is also subjective, and closely aligned with the doubting Father Karras, making us privy to his visions and dreams. Since neither Rosemary nor Karras understands the forces opposing them, we never understand them, either; those forces remain foreign and opaque. In fact, *The Exorcist* goes out of its way to demonstrate that its demons are beyond the detective powers of science. In a harrowing scene, Regan is subjected to a battery of painful medical tests that turn up nothing. Pazuzu can't be picked up by X-rays.

In the case of *2001*, there's presumably a practical explanation as to how the monoliths wound up on the Earth and on the moon, as well as to what the Star Gate is, and what precisely happens to the astronaut Dave Bowman after he travels through the colorful thing, but Stanley Kubrick wasn't interested in explaining any of that. If anything, Kubrick went out of his way to make the movie *more* cryptic, *more* inscrutable, which is why multiple viewers have found themselves wondering, as Rock Hudson famously did at the film's Los Angeles premiere, "Will someone tell me what the hell this is about?" As any geek will gladly inform you, the film's cowriter, Arthur C. Clarke, argued that "any sufficiently advanced technology is indistinguishable from magic," and so the monolith and the Star Gate might as well *be* magic, the product of divine forces. The humans in *2001* are capable of building a computer that's self-aware, HAL, and the spaceship *Discovery One*, and of thereby traveling to Jupiter and "beyond the infinite," but those of us watching in the theater feel as befuddled and unnerved as the hominids scampering around the base of the monolith back at the Dawn of Man.

Lucas adored *2001* as a technical triumph, but he agreed in part with Rock Hudson, supposedly finding the movie "too obscure and downbeat for his tastes." He wanted a different kind of motion picture entirely, one that would satisfy his inner geek. Lucas was always technically minded, having been a gearhead as a teen. Later, he went on not just to write and direct films, but to help create Industrial Light & Magic, the THX sound system, Pixar, computer-generated imagery (CGI), and more. As such, he preferred to approach the supernatural and the fantastical the same way he approached everything else: scientifically, as an engineering problem to be solved. In making *Star Wars*, Lucas, like all geeks, wanted to transform the irrational into the rational. He desired neither the mystical nor the divine, but their obliteration.

MIND YOU, LUCAS hardly invented this approach. Long before his birth, philosophers and scientists had already created the intellectual practice of world-building, a kind of thought experiment in which one invents a fictional world in order to test abstract concepts. For instance, Immanuel Kant used world-building in the late 1700s to make ethical arguments. In a famous example, he proposed that one has a moral obligation to repay loans, because if everyone chose not to repay, then the result would be a world where no one ever lent anyone money. Scientists since then have used world-building to see how natural laws might work, whether real or imaginary—for instance, what other planets might be like. By the late 1850s, a fictionalized version of this practice had split off from philosophy and the sciences, becoming science fantasy, then modern science fiction literature, resulting in works like Edwin Abbott Abbott's *Flatland: A Romance of Many Dimensions*. That novel, first published in 1884, is many things, including a satire of Victorian social customs. But it also imagines different dimensions in order to demonstrate concepts of space and time, telling the story of a square that inhabits a two-dimensional world (Flatland), but winds up visiting a one-dimensional world (Lineland), then meets a sphere from a three-dimensional world (Spaceland).

The physicists on *Big Bang Theory* are passionate fans of sci-fi, and in that sense, little has changed since the Victorian Era. There has always been a great deal of cross-pollination between science and science fiction. In his 1920 volume *Space, Time and Gravitation*, Sir A. S. Eddington, Plumian Professor of Astronomy and Experimental Philosophy at Cambridge, tries to explain how moving in spherical space might cause distant places to appear frozen in time. To help the reader envision this, he appeals to the "fantastic world-building" in a 1901 story by H. G. Wells, "The New Accelerator," in which a fantastical drug allows a person to live and move so quickly that the rest of creation seems to crawl to a halt. Indeed, for many geeks, the whole purpose of science fiction is the illustration and explanation of scientific concepts.

Prior to Lucas, the most famous world-builder was probably J.R.R. Tolkien, who celebrated the practice in his 1939 lecture "On Fairy-Stories." There he defined and defended fantasy literature as being stories about other realms—"faerie," or "Secondary Worlds"—via which authors and readers engage in imaginative and linguistic play. Just as in the case of science fiction, these stories create realities other than our own, enchanted realms where the sun might be green instead of yellow. Tolkien defended this practice on practical grounds, claiming that it allowed us to refresh our perception of reality. Essentially, reading fantasy lit allows us a break from the everyday, the chance to go on a mental vacation, after which we return to the real world and see it anew. Tolkien further argued that in order for this experience to succeed, in order for faerie to be able to work its magic, the secondary worlds must be credible enough that we fall completely under their spell, to which end authors must give them "the inner consistency of reality."

Tolkien delivered his lecture right after he started work on the sequel to his popular 1937 children's book *The Hobbit*. Today we know that sequel as *The Lord of the Rings*. Rather than writing "*The Hobbit*, Part 2" as his publisher originally requested, Tolkien expanded his quaint children's tale into an epic account of a war involving hundreds of characters. To do so, and in order to illustrate his ideas about fantasy writing, he devised an elaborate mythology of the "Secondary World" of Middle-earth, complete with its own geography, plus detailed accounts of all its peoples: humans, Elves, Dwarves, Orcs—and Hobbits. In doing so, Tolkien updated the concepts of fairy tales. Those stories traditionally depict fanciful species as needing to abide by peculiar rules. Fairies can't tolerate the feel or sound of cold iron, and brownies will flee if you reward them for their work. Holy water and crucifixes repel vampires, and only silver bullets can slay werewolves. But Tolkien, being an Oxford professor of language and literature, went much further than any of that, creating respective kingdoms with lineages and histories and dietary norms and architectural preferences—and languages. Which is to say, he made his fantastical cultures more like human cultures, the same way that Lucas made spaceships more like cars. Tolkien went so far, in fact, that not even *The Lord of the Rings* and its appendices could contain all his world-building, which is why his son Christopher was able to collect and publish, four years after Tolkien's death, *The Silmarillion*, a multivolume "backstory" that reveals that the Quest to destroy the One Ring was but one event in an epic struggle lasting thousands of years. (It involves magical jewels.)

Through world-building, geeks redefine the supernatural as the product of alternative natural laws that are themselves subject to discovery and documentation via the tools of science and reason. Which is to say, in world-building, there isn't any supernatural, not really—just a different order of the natural. Dwarves and elves, planets where time runs backward, self-aware computers that go rogue and murder astronauts—all these things and more can be posited via world-building, an elaborate game of "what if?" that gives those fantasies and others their time in the sun, where they're treated as something real, beings and objects as mundane as umbrellas and batteries, as normal as earthworms and pots of coffee.

For philosophers and scientists, and for Tolkien, world-building had a practical function, and some still use it that way today. But many engage in world-building now for purely artistic reasons, or simply because it's fun. Humans have always felt compelled to imagine things that aren't real, then devise elaborate mythologies around them—hence the elaborate pantheons that define so many religions past and present. Geeks differ from mystics, however, in knowing that their invented worlds aren't real, even as they want their fantasies to seem as real and as believable as possible.

The geek mantra might prove the same as the tagline for *The X-Files*: "I want to believe." What makes the game they're playing engaging and challenging is the inherent tension in making the imaginary seem nonimaginary. What does a blue whale look like? One can just go look. But what does a dragon look like? Ah, that presents a problem. Since dragons don't exist, and never will exist, one is forced to dream up an answer. The challenge for geeks, then, is to produce an illustration or a movie that looks as convincing as the blue whale does when drawn or photographed, as well as to explain what impact a dragon would have on its environment, from the food chain to the local economy.

Lucas absorbed the tenets of world-building from the fantastical works that he adored as a child, including his beloved *Flash Gordon*, which featured its own strange Martian species, such as the Clay People and the Forest People. Edgar Rice Burroughs's *John Carter of Mars* and Frank Herbert's *Dune* are other clear influences. So when Lucas couldn't get the rights to *Flash Gordon*, and decided to make his own version, he imagined not only a fast-paced adventure set in space starring Luke and Han and Leia, but an elaborate backstory—his own batch of world-building. Lucas's biographer Dale Pollock reports that even in the first treatment of *Star Wars*, finished in May 1973, every "person, beast, and structure was explicitly named and described in detail." Lucas worked out detailed histories and cultural traditions for the Wookies, as well as all of C-3PO and R2-D2's owners. This wealth of material eventually proved far too much for a single film, leading Lucas to cut his treatment in half, then into thirds, finally focusing on the middle third, the portion that would become, in 1975, recognizable as *Star Wars*. But Lucas retained his ambition of telling a larger story, a saga, which is why he went on to make two sequels as well as the prequel trilogy. Along the way, he also toyed with making smaller spin-off films that would showcase the elaborate world that he'd created: a movie with nothing but droids, and another with nothing but Wookies, speaking their native language. (Lucas initially conceived of Luke's Uncle Owen and Aunt Beru as anthropologists studying the Wookies.) Indeed, it's possible that the concept of a Wookies-only movie served as the basis for three later works for television: the 1978 *Star Wars Holiday Special*, the 1984 *Caravan of Courage: An Ewok Adventure*, and the 1985 *Ewoks: The Battle for Endor* (Ewoks being a diminutive version of Wookies). This ambition might have also fueled the animated *Ewoks and Droids Adventure Hour*, broadcast from 1985 to 1986.

All of these TV programs are instructive, offering insight into what *Star Wars* might have looked like minus its New Hollywood realism. The *Star Wars Holiday Special*, for instance, is thoroughly fake-looking, having been shot quickly and cheaply on obvious television soundstages, using shoddy costumes and makeup. It's also bewilderingly episodic, emphasizing older TV guest stars like Harvey Korman, who does a manic Julia Child impression, instructing Chewie's wife, Malla, on how to prepare "Bantha Surprise," and Bea Arthur, who turns out to own the Mos Eisley Cantina, where she sings a cabaret number. Over two tedious hours, we're treated to colorfully decked-out acrobats, a sultry serenade by Diahann Carroll, vaudevillian improvisation, and cartoonish matte paintings that look like paintings, not actual treetop Wookie homes. At one point, Jefferson Starship turns up, presumably because the band has *starship* in its name. All of which is to say, that while the *Special* features world-building—we meet Chewie's family conversing for long stretches in their native grunts and growls while romping about their cozy tree house on Kashyyyk as they prepare to celebrate a holiday known as "Life Day"—it's much more like a bad late-seventies variety show than it is like *A New Hope*.

Star Trek's original TV series is similarly instructive. There's no doubt that from its first appearance in the 1960s, *Star Trek* was deeply committed to world-building. Episodes frequently saw Kirk and his crew reach regions of space where the laws of physics got turned upside down, and the design of the USS *Enterprise* was anything but arbitrary. Its designer, Matt Jefferies, who was a pilot, based the ship's designation, "NCC-1701," on aircraft registration codes, and angled the twin sweeping nacelles away from the rest of the craft with the logic that they project their warp field backward, allowing the ship and its crew to ride in front of it. The ship's layout is similarly logical, its sections defined and mapped out in relation to one another. When Kirk and the others ride the elevator-like Turbolift from engineering to the bridge, for instance, their car's pulsing lights and corresponding sound effects indicate each time it changes direction, running first horizontally, then vertically, then horizontally, then vertically again.

Star Trek also regaled its viewers with an expansive mythos of alien worlds and species. While many of those aliens were obvious metaphors for rival nations involved in the Cold War, and depicted with little more than simple prosthetics and face paint, the Vulcans, Klingons, and Romulans each possessed unique anatomies and physiologies and psychological profiles, not to mention unique languages, histories, calendars, and mating customs. Being a lifelong fan of *Star Trek*, I know that Vulcans have green blood, a heart where a human liver is, and no appendices, while Klingons have reddish-pink blood and multiple organ redundancy (which even has a Klingon name: *brak'lul*). Vulcans also mate every seven years, in a ritual known as *pon farr*, while Klingons—well, let's just say it gets intense.

But while *Star Trek* featured oodles and oodles of worldbuilding, it's remembered just as much today for its cheap sets and cheesy special effects, not to mention its melodrama and heavy-handed allegories. While many of its episodes are undeniably classics, a fair amount of the show was always hokey. Even a brilliant episode like "The City on the Edge of Forever," which is gripping, dramatic television, includes an alien planet with obviously fake rocks, a city with obviously fake streets, and a delusional Dr. McCoy with obviously fake "disease" makeup plastered all over his face.

As we've seen, in making *Star Wars*, Lucas brought New

Hollywood realism to bear upon the science fiction practice of world-building. The result is especially evident in the movie's cantina scene, a favorite of many a geek. Before that scene, which starts about forty-five minutes into the film, we see Jawas and droids, as well as Tusken Raiders. But it isn't until Luke journeys with Ben Kenobi to Mos Eisley, a "wretched hive of scum and villainy," that we truly get a sense of the scope of the galaxy that *Star Wars* represents. Stepping into that bar, our eyes adjusting to the light, we, like Luke, are overwhelmed by the sheer number of weird aliens on display, from creatures that look like werewolves and horned devils, to sultry twin ladies in long braids, to a dwarfish bat thing chirping for more booze, to a hammerhead-like beast decked out in a robe, all of them jabbering in foreign tongues, quaffing drinks while kicking back to space-age jazz. *Star Wars* boldly and confidently presented its viewers with a secondary world (à la Tolkien) with more inner consistency than ever seen before—a more convincing vision of fantasy, *Flash Gordon* "done very well." The achievement of *Star Wars*, then, as far as geeks are concerned, is that it opened the gateway to reimagining *all* science fiction and fantasy in the same way.

Which is what they've been busy doing ever since.

FOR GEEKS, forty years after *Star Wars*, it is no longer enough to make a work of fantasy; one must make a world. World-building has become the essential foundation of geek artworks, so much so that in 2013, the science fiction author Charlie Jane Anders called it "an essential part of any work of fiction" (!), and "the lifeblood of [science fiction and fantasy] storytelling." In order to appeal to geeks, fantasy artists today are obliged to create not just movies, novels, or comics, but entire fictional cultures, languages, species, landscapes, histories, mythologies—sprawling alternative earths, strange other places that can be described so confidently and so thoroughly that their flora and fauna and machinery seem as solid and convincing as our own. This is why while the first *Alien* movie featured a very scary monster, later installments have featured Xenomorphs, "eusocial life-forms with a caste system ruled over by a queen," and whose intricate life cycle can be described from beginning to end in grisly detail.

But that's not all. Geeks also want those worlds to be presented via realist techniques derived from *Star Wars* and the New Hollywood, and that render marvelous things like lightsabers and the Starship *Enterprise* with the appearance that they're as real as coffee tables and Chicago and aunts and uncles. Indeed, for geeks, most if not all of the fun of fantasy is investing countless hours in producing and consuming a realist other world. In an interview about his film *Elysium*, the writer-director Neill Blomkamp describes how he could never make a "straight drama," but would have to make sci-fi or horror or fantasy, genres that involve inventing "crazy amounts of design that you can get into, and creating a world for people to go to." His colleague the actor Sharlto Copley chimes in to enthuse about his character's "flying vehicle," the *Raven*, explaining how obsessively

Blomkamp labored over the craft, including "amazing levels of detail"—little features like labels and vents that wouldn't even be visible in the film—all to make the *Raven* look like it actually worked. Blomkamp follows up Copley's trivia by declaring that the purpose of cinema "is to take the audience to a place," and that "without all that design, you're not taking them anywhere."

But of course *any* kind of filmmaking, any art making, allows its creators to obsess over "crazy amounts of design." Westerns and period drama are often thoroughly researched and meticulously manufactured. A police procedural or gangster film might necessitate extensive research into the criminal underworld; a war movie might require precise knowledge of weapons, tactics, and slang. And even "straight dramas" are artificial and contrived. Filmmakers don't just plunk down their cameras and microphones and start filming, even when they make it look as though that's exactly what they've done. What appears to be a real location can turn out to be studio trickery, such as the *Washington Post* newsroom set in *All the President's Men*, which was meticulously re-created on a Hollywood soundstage. Even real locations are often modified to produce particular artistic effects. Ellen Burstyn praised Toby Rafelson's production design on *Alice Doesn't Live Here Anymore*, as well as Polly Platt's production and costume design on *The Last Picture Show* and *Paper Moon*, telling Peter Biskind that "they both had an incredible eye for detail, from the right doorknob on the door to the clothes." But while obsessive research and manufacturing can be geeky, *All the Presi-*

dent's Men and *Paper Moon* aren't geeky artworks, the same way that *Breaking Bad* and *The Lone Ranger* aren't. What nerdy directors like Neill Blomkamp really want is to apply "crazy amounts of design" to purely imaginary things—to aliens and robots, to futuristic weaponry and vehicles.

Some geeks even understand that following in the footsteps of George Lucas means following in the footsteps of the New Hollywood. The writer Jeph Loeb told a reporter at *Entertainment Weekly* that his inspiration for Netflix's *Daredevil* series was movies like "*The French Connection, Dog Day Afternoon, Taxi Driver*," films that would help the series feel "very, very grounded, very gritty, very real." The actor Mike Colter, star of the *Daredevil* sister series *Luke Cage*, echoed this sentiment, claiming his show would be "geared towards an adult audience" and "very detailed, gritty." The producer and director Matthew Vaughn has said that his original treatment for *X-Men: Days of Future Past* was to "do the *Godfather II* of the X-Men world, and bring all of them together" (though he later left the film to make *Kingsman: The Secret Service*). Joss Whedon similarly looked to the second *Godfather* film for inspiration when directing *Avengers 2: Age of Ultron*, calling it his "guiding star" in that he wanted *Age of Ultron* to be "darker," as well as to convey the sense that "a ton has happened in-between and it's a very different movie, but you don't need any information." Years before that, he declared his aim with the science fiction TV series *Firefly* to be crafting a work of "gritty realism that wasn't an *Alien* ripoff [*sic*]," which led him to draw on the "rough-and-tumble" look of "'70s Westerns." Meanwhile, *Captain America: The Winter*

Soldier drew comparisons with 1970s "paranoia thrillers" like *The Parallax View*, *Three Days of the Condor*, and *All the President's Men*, comparisons aided by its inclusion of Robert Redford, who'd starred in the latter two films. What's more, all these geeky films and series are dark, moody, and character-driven—rather like *The Empire Strikes Back*, which remains a touchstone of geek culture, the film that just about everybody wants to re-create.

No doubt these comparisons would piss off Peter Biskind, and set his teeth on edge. But in his criticisms of *Star Wars* and geek culture, he misses a fundamental point. Biskind claims that filmgoers today are the children of Lucas, not Coppola, but the children of Lucas turn out to be not so different from the children of Coppola. Whereas Biskind wants a realist film about cops and robbers in New York City, geeks want a realist film about Batman and the Joker in Gotham City. The two sides differ mainly in terms of subject matter—genre, not approach. Rather than being a betrayal of the New Hollywood, *Star Wars* was in fact one of its greatest achievements. And in their fervent commitment to *Star Wars*, geeks turn out to be not the opposite of the New Hollywood but the movement's legitimate heirs. The New Hollywood is their birthright, the same way the Force is Luke Skywalker's birthright. Ever since 1977, the geeks have been keeping the movement's faith.

three.

GEEK GOES MAINSTREAM

The blockbuster success of *Star Wars* led to more than kitschy disco remixes and William Shatner covering Elton John in his own inimitable manner. The following years saw a boom in fantastical art of all kinds. Some works were obvious attempts to cash in on *Star Wars'* millions of fans, such as movies like *Battle Beyond the*

Stars and *The Last Starfighter*. On TV there were programs like the original *Battlestar Galactica* series, whose special effects were produced by John Dykstra, the original director of Industrial Light & Magic. (Lucas, upset by what he perceived as Dykstra's betrayal, got 20th Century Fox to sue Universal over that show.) Other artists pursued different angles, creating horror films like *Alien* and *The Thing*, children's films like *E.T. the Extra-Terrestrial* and *The Dark Crystal*, sword and sorcery franchises like *Conan the Barbarian* and *Masters of the Universe*, and, in 1980, a decade after Lucas inquired about the rights, a big-budget, big-screen adaptation of *Flash Gordon*. ("Gordon's alive?!") For a while, nothing could escape the influence of *Star Wars*. James Bond ventured into space in *Moonraker*, and Hasbro reinvented its defunct *G.I. Joe* toy line, shrinking the twelve-inch-tall toys down to the same size as *Star Wars* action figures, and outfitting them with colorful costumes, fantastic vehicles, and laser guns.

Even *Star Trek* got revived, first as a string of motion pictures, then as three successive television series, the last of which went off the air in 2005. Those movies and TV shows refashioned *The Original Series*, dropping its penchant for naked, heavy-handed allegory to instead delve deeper into psychological realism. Whereas Captain Kirk, Mr. Spock, and Dr. McCoy started out mostly as characters of type, a single human psyche split into three individuals, *Star Trek II: The Wrath of Khan* portrayed each man as his own person, containing a mixture of attitudes and emotions, as well as deep anxieties about inadequacy and aging. That approach to character was developed further between 1987 and 1994 by the sequel series *Star Trek: The Next Generation*, via characters like Data, Worf, and Picard, then by *Star Trek: Deep Space Nine*, which in its third season (1994–95) began spinning a labyrinthine plot about political intrigue during wartime, featuring dozens of nuanced characters caught up in morally complex situations. *Star Wars* also inspired *Star Trek* to give its aliens and starships a thorough makeover. Starting in 1979, the Klingons who showed up to menace Captain Kirk and his crew in the *Star Trek* feature films not only looked more alien, with pronounced forehead ridges and costumes modeled on samurai armor, but spoke an actual language, invented for the film by Marc Okrand, based on a dozen or so words whipped up by none other than the actor who played Scotty, James Doohan.

By and large, artists and entertainment companies were vying to create franchises that would appeal to just about everyone, young and old, nerdy and non-nerdy alike—but especially to little kids always crying and tugging hard at their parents' sleeves, begging for toys. This is the situation that Peter Biskind and so many others have decried, an endless wave of mindless fun and unchecked consumerism that washed away the New Hollywood, leaving its auteurs bereft of funding and filmgoers. Shiny objects and flashing lights lured patrons away from art-house fare, drawing them into a three-ring circus that promised aliens and robots and other exotic ephemeral thrills. To make matters worse, as the eighties progressed, even *Star Wars* went downhill. The final film in the trilogy, *Return of the Jedi*, was lazily shot in Arizona and California—no more Tunisia or Guatemala standing in for other worlds. Carrie Fisher, God rest her soul, looks as high as a kite, and Harrison Ford looks mostly embarrassed to be stuck in Redwood National Park, surrounded by chubby teddy bears. After that came those kiddy-centric Ewok TV specials, followed by cartoons starring Artoo and Threepio, as well as more Ewoks.

None of it lasted. It might be hard to believe this now, but by 1987, *Star Wars* was mostly moribund. Adults were flocking to films like *Three Men and a Baby*, *Fatal Attraction*, and *Beverly Hills Cop II*, while kids, ever fickle, chased other newfangled fads: Cabbage Patch Kids, Garbage Pail Kids, Transformers, the Teenage Mutant Ninja Turtles. The *Star Wars* franchise, despite its kiddification with *Jedi*, fizzled out. Kenner stopped making the plastic toys. Marvel stopped making *Star Wars* comics. *Droids* and *Ewoks* signed off in 1986. Even George Lucas moved on, busying himself with other projects like ILM and CGI and Pixar, and movies like *Howard the Duck*. As far as he was concerned, as far as everyone was concerned, the market for his magnificent space opera had gone as dry as Tatooine, people having had their fill of Luke, Han, and Leia.

But what George Lucas didn't realize—what no one had yet realized—was that there were still fervent *Star Wars* fans out there, scattered but obsessive, and hungry for more. These fans not only yearned to watch the movies on repeat, but to explore more of the worlds they depicted. They wanted to know who all those background aliens were, and how they got caught up in the saga. They wanted to see young Anakin Skywalker train with Obi-Wan Kenobi, growing up to swing a lightsaber by his side during the Clone Wars ("He was a good friend"), only to be seduced by the Dark Side and betray his fellow Jedi, becoming Darth Vader. And that's not all. These fans were desperate to know what their heroes did after the closing shots of *Jedi*, after the "Yub Nub" song and the party with the Ewoks. Did Leia and Han go on to marry and have kids? If so, could those children use the Force? Did Luke train a new generation of Jedi? Was the Empire gone for good, or did it hang on, forcing more battles with the Rebels? What other strange worlds remained to be visited, harboring what new friends and foes? What happened next?

These fans weren't satisfied by the *Droids* cartoon or by the *Ewoks* cartoon, slapdash diversions. They wanted something more substantial, something realist and immersive. Nor did they care if others were sick to death of *Star Wars*. They weren't about to let it die, just as how, two decades prior, they hadn't let *Star Trek* die, keeping its spirit alive through an underground network of zines, conventions, role-play, fan art, and fan fiction. If Lucas wanted to walk away, and not make the content that they craved, then fine. The geeks knew what to do. They would make it themselves.

I GREW UP in the 1980s, and I remember being puzzled toward the end of that decade by how *Star Wars* disappeared. By the late 1980s, I was head over heels for the franchise but didn't know anyone else who shared my passion. I didn't get it. How could my parents, who'd gone to see *Star Wars* when it came out (so lucky), and who'd taken me to see *Jedi*, and bought me the action figures, not want more installments? Didn't they want to see Obi-Wan duel Anakin on a planet covered with lava, during which Anakin fell in the lava, and got all burned, and had to don the Darth Vader outfit? I mean, who wouldn't want to see that? And who wouldn't want to see the Clone Wars, in which Obi-Wan and Luke Skywalker's father, as well as the other Jedi Knights, fought either alongside or against clones? Why wasn't the culture committed to selling me these adventures?

But in the 1980s and even the 1990s, geekdom remained on the margins of the culture, stigmatized and deeply unappealing to most people. No matter how marvelous *Star Wars* had been, no matter how many tickets it had sold, most people weren't geeks, and still thought adult geeks like me very weird. Only after 1999 would geeks be able to let their freak flags fly by wearing Chewbacca shirts in public, reading comic books on the train, and admitting while on dates that they collected superhero figures. Which raises the question: What changed, two decades after *Star Wars*, that resulted in our current Golden Age of Geekdom? What caused geek culture to rise so suddenly to the fore? Why geek culture *now*?

THE FIRST AND most obvious answer is the proliferation of Internet access, which began with the invention of the World Wide Web in 1993. Before that, geeks were largely scattered and disconnected, meeting up only at places like science labs and *Star Trek* conventions. Growing up in Scranton, Pennsylvania, I knew hardly anyone who shared my interests in animation, fantasy, and science fiction—just one schoolmate, and the older guy who ran the comic book store in the town across the Susquehanna River.

All of that changed for me, as I wrote at the start of this book, when I went to college and took up residence in the Geek Dorm. I remember very clearly the day I realized how my situation had changed. Early on in my freshman year, I attended the first Penn State home football game, joining a hundred thousand people, if not more, outside Beaver Stadium to tailgate, then file inside to wave and scream as the Nittany Lions took the field. Bored to tears, I left during halftime, walking back through a campus as desolate as any ghost town. When I entered Atherton Hall, I was astonished to find the Geek Dorm the same as always. The lobby was full of people in robes playing *Dungeons & Dragons*, while others watched the *Star Wars* trilogy yet again on the big-screen TV. None of them cared that the football game was going on. Some of them probably didn't know there *was* a game.

I can't tell you how refreshing it was to find myself in their company, to at last be surrounded by fellow weirdos who felt no need to hide their eccentricities. I sold my remaining football tickets and embraced my inner geek, befriending a guy who liked to pretend he was Spider-Man, and dating a woman who taught me how to play *Magic: The Gathering*. She and I dressed up as Princess Leia and Han

Solo for Halloween. One year prior, back in high school, I'd been teased by my classmates for dressing up as a ninja for that holiday's school dance. But at the Geek Dorm, everyone told me that my Han Solo costume was cool. I had finally found my kind. Being accepted for who I was, with all my pimples and geeky passions, had a profound effect on me. I loosened up, came out of my shell, became more social. I became me.

The Internet is the Geek Dorm times a thousand, a place where anyone, not just geeks, can encounter others who share their interests, no matter how obscure: home-brewing, raising spiders, performance art. What's more, as people coalesce around previously obscure topics of interest, they bring them to light, raising awareness, creating incentives for others to join them. Thirty years ago, if you wanted to learn how to brew beer—well, I don't have the first clue how you would have done that, other than getting a job at a commercial brewery. Today, you can watch a few videos on YouTube, then order a kit through Amazon Prime. If you wake up wanting to brew beer, if that desire's strong enough, and if you can afford it, then by evening, you can be brewing.

In the same way, the Internet has lowered the barrier of entry for being a geek, which was previously a specialized activity, a lifestyle that had to be actively pursued. While I was in middle school, I somehow picked up and read an issue of *Uncanny X-Men*—I think I bought it at the Waldenbooks at the mall, or maybe a Rite Aid. I distinctly remember it being #236, "Busting Loose!," published in May 1988 (a fact I can check in seconds, thanks to the Internet). As it happened, the issue made for a good jumping-on point, since it focused on just two characters, Rogue and Wolverine (both stark-naked!), as they battled a new batch of villains: the Genoshan Magistrates, inhabitants of a (fictional) island nation off the coast of Africa, "a green and pleasant land" where mutant citizens were slaves. (The writer Chris Claremont was making a point about the evils of apartheid.) New though I was, I got the gist of the proceedings fairly quickly, even if the issue alluded to matters I didn't understand, such as Rogue having an alternate personality, Carol Danvers; as well as a subplot depicting Madelyne Pryor's transformation into the Goblin Queen. (If you don't know who Carol Danvers is, or who Madelyne Pryor is, or what a Goblin Queen is, well, then you're just like I was at that time.) I wanted to know more, but I didn't have Internet access, and none of the libraries near me stocked comic books. In fact, Marvel was only just starting to reprint famous back issues as graphic novels, as is common practice today.

So I did the only thing I could do: save the money I made cutting grass and shoveling snow, and buy back issues at my local comics shop (the one across the Susquehanna River). But first I had to find that shop, a hurdle that, while minor, shouldn't be overlooked. People tend to avoid unfamiliar places, preferring not to be seen outside their comfort zones, looking lost. Just think of how hard it is to start going to a new gym, or to any gym at all. Any kind of specialized business intimidates nonspecialists, and comics at that time were only for dorks. In retrospect, my being geeky probably helped me get into comics, since I was more interested in the *X-Men* than I was in looking cool. I already wasn't popular, so I didn't have anything to lose.

Through the comics shop I gradually tracked down and purchased *Uncanny X-Men* #200 through #235. I also bought the companion titles: *X-Factor*, *Wolverine*, *The New Mutants*, *X-Force*, *eXcalibur*—any X-Book that Marvel published. But still there were limits. Older issues of *Uncanny X-Men* were prohibitively expensive. I could justify spending $5 on a comic, and sometimes more, but not much more, and not very often. So for the most part, I stared at those pricier back issues, sealed in plastic and under glass, dreaming of someday finding out what had happened to the Children of the Atom before the mideighties.

Around this time, I also fell in love with *Star Trek: The Next Generation*. That was easier to get into, since I could watch it on TV. But I still had to prioritize doing so, since no one else in my family cared about the show. And as with *X-Men*, I was starting out from zero, not always understanding allusions to series lore, such as who the Romulans were, or the Klingons. I had just vague ideas, impressions. That's why I started taking notes: I was looking for connections, trying to puzzle out the series' deeper secrets. It wasn't until I went to college that I met someone whose family had videotaped every episode of both *The Next Generation* and *The Original Series*. I was blown away. A *whole family* that was into *Star Trek*? How lucky was that?

This undoubtedly sounds quaint now, but that's the point. Being a geek a mere generation ago meant going to sometimes extravagant lengths in order to watch a show or read a comic. Before the Internet, geek artworks—artworks in general—were more ephemeral, especially if they weren't very popular. They disappeared, went out of print. Any reader who belonged to a subculture last century will relate to this, from fans of cult movies or esoteric music subgenres or experimental fiction, to people marginalized by politics, such as queer and transgendered folk.

Before the Internet, when information was less free, if you wanted to be a geek, if you wanted admission into that guild, you had to do a lot of legwork and research yourself. Nobody else would do it for you. To this day, I still pride myself on my ability to recall the title of any episode of *The Next Generation*, although that knowledge is now slipping. And it's slipping because of the Internet. When I want to remember a title, I can just look it up—on my cell phone! Where I can watch the episode, too! Anytime that I want! And not just *TNG*, but any *Star Trek* series, including the short-lived Saturday morning cartoon from the early seventies! It feels like a childhood dream come true, like I'm finally living aboard the Starship *Enterprise*, whose inhabitants could ask its mighty computer any question they wanted whenever they felt the urge.

In the mid-2000s, I downloaded digital editions of every issue of every X-Book, all the way back to the very first issue of *X-Men*, published on September 10, 1963. I read them all, from classic story lines like the Dark Phoenix Saga, to bizarre single issues that have been mostly forgotten, such as the time in 1982 when Storm got bitten by Count Dracula (yes, Count Dracula) and became a vampire for all of seventeen pages. (Aided by Kitty Pryde, as well as her own indomitable will, Storm eventually fights free of Dracula's control, boldly crying: "I was born free, vampire, and free I will remain!" Dracula, bowing, compliments the woman's "rare beauty, rare courage, rare strength," then transforms into a bat and flutters off, intoning as he does so, "You have earned Dracula's respect—and hence, your life." I don't think the X-Men ever crossed paths with the Count again.)

The Internet has made geek culture less scarce and more accessible since the turn of the century. What's more, the Internet was largely built by geeks, who right from the get-go used the network to play text-based games like *Colossal Cave Adventure* and *Zork*, created in the late 1970s. The Internet's pro-geek bias persists to this day. At Wikipedia, the article on cobras (the venomous snakes) is, as I write this sentence in the spring of 2017, about 300 words long. The article on Cobra, the ruthless terrorist organization in *G.I. Joe*, is well over 5,000 words, and was updated more recently. And the article "List of *Teen Wolf* characters" (about the MTV series) is 86,665 words long, a full third longer than this book.

The doors of the geek guild have been thrown open, its mysteries made accessible to all. Just as anyone can be brewing beer by nightfall, anyone can spend a day reading Wikipedia about *Star Trek* or *Doctor Who*, plus watching those programs via streaming services like Amazon Prime and Netflix. Thirty years ago, if you liked a TV show, you had to watch it when it first aired, or else as reruns. VCRs helped some, but not everybody had one, or knew how to program one. (Remember how tough that was?) Not only was this another barrier to entry, it meant that the people making TV could never be sure that viewers would see every episode, or see them in broadcast order. This incentivized creators to make their series episodic, organizing them around situations (hence situation comedies), resetting the show to default norms at the beginning of each episode. *Seinfeld*'s show runner Larry David gave his writers two rules, "no hugging, no learning," to keep the show consistent, year in and year out. The final scene of the final episode embodies that instruction. Jerry, sitting with the others in a jail cell, begins critiquing the second button on George's shirt, which for him is "in the worst possible spot." George senses that he and Jerry have already had this conversation. Ironically, most of the 76.3 million people watching "The Finale" didn't know that George was remembering the very first scene of the series premiere, which, when it aired on July 5, 1989, was viewed by only 15.4 million. (I know that David's joke was lost on me at the time.)

This situation started changing in the late 1990s, with the widespread adoption of DVDs, plus the founding of Netflix in 1997, which enabled viewers to watch not only movies but television series on demand. The advent of streaming over the past ten years has only made serial viewing easier. Now people who come late to a show can still watch the episodes in order, binge-watching to catch up with other fans. As a result, it's possible for someone like Vince Gilligan to make a show like *Breaking Bad*, whose sixty-two episodes depict Walter White's gradual transformation from Mr. Wizard into Scarface. And if you haven't seen every episode, so what? I first watched *Game of Thrones* at a viewing party some friends threw for the fifth season's premiere, during which I skimmed Wikipedia articles on my phone, getting the gist, more or less, of who each character was, and what part they played in the sexy but deadly political landscape of Westeros.

THE RISE OF the Internet had caused the rise of geek culture, its going mainstream, a transition that can be measured by attendance at the San Diego Comic-Con. That convention started in 1970 with a mere 145 fans in attendance. By 1978 it was drawing 5,000, many no doubt driven there by the recent success of *Star Wars*. But the Con remained at that size until the late eighties, when it experienced a growth spurt, reaching 40,000 attendees by 1997. My guess is that the Web was working its magic on college campuses and at tech companies. But that was nothing compared with what happened next. Between 1999 and 2008, the convention's attendance tripled, skyrocketing from 42,000 to 126,000. The rise of the World Wide Web not only made it easier for fans to converge in one place (recall the flash mob fad that happened during that time), it made it easier for advertisers to find them, which is why the San Diego Comic-Con has become such a crucial marketing event for Hollywood studios and other corporations.

That brings us to the other reason why geekdom has

saturated the culture, transforming American life into an ongoing comic-con, camped out at the multiplexes and the toy aisles at Target, as well as why every movie made these days seems to be a sequel or reboot, regardless of whether the film is geeky or not. (As I write this, my local theaters are showing *Power Rangers*, *Beauty and the Beast*, *Ghost in the Shell*, *T2 Trainspotting*, and *Chips*. As I saw somebody say on Twitter, what year is this?)

Historically, Hollywood has relied on commercial genres and stars to sell tickets. Obviously that's still the case, which is why there are so many horror films, which are cheap to make and appeal to younger viewers. It's also why hot stars like the Rock show up in so many movies each year. But fans won't necessarily turn out for every film of a given genre, and even the biggest movie stars have appeared in flops. *Jupiter Ascending* was a sci-fi action film from the creators of *The Matrix*, Lilly and Lana Wachowski, and starred Mila Kunis, Channing Tatum, Eddie Redmayne, and Sean Bean. It cost $176 million to make, and went on to gross just a little over that—$184 million worldwide—putting it solidly in the red, after accounting for marketing. I enjoyed the movie myself; it's not especially good, but it is charmingly hokey and offbeat, a modern *Flash Gordon*. But I'm not holding my breath for a sequel. (The Wachowskis have migrated to TV, where their program *Sense8* has met with a much more welcome reception.)

Since neither genre nor star presence guarantees success, entertainment companies are increasingly turning to the franchise model in order to minimize risk—franchises are their new hope, so to speak. *Star Wars* wasn't just the biggest movie ever, and didn't just spawn sequels and TV specials and spin-off series, it generated massive profits through extensive merchandising—the licensing of the brand to a variety of other products and experiences such as action figures, novels, comic books, records, breakfast cereals, trading cards, amusement park rides and attractions, and much, much more. While Lucas claims to have initially limited *Star Wars* merchandising, approving only licenses of the highest quality, forty years later, fans of the franchise can buy just about anything with a *Star Wars* tie-in, including boxes of Jelly Belly jelly beans bearing Darth Vader's image, as well as USB sticks in the shape of Yoda. You probably won't be surprised to hear that the merchandising revenue for *Star Wars* quickly surpassed the film's box office receipts, and became the engine driving Lucasfilm (which Lucas sold to Disney in 2012). Other companies immediately began trying to copy this success; hence the plethora of toys and products that defined the 1980s, and that littered so many homes, from *Masters of the Universe* play sets and figures to *Muppets* lunch boxes, from *Strawberry Shortcake* coloring books to *My Little Pony* Colorforms.

Providing additional incentive is the fact that entertainment companies today are usually owned by larger corporations. In 1968, DC Comics became a subsidiary of Kinney National Service, Inc., which itself was the result of various mergers, including the Kinney Parking Company and National Cleaning Contractors. That same year, Kinney also bought Panavision, and one year later, it bought Warner

Bros.–Seven Arts, which itself had recently purchased Atlantic Records. In 1971, the conglomerate shed its non-entertainment holdings and rebranded itself as Warner Communications. In the late 1980s, Warner merged with Time Inc., becoming Time Warner in 1990. Today, that massive company owns not only Warner Bros. and DC Comics, but HBO and the Turner Broadcasting System, which includes Cartoon Network, CNN, and a 10 percent share in Hulu. (Interestingly, Time Warner no longer owns Time Inc., which it spun off in 2014. It's also currently in the process of trying to merge with AT&T.) This is why the artists at Williams Street, the company that programs Adult Swim, are able to make ironic cartoons like *Space Ghost Coast to Coast*; *Harvey Birdman, Attorney at Law*; and *Sealab 2021*: they're owned by the same company that owns the former Hanna-Barbera Productions, which Ted Turner bought in 1991, and was then absorbed into Warner Bros. Animation.

The upshot of all of this is that, rather than making a single TV show or movie, companies are looking for brands that they can exploit through a variety of products, ideally produced by their subsidiaries. An added benefit is that franchises transcend both genre and stars, which is why, in the words of the film scholar Kristin Thompson, "today, the franchise is often the star." Fifty years after Gene Roddenberry dreamed up a show that was "*Wagon Train* to the stars," *Star Trek* is still cruising along, having survived not only the original show's cancellation but the death of its creator, as well as several of its actors. Along the way, it's been a Saturday morning animated cartoon, a long-running film series, and four other live-action television series, all of them featuring new characters and, more recently, an entirely new cast portraying the original *Enterprise* crew. There's also been more merchandise than a Galaxy Class starship could carry: the usual novels and comics and video games and T-shirts, as well as novelty products, such as pizza cutters shaped like the Starship *Enterprise*, and light-up Borg cube Christmas tree ornaments. And while the franchise has remained, at its core, science fiction, it's also produced hybrid works that range from the lighthearted *Voyage Home* to the more action-oriented *First Contact* and J. J. Abrams flicks.

Franchises aren't synonymous with geek culture. The longest-running movie franchise is James Bond, which turned fifty in 2012, and was based on a series of novels first published in 1953. James Bond, so dapper and suave, is hardly a geek, and his franchise isn't geeky. With the exception of the voodoo on display in *Live and Let Die*, the series isn't supernatural, just preposterous. And yet nobody except Auric Goldfinger expects Mr. Bond to die, despite the end of the Cold War and the rise of feminism. Seven different actors have portrayed 007 so far, and there have been new novels, a newspaper comic strip, video games, a series of "Young Bond" young adult novels (set in the 1930s), plus hundreds of tie-ins with relevant brands. The website Bond Lifestyle documents a wide variety of products on sale to anyone who wishes to pretend they're the superspy, from colognes to limited-edition laptop computers. And while James Bond may prefer to drive Aston Martins and drink martinis (shaken, not stirred), he's driven all manner of other cars, ranging from a Lotus Esprit to BMWs, and he's shilled for many other adult beverages, from Macallan 18-Year-Old whisky to Heineken. As Bond himself might say, "The world is not enough."

Any franchise can inspire sequels and prequels, sister series, theme park attractions, and other merchandise. But the franchise model does line up very well with geeky interests, because geeks are looking for something particular from the artworks that they consume, something that franchises are well-suited to provide. In order to understand why that is so, we must first understand why geeks behave the way that they do—why they read and write fan fiction and flock to conventions in costumes that they've sewn, all the while conversing in made-up languages like Elvish and Klingon. The past twenty years have seen the spread and mainstreaming of these pastimes—why? What's been driving them? What's their appeal? And what are geeks hoping to find?

WHAT EVERY GEEK WANTS

PART II

four.

DO YOU BLEED?

By 1985, *Star Wars* wasn't the only franchise in decline. Batman was also in deadly peril, confronting a foe more troublesome than any member of his formidable rogues' gallery. Whereas in 1966 the character had sold upwards of a million comic books, by the mid-1980s, he was moving less than a tenth of that, an all-time low. The Caped Crusader was nearly fifty years old and mostly a joke, best remembered for having been played by—WHAM! OUCH! KAPOW!—Adam West. Perhaps his time had passed?

But before consigning Bats to the dustbin, DC decided to give an up-and-coming comics writer and artist, Frank Miller, the chance to reinvent the character. This was logical: Miller had risen to prominence at DC's rival, Marvel Comics, by reinventing *Daredevil*, a comic that featured a Batman-like vigilante and whose sales, at the beginning of the decade, had similarly been in the gutter. Between 1981 and 1983, Miller's new approach steadily revitalized *Daredevil*, making it one of Marvel's bestselling titles. Miller's method was akin to the one Ellen Burstyn and Martin Scorsese had used on *Alice*, a "roughing up." He transformed Daredevil—the blind crime-fighter Matt Murdock, "The Man Without Fear"—from an idealized hero for kids into something more plausible, a real flesh-and-blood person leading an actual life, both his mind and his body affected by the battles he waged. Among other things, Miller limited the range of Daredevil's heightened senses, and eliminated his swinging around Manhattan like Spider-Man via a rope attached to his billy club. He also beat him up a lot. As Miller put it at the time, "Part of Daredevil's appeal to me is that he loses one fight out of every three." This more practical approach extended to the other characters in the book, such as the ninja assassin Elektra, Miller's own creation, whom he armed with a sai (an Asian piercing weapon) in order to amplify the force of her blows and extend her reach.

And famously (or notoriously), after making Elektra a fan favorite, Miller killed the character off in *Daredevil* #181 (April 1982), a mere fifteen months after her debut.

DC wooed Miller away from Marvel, first by allowing him to make the experimental miniseries *Ronin*, in which he explored his growing interest in Japanese comics, then by letting him do whatever he wanted with Batman. What was the risk? If the hottest artist in comics could get folks excited about Batman, wonderful. And if not, then Batman would sleep with the fishes.

As it turned out, Miller proceeded to make the comics miniseries that defined his career, if not the decade: *Batman: The Dark Knight Returns*, published in four parts between February and June 1986. Just as he'd done with *Daredevil* and *Ronin*, Miller used the opportunity to push the limits of comics by assailing what he regarded as the medium's two worst foes. The first was the Comics Code Authority, a self-imposed form of censorship adopted by the major comics publishing houses in 1954 in response to parent outcry and congressional hearings. Just as with Hollywood's Hays Code, the Comics Code Authority limited for decades what artists could make, drastically toning down depictions of sex and violence, mandating respect for parents and law-enforcement officials, and insisting that crime always be portrayed as sordid and self-destructive. Criminals weren't even allowed to murder cops. Another section of the Code outlawed "walking dead, torture, vampires and vampirism, ghouls, cannibalism, and werewolfism." In 1971, the Comics Code was softened somewhat. Classic undead monsters like Count Dracula were let back in (which is why Storm could later meet him), though zombies remained beyond the pale. Cops could also be shown as corrupt, and get killed by crooks, as long as things turned out well in the end and kids weren't seduced by sin.

Miller's second opponent was the inferior printing quality that had characterized comics ever since their birth in the late 1930s. In his view, those two traditions, cheap printing and the Code, reinforced one another, creating the widespread perception that comics were nothing more than disposable trash for children, rather than a serious art form. As he put it in an interview to *The Comics Journal* in 1985, "You've got to overcome all the public prejudices, justified as they are. We've got a lot of bad momentum. We've got fifty years of crap, and people talk as if we've got a heritage behind us. We've got a lot of bad stories, just one after another." Rather than make such crap himself, Miller yearned to produce ambitious "romances," or fantasies for adults, driven by his desire to emulate advances in European and Japanese comics, commercial art, and Hollywood cinema (which had recently become unshackled from its own self-censorship). To that end, Miller insisted that his comics be printed on higher-quality paper via better printing processes, and that he be allowed to put Batman through his paces. DC agreed, publishing the miniseries in a new "prestige format," with heavier, glossier paper stock, sturdier covers, square bindings, more pages, and no ads—plus a heftier price tag: $2.95, as opposed to 75 cents.

Just like George Lucas, Miller was wondering what

fantasy might look like if it weren't something shoddy and cheap but "well done," which once again involved reimagining it as realist. This wasn't mere coincidence. Miller was a lifelong fan of *Dirty Harry*, a franchise with deep roots in the New Hollywood. The first film in that series was rewritten by George Lucas's close friend John Milius, who then coauthored the sequel, *Magnum Force*, with fellow New Hollywood wunderkind Michael Cimino. In particular, Miller admired the qualities that Milius had brought to the character, such as his "attitude," and "being a cop who was ruthless [and] the same as the killer except he has a badge. And being lonely." Dirty Harry is willing to do what no other cop will dare: to go outside the law, blasting his way through the red tape that hamstrings the rest of the force. In the first film, he tortures the injured Scorpio in order to find out where that serial killer has buried alive a young girl, then shoots him after he kidnaps a busload of kids, knocking him backward into a pond. The final shot shows Harry flinging his detective's badge after Scorpio, an homage to the ending of *High Noon*. Presumably Miller was tickled by that parallel in addition to all the violence: the villain of *High Noon*, as it happens, is named Frank Miller.

In creating *The Dark Knight Returns*, Miller applied the same logic he'd used on *Daredevil*, stripping the character down, going back to basics. He made Batman his actual age at the time, forty-six, as well as retired following the death of Jason Todd, the second Robin. Bruce Wayne claims to Commissioner Gordon at the outset of the first issue that his crime-fighting days are behind him, but we quickly sense that Wayne, rather than being happy, is paralyzed with grief, battling an inner demon that he blames for the death of a kid. Wayne tries to drown that demon with booze and late-night TV, but he can resist it for only so long. Miller likens the man's being Batman to a kind of addiction, akin to Dr. Jekyll's Hyde. Gradually, the crime-ridden nature of Gotham City, as well as a chance viewing of a television broadcast of *The Mark of Zorro*—the movie that Wayne saw with his parents the night they were killed—triggers the billionaire's childhood trauma, causing him to relapse. The more dominant as well as more sadistic Batman persona bursts free, wholly subsuming Wayne, which Miller associates with the image of a bat crashing through a closed window. That image echoes throughout the series, as Batman's arrival at different crime scenes is repeatedly accompanied by shattering glass.

Over the course of the story's 188 pages, Miller takes a practical approach to Batman, eliminating the character's goofier aspects, and asking how Bruce Wayne might reasonably wage his one-man war on crime. (The series' title signals this, promising the return of a grimmer, grittier version of the character after intervening decades of kid-friendly camp.) For starters, Miller refashions the Batsuit, transforming it from the blue "New Look" costume popularized in the sixties and seventies, with its yellow chest insignia, into a black-and-gray costume more reminiscent of Batman's earliest days as a crime-fighter. In the first issue, Miller has Batman explain the presence of the yellow chest insignia as a tool for drawing gunfire away from his more vulnerable head, and toward a body part that he can shield with armor. (The bright oval disc gets blown apart by a shotgun blast.) Everything about this Batman is deliberate, a tactic. Even so, he stumbles and falls, suffering, just like Daredevil did, tremendous bodily damage. A severe beating at the hands of a vicious gang leader results in his needing to wear an arm brace, and various punches, kicks, gunshots, and stabbings all take their toll on the middle-aged Wayne, who ages rapidly throughout the series, his hair graying, his facial features becoming deeply lined.

In taking Batman seriously, Miller also explored the character's effect on Gotham City and its inhabitants, a bit of world-building in which he strove for his own version of Tolkien's inner consistency. While the series starts out tightly focused on Bruce Wayne, the following issues steadily expand their scope, drawing in other narrators: Commissioner Gordon, Carrie Kelley (the new Robin), Superman, and the Joker. Television reporters and commentators, meanwhile, provide a chorus as the comic shifts from being a portrait of a single man into a portrait of Gotham City, which Miller depicts like a real U.S. city—NYC in the 1980s. Here Miller is once again drawing on *Dirty Harry* and other 1970s exploitation films, such as *Death Wish* and *Taxi Driver*. Miller also integrates Batman into a larger history. Ronald Reagan appears as president, busy waging a proxy war with Soviet forces in the fictional island nation of Corto Maltese. That battle culminates in the detonation of a nuclear missile, after which Batman must (literally) ride to the rescue of Gotham, galloping in on horseback to reimpose order as the city succumbs to rioting and looting. Which is to say that, after conquering Two-Face and the Joker, Batman comes to wage war with society itself, and with history itself, the sources of crime. That battle proves too great for a single man, even a billionaire who wears a scary costume, so Batman gathers other combatants under his scalloped cape, including former gang members, rechristened as "the Sons of Batman." Whereas the series opens with Alfred chiding his master for displaying no interest in marriage or children, it ends with Bruce Wayne reproducing after a fashion, creating an institution that will survive him, an underground shadow society that will wage ongoing war with the world up above.

But before that happy ending (if you can call it that), the conflict between Wayne and the world comes to a climax in a battle between Batman and Superman. In Miller's hands, Superman comes to represent traitorous submission to the false authority of the state, the same blind subservience to an inept bureaucracy that Dirty Harry couldn't stomach. Deep in Crime Alley, at the base of the very streetlight where Bruce Wayne watched his mother and father die, Batman unleashes every ounce of his pent-up, ingenious rage upon Superman, assailing Reagan's puppet with hunter missiles, a sonic gun, a Kryptonite arrow, and Gotham City's electrical grid. In what is surely the most famous panel of the series, if not of the past three decades of superhero comics, Batman stomps the Man of Steel into submission, his spiked boot drawing blood from the Last Son of Krypton's dimpled chin, telling his foe to "remember . . . my hand . . . at your throat . . . remember the man who beat you."

There's a great deal going on here. First off, Miller is pursuing his revisionist logic to its necessary conclusion. As he explained to *The Comics Journal* at the time, "Kids with a sort of happy, benevolent view of the world tend toward Superman, and kids who find the world a big, scary place go for Batman." Miller's keen insight is that while Superman and Batman are both orphans, Superman was adopted by a kindly couple from Kansas, gaining fantastical superpowers in the process (from the sun), while Bruce Wayne was left alone in the dark, consumed by rage and driven to train himself to the peak of human perfection. Superman is daylight and the order of the state, while Batman is night, and the enemy of the state. But even beyond that, Miller is making a larger, more symbolic point about comics. In having Batman defeat Superman, Miller is having his new order of comic book art—artistically daring, adult-oriented adventure—defeat the kiddy-centric, censored, obedient years of the medium, those "fifty years of crap" that he deplores.

The Dark Knight Returns was the ultimate Batman story, the character's Omega. But Miller wasn't finished yet with his realist revision of the character. One year later, he teamed up with the artist David Mazzucchelli to provide Batman's Alpha, *Year One*, a four-issue arc in the monthly *Batman* comic. (It has since been reprinted as a stand-alone graphic novel.) Those four comics, issues #404 to 407, tell the parallel stories of a young Bruce Wayne and Lieutenant Jim Gordon as they struggle to find their footing in Gotham City and wage their respective wars on crime. (Of course their paths merge by the end.) As before, Miller approaches the characters practically, drawing on 1970s crime films like *Dirty Harry* and, this time around, *Serpico*. Gordon deals with being the only honest cop on a corrupt force that's epitomized by his sleazy partner, Detective Flass, who's on the take, working for mobsters like Carmine "The Roman" Falcone. Bruce Wayne, meanwhile, invents a double life as a drunken playboy while constructing his terror-inducing costume and honing his skills, learning from the many mistakes he makes along the way—mistakes that, as is par for the course with Miller, subject the man to multiple brutal injuries. Gordon also slips up, cheating on his heavily pregnant wife, Barbara, with fellow cop Sarah Essen, which makes him vulnerable to blackmail by the bent Commissioner Loeb. Other familiar characters also appear, refashioned: Harvey Dent is an assistant district attorney held back by his own ideals; Selina Kyle is a sex worker turned cat burglar; and Alfred is a former soldier with training in combat medicine.

After that comic, at the end of the 1980s, Miller tried to make a go of it in Hollywood, working on the script for *RoboCop 2*. (He has an amusing cameo in that film, as a chemist who manufactures a strain of drug—called Blue Velvet of all things—for Tom Noonan's sociopathic drug lord.) Later, he went on to create a number of important comics, namely *Sin City* and *300*, in which he explored a more cartoonish, expressionistic style. But he's best remembered for bringing gritty realism and adult themes to comics, and his influence is obvious to anyone who's read superhero comics, or watched movies and TV shows based on superhero comics, over the past twenty years—such as Marvel's *Daredevil* Netflix series, which was largely inspired by Miller's run.

Miller's work on Batman succeeded commercially, too, exceeding DC's hopes and revitalizing the character. Today, it's arguable that Batman has eclipsed Superman to become the company's flagship superhero, a massive franchise unto itself. That said, not everyone who's followed in Miller's wake has shared his fondness for realism, as can be seen (for example) from the two Batman movies that Tim Burton made as the 1980s gave way to the 1990s. Burton, like Miller, aspired to make adult-oriented fantasies, and his 1989 *Batman* briefly alludes to *The Dark Knight Returns* by having the photojournalist Vicki Vale arrive in Gotham City by way of Corto Maltese, where she was documenting a war. But Burton was not and has never been a realist, and his take on Batman was singularly his, more comparable to his other films, such as *Beetlejuice*, than to the respective works of either Miller or Lucas.

This is especially evident in Burton's 1992 sequel *Batman Returns*, which forgoes realism in order to revel in self-conscious artifice. Burton shot the film entirely on Hollywood soundstages in the manner of German Expressionist films from the 1920s like *Nosferatu*, *Faust*, and *Metropolis*. The exterior of Wayne Manor is clearly a model, surrounded by obviously fake, bare twisted trees that pay homage to the forest in the 1920 film *The Cabinet of Dr. Caligari*. Even the park at the beginning of *Batman Returns* is wholly fake, as is the snowfall that blankets Gotham. That snow falls gently and evenly throughout the film, never accumulating or blackening from car exhaust, being the ideal, perfect snowfall of a fairy tale, just as in Burton's previous movie, *Edward Scissorhands*. The result is a timeless, static world that can be neither entered nor departed. Watching *Batman Returns*, I always get the impression that it's taking place inside a snow globe, a perfect little world, not unlike the dollhouse that Selina Kyle owns, or the Halloween Town in *The Nightmare Before Christmas*. Everything looks "just so," mannered and carefully poised, neither haphazard nor accidental, and never gritty or disheveled the way that realism requires. Every shot is composed, every item and costume the product of a single mind (Tim Burton's), which is why geeks today routinely describe the film as "a Tim Burton movie" and not "a *Batman* movie." In downplaying signs of artifice, realism downplays more eccentric artistic styles, self-conscious quirks that we associate with artists such as Burton, whose love of 1950s kitsch and German Expressionism make all his films look like *his* films, drawing our attention to the man behind the curtain.

Batman Returns is also ribald and politically provocative, and thereby ran afoul of mainstream consumers, who in 1992 still thought of Batman as a family-friendly franchise. Warner Bros. agreed; they wanted a franchise aimed at kids, so they could sell toys and Happy Meals and comic

I FIND YOUR LACK OF FAITH DISTURBING

books, which were still under the jurisprudence of the Comics Code Authority. So they fired Burton and turned to someone else for the sequels, the director Joel Schumacher. His installments, *Batman Forever* and *Batman & Robin*, were neither realist nor adult; instead, they're mostly buffoonery pitched at little children, made in the style of the 1960s TV show, featuring canted angles, purplish prose and cheesy puns, melodramatic death traps, and villains who cry "Curses!" The preposterous action sequences flaunt the laws of physics and lack any genuine sense of peril. There's no sense that the punches and kicks, accompanied by brass stings, leave as much as a bruise, and the worst thing that happens to Robin in the second film is that he gets frozen, then has to sit with his feet in a bucket of hot water. Throughout, Schumacher irreverently exaggerates the material, rendering Gotham City as a loud, bright, neon-colored nightclub, and Batman's and Robin's costumes as kitschy tributes to antique statuary, with enlarged codpieces and nipples. Unsurprisingly, his movies incensed the geeks, but they also didn't fare that well with critics or mainstream audiences. It was a sign that, even in the five years between *Batman Returns* and *Batman & Robin*, tastes were changing. George Clooney, the star of the latter film, later apologized for having made it, lamenting, "We might have killed the franchise."

Instead, it took the Dark Knight just eight years and a different tone to get back out on the streets. When *Batman & Robin* failed to impress, Time Warner started casting about for a new hot young director willing to try a different approach. At that time, mind-bending independent crime films were all the rage, as studios rushed to copy the sur-prise success of Quentin Tarantino's *Pulp Fiction*. Bryan Singer's *The Usual Suspects*, Alex Proyas's *The Crow* and *Dark City*, David Fincher's *Fight Club*, Darren Aronofsky's *Requiem for a Dream*, and even the Wachowskis' *The Matrix* all be-longed, in one way or another, to this noir revival. The time seemed right to return Batman to his roots. After all, wasn't he the world's greatest detective? Time Warner entered talks with Aronofsky and Miller concerning an adaptation of *Year One*. That project stalled out, after which the company pursued other options, including a Batman/Superman team-up, and a *Catwoman* solo film that had been stuck in development hell since *Batman Returns*. (It finally came out in 2004, starring Halle Berry, and was as hokey as *Batman & Robin*. It flopped.)

By 2003, superhero movies were back in fashion, and Time Warner settled on a different emerging artist: Chris-topher Nolan, hot off his own heady crime films *Memento* and *Insomnia*. Nolan, like Miller, used the opportunity to ap-proach the Dark Knight from a practical, realist angle, ask-ing how a billionaire orphan might plausibly don a batty outfit and beat up crooks. Nolan used his first film, *Batman Begins*, which was heavily inspired by *Year One*, to show us how Bruce Wayne assembles his costume piece by piece while at the same time inventing his playboy act and suffer-ing injuries, which are tended to by Alfred. The film imports whole scenes from Miller and Mazzucchelli's comic, like the one where Batman escapes a SWAT team by summoning a flock of bats, as well as the ending, in which Gordon tells

Batman about the appearance of the Joker, who's announced his presence by means of an old-fashioned playing card. Nolan's Gotham is also a modern U.S. city, devoid of the Gothic and Art Deco elements that Burton overexaggerated, as well as the garish neon and chrome additions that Schumacher installed.

To accomplish this, Nolan took a page from the New Hollywood, shooting on location. In *Batman Begins*, Bruce Wayne scales mountains and ice fields in his journey to find Ra's al Ghul. The sequel, *The Dark Knight*, is even more brazen, opening with a striking helicopter shot set at midday in downtown Gotham. The impact is immediate and visceral. In lieu of the overt artifice of *Batman Returns* or *Batman & Robin*, we're given the look of reality itself, which is big and complex, too big and complex to ever have been faked. This Gotham City exists in our landscape. We could travel there if we wanted to, the way Bruce Wayne goes to Ladakh, Hong Kong, and, eventually, Alfred's favorite café, a pretty bistro by the Arno, in Florence. And while Nolan used soundstages for locations like the Batcave, just like George Lucas before him, he took care to make them look convincingly real. For once, the Batcave resembles an actual cave, jagged and angular and flooded. Watching the film, one can't tell that it isn't a real location.

But Nolan did more than just adapt Frank Miller. Without doubt, his trilogy is best remembered for its redesign of the Joker, whom Heath Ledger portrayed less as a "clown prince of crime," and more as a deranged madman who does things like ram pencils through people's heads and hang amateur vigilantes from rooftops. The character, re-conceived as a vagrant, physically embodied griminess and grittiness. The costume designer Lindy Hemming claimed that the goal was to make a "scruffier, grungier" version of the Joker whose appearance and demeanor was rooted in real-world performers like Johnny Rotten. The result can almost be seen to reek. His hair is matted and stringy, and he rarely changes his clothes, let alone showers. He also wears makeup, which always looks as if it's coming off, as op-posed to his skin having been bleached white during a mis-hap at Ace Chemicals. And while the movie only hints at the Joker's past, we're given the sense that he, like Wayne, is the victim of some horrible trauma. Supposedly, Ledger prepared for the role by living alone in a London hotel room for a month and keeping a diary while in character. The result was a far more plausible creation than Nicholson's take, or Cesar Romero's portrayal on the TV show, where he famously refused to shave his mustache for the role, simply slathering greasepaint over it.

Nolan extended this practical approach to other mem-bers of Batman's rogues' gallery, revamping them to be more plausible both physically and psychologically. Ra's al Ghul is immortal more in concept than in fact, being the latest leader of the League of Shadows. The Scarecrow, Dr. Crane, mostly wears a business suit, and when he does don his terrifying mask, it's to enhance the effects of his fear toxin. Anne Hathaway's Catwoman is never referred to by that name, and she doesn't go slinking about in the cat-suit made so famous by Julie Newmar, Lee Meriwether, and Eartha Kitt; nor does she speak in *purr*-fect puns. Bane isn't a supersoldier empowered by an experimental serum, and while he struts around acting the part of a socialist revolutionary, in fact he's the servant of Talia al Ghul, who inherits what remains of the League of Shadows from her father. None of these foes are sneering, mustache-twirling villains, but human beings, with understandable and sometimes even sympathetic motivations. They're neither flamboyant nor self-conscious, and they don't turn up in Gotham just because Batman needs people to fight—or, at least, that's not the impression we get. Nolan instead downplays the formula, making the characters seem a part of a larger *history*, players on a world stage that includes recognizable forces like terrorism and economic downturns.

In which regard, Batman's no different from his foes. Being a businessman, the CEO of Wayne Enterprises, he exists in a web of global capital, contracting with the U.S. military and other corporations. He also has flaws, being more akin to 1970s antiheroes than to his squeaky-clean counterpart on the 1960s TV show. He and Commissioner Gordon conspire to conceal the crimes committed by Harvey Dent, as well as the details of that district attorney's death. And despite his armor and weapons, he falters and fails, suffering grievous injuries. In order to wage his war on crime, he must enlist the help of others, forging alliances not only with Jim Gordon and Alfred and Dent, but Lucius Fox, Rachel Dawes, and eventually the young police officer John Blake. Their struggle turns out to be not just a matter of punching and kicking crooks, but remaking Gotham City, which they win back, city block by city block, from the mafia, corrupt city officials, mercenaries, warlords, and shadowy cabals. Each victory gives rise to new threats, as when the Joker rushes in to fill the power vacuum created by the weakening of the mob. As Jim Gordon puts it at the end of *Batman Begins*, "We start carrying semi-automatics, they buy automatics. We start wearing Kevlar, they buy armor-piercing rounds." By this logic, Batman's appearance, his dressing up like a giant bat to inspire fear, drives his foes to adopt their own theatrical appearances and terrorist techniques. In the end, in a last-ditch effort to save the day (at least for now), Batman fakes his death and donates his mansion to Gotham as an orphanage, and passes the mantle of the Dark Knight on to Blake, who's revealed in the film's final moments to be a stripped-down, practical version of Robin. Having been produced by history, Batman, Bruce Wayne, enshrines himself in history, even legend.

NOT UNLIKE *STAR WARS* in 1977, Nolan's *Dark Knight* trilogy took the culture by surprise. Even in 2005, twenty years after Frank Miller, most people still thought of superheroes as pulp intended for children. (Schumacher's two Batman films didn't help.) In particular, *The Dark Knight*'s release in 2008 opened many an eye to just how grown-up comic book superheroes could be.

But Nolan's work is hardly unique in its commitment to adult themes or to realism. As geek's gone mainstream, and as artists have wriggled free of the Comics Code Authority, which officially came to an end in 2011, geeky readers of comic books have been demanding characters that are less like abstract archetypes and more like regular folks who are leading regular lives, lives that seem to extend beyond the funny pages, or the beginning and end of the TV show or movie. Over the past thirty years, superheroes have become less iconic and less idealized, no longer running around in brightly colored outfits made from magical substances like "unstable molecules," but sporting more practical costumes that, like Batman, they tend to assemble from the materials around them. They also screw up, bleed, and scar. The Marvel Cinematic Universe sees its characters struggling to control their weapons and powers, and nearly every member of the Avengers suffers from trauma, whether it's Tony Stark's PTSD in *Iron Man 3*, caused by the events in *The Avengers*, or Black Widow's being haunted by her conditioning as an assassin, which was made a plot point in *Avengers: Age of Ultron*.

The geeky penchant for realism has been steadily transforming superheroes, no matter how cartoonish they once may have been. Rocket Raccoon was created in 1976 as something of a joke, being a walking, talking raccoon named after a silly Beatles song. As Sean T. Collins noted in the pages of *Rolling Stone*, "Rocket was a punchline, putting in brief comic-relief cameos in titles like *Incredible Hulk* and *She-Hulk*; he appeared in 10 comics *total* over 30 years." But since 2006, he's been reimagined as something else, something much geekier. In making *The Guardians of the Galaxy*, the director James Gunn went to great lengths to refashion the critter, who's no longer called Rocket Raccoon but simply Rocket. Indeed, when Star-Lord says that Rocket looks like a raccoon, the creature doesn't know what he's talking about, asserting, "Ain't no thing like me, except *me!*" Later, in a touching scene at a bar, a drunken Rocket lets his gruff demeanor slip, revealing how he's the product of scientific experimentation that ripped him apart and reassembled him in his current bionic form, becoming in the process a tragic creation that James Gunn describes as "a real, little, somewhat mangled beast that's alone." That last detail echoes Dirty Harry, while other elements embellish Rocket's past and mortality, like when the Nova Corps read his rap sheet, and when Rocket bemoans his short life expectancy. Adding further plausibility is the fact that Rocket's performance was modeled on Bradley Cooper's voice and facial expressions, while James Gunn's brother Sean stood in for Rocket on set. We are meant to believe that Rocket inhabits the same space as the other characters, and is subject to the same laws of physics, despite his being made of pixels, not flesh and blood and bionic bits. The CGI comprising him is finely textured and delicately shaded to appear three-dimensional, lit by the same light sources as his human costars, unlike the Toons in *Who Framed Roger Rabbit*, who always appear two-dimensional and lit up from within. All in all, Rocket is meant to appear as substantial and as present as any human in the film. It wouldn't do for him to look like Roger Rabbit, or like Bert Lahr's Cowardly Lion, a man in face paint and a lion suit. As James Gunn put it, "It's really, really important to me that Rocket . . . is not a cartoon character, it's not Bugs Bunny in the middle of *The Avengers*."

IN BEING A DESCENDANT of Miller's Batman, Rocket is certainly no Bugs Bunny. But he's also a descendant of Mickey Mouse, whom Walt Disney, an early geek, portrayed not as a fictional character but as a being that really exists, capable of appearing in a variety of roles, and working a variety of jobs, wearing different costumes. Mickey's a steamboat captain in *Steamboat Willie*, a sorcerer's apprentice in *Fantasia*, and an assistant to a mad scientist in *Runaway Brain*. At Disneyland and Disney World, the person playing him is always in costume and in character. The illusion must be complete.

Other puppeteers and animators have followed Disney's example. Paul Fusco, the man behind the popular 1980s character ALF, went to great lengths to disguise the fact that his creation was a puppet, insisting the creature really was an Alien Life Form. ALF appeared not only on his own TV show, but on *Matlock*, the 1998 Emmys, and a roast for Bob Hope, and as a guest host for Johnny Carson. Similarly, Jim Henson's Muppets (now owned by Disney) are never presented as marionette-puppets, but as real living beings. Watching *The Muppet Show*, we see not only their nightly vaudeville revue but its production, peeking behind the scenes as everything goes wrong and Kermit the Frog valiantly struggles to maintain control. Not one to let ALF get the better of him, Kermit has guest-hosted for Larry King (on his April Fool's Day programs in 1994 and 2002), and appeared with Pepé the King Prawn and later Miss Piggy on two episodes of the *Empire Podcast*. After making *The Muppets*, Jason Segel described the precautions taken to prevent children from seeing the Muppets in their cupboards, in order to not "spoil the illusion." Segel then added that "even as an adult" to see the Muppets lying motionless "breaks your heart a little." His costar Amy Adams agreed: "To see them when they're not animated was really upsetting." And while the Muppets may be immortal, and immune to the ravages of aging, time still passes for them at the same rate it does for us. The recent movie *The Muppets* accounts for the dozen years since *Muppets from Space*, inventing a fictional backstory in which the gang disbanded to pursue their individual interests. Fozzie became a stand-up comedian in Reno, while Miss Piggy edited *Vogue* in Paris. Whenever the artwork ends, the Muppets keep living their lives, failing and succeeding on their own merits. Along the same lines, the recent prime-time *Muppets* TV show was sold as a "documentary-style" program exploring "the Muppets' personal lives and relationships, both at home and at work, as well as romances, break-ups, achievements, disappointments, wants and desires." The pilot episode revolves around the fact that Kermit and Miss Piggy have broken up, with Kermit finding solace in the arms of another pig.

Star Wars, too, has dabbled in this sort of realism. George Lucas reportedly annoyed the actors Anthony Daniels and Kenny Baker by forgetting that C-3PO and R2-D2 weren't real, repeatedly leaving them stuck inside their costumes.

Later, Lucasfilm made an Artoo mockumentary, *Beneath the Dome*, a series of interviews and altered archival footage that relates how the astromech droid rebelled against his conservative British upbringing, becoming an experimental dancer in late 1960s Swinging London. The little robot then supposedly traveled to Hollywood, where he dated Candy Clark and considered playing Michael Corleone in Francis Ford Coppola's adaptation of *The Godfather*. As the story goes, that's where Lucas met the droid, leading to the "actor's" casting in *Star Wars*.

I want to believe. The first film I saw, when I was a toddler, was *The Muppet Movie*, and it thoroughly bewitched me. Even today, I find it impossible to fully comprehend that the Muppets aren't really alive, that Kermit isn't right now running around in some old theater, waving his arms above his head, leading his troupe in a rehearsal of their show. The alternative is too painful to contemplate. Jim Henson worked his magic well, and the spell that he cast, like all good spells, is ever subtle, containing layers we've yet to unravel, layers perhaps beyond even Henson's own realization. The potent enchantment that is realism, once set in motion, is not easily checked, but continues radiating outward, captivating us, beguiling us, dissolving any and all signs of artifice that it encounters.

five

HISTORICAL DOCUMENTS

Reality itself, however, makes its own demands. Jim Henson passed away suddenly on May 16, 1990, of complications from a bacterial infection. Six months later, CBS aired a one-hour special dedicated to the man, entitled *The Muppets Celebrate Jim Henson*. It sees the Muppets not only planning a tribute to their creator, but trying to figure out who "this Jim Henson fellow" was. Kermit's nephew Robin remembers that Henson was always hanging around, down under the floorboards, having a great time. Neither he nor his companions seems to have any idea what a puppeteer is, let alone a puppet. Though they can see people underneath them, people who move whenever they move, they find this more curious than anything, and decide not to dwell on this fact. "Let's stop looking at them, even," Fozzie Bear says. "It's too weird." Later on in the program, Rizzo the Rat claims to have uncovered the truth of the matter, after happening upon one of Gonzo's old paychecks while nosing around in the back office. ("I always forget to cash those things," Gonzo admits. "We artists and madmen are like that.") "But just look who signed it," Rizzo tells him. Gonzo squints: "Jim Henson! But that must mean he was—" "An accountant!" Rizzo cries. Only toward the end of the show do the Muppets realize, after reading letters sent in by mournful fans, that Jim Henson has died. Gonzo gasps: "We were just starting to get to know him!"

This tribute special is tender and touching. I well remember being moved to tears upon its initial broadcast, and even now the thought of it causes me to choke up. The show's power stems from its commitment to realism, from how thoroughly it creates the illusion that the Muppets are more than the product of their creator. Despite the sad fact of Henson's passing, his Muppets are still there on the TV, discussing the man, who is made to seem less like a distant god, living on high, outside the artwork, and more like a person who dwelled in the same reality as them. Or, rather, the Muppets are made to seem to exist in the same reality as Henson, and therefore us. Saddened by the discovery of Henson's passing, Fozzie Bear breaks into song, then is slowly joined by his fellow Muppets, as well as characters from *Sesame Street* and *Fraggle Rock*. As the number swells, Kermit enters silently and observes. When they finish, he congratulates his companions: "What a good song. I knew you guys could do the tribute for Jim." His froggy voice sounds slightly different, but it's still Kermit, recognizably thoughtful and awkward and lovable. Henson's passing, as it turned out, wasn't also Kermit's demise, or the death of any of the Muppets. Instead, Kermit promises the viewers, "We'll be seeing you soon with more Muppet stuff, because that's the way the boss would want it." The credits roll, and we're left feeling reaffirmed that these creatures are moving about of their own volition, alive and independent.

This is the logic of realism, which conceals signs of the artwork's artifice, evidence of the artwork's creator's hand. By this logic, if the artwork isn't artifice, then there isn't any artist. No real-life person can be found behind a curtain, pulling the strings. There isn't a curtain; there aren't any strings. No one is making the characters say the things they say, or do what they do; no one is making the whole thing up with paint on a canvas, or words on a page, or actors and pixels committed to video or film. The artwork isn't manufactured, but life, authentic and unfeigned. Why, just look at it! It has the look of life itself, the look of truth.

Geeks like this approach because it makes fantasy look

real. Their commitment to realism leads them to oppose any sign of artifice, any evidence of fakery that takes them out of the artwork, any clue that reminds them the artwork *is* an artwork. (They don't want the artwork getting in the way of their enjoyment.) To this end, they want fantastical art with not only the look of life, but the look of *history*, because history has no author, being instead the product of competing desires and ideologies. For example, because Tony Stark invented Ultron (trying to do good), his fellow Avengers were forced to battle that runaway robot in Sokovia, destroying that country's capital city in the process. And because that tragedy occurred, the UN drafted the Sokovia Accords, a plan to regulate Earth's Mightiest Heroes, a plan that Tony Stark, freshly humbled by his failure, agreed to honor. But Steve Rogers, Captain America, still recovering from his discovery that the fascist Hydra had infiltrated S.H.I.E.L.D., refused to submit to the UN plan. The conflict between him and Stark escalated, dividing the Avengers down the middle, a schism that culminated in a massive fight at an airport in Germany . . . This is a story intended to look less like a story, less like a narrative fashioned by an author, or different authors, and more like history, events on a planet that looks like Earth but isn't *quite*, where events are unfolding in real time, unscripted and uncontrived, driven by the characters themselves, who exist amidst larger social forces.

Which is to say that in pursuing their game of make-believe, geeks wind up behaving like the aliens in the movie *Galaxy Quest*, Thermians from the Klaatu Nebula, who have no concept of fiction, and who therefore mistake Earth television broadcasts for reality—for "historical documents." (When someone complains that the Thermians can't honestly believe that *Gilligan's Island* really happened, the aliens hang their heads and moan, "Those poor people . . .") Naïve and trusting, the Thermians have fallen in love with a chintzy early-1980s science fiction TV series, *Galaxy Quest*, which is clearly meant to remind us viewers of 1960s *Star Trek*. The Thermians have become the ultimate fans of *Galaxy Quest*, modeling their entire culture on it. One of the Thermians, Quellek, tells Alan Rickman's character, Alexander Dane (an obvious stand-in for Leonard Nimoy), "I have lived my life by your philosophy, by the code of the Mak'tar." This declaration horrifies the classically trained Dane. Just like Nimoy, who once declared he wasn't Spock, Dane has spent the years since *Galaxy Quest*'s cancellation trying to distance himself from the role of "Dr. Lazarus of Tev'Meck." (He grits his teeth whenever fans compel him to recite his famous catchphrase, "By Grabthar's hammer, by the suns of Worvan, you shall be avenged!") But Dr. Lazarus's fictional history has become poor Quellek's *actual* history, to the point that Thermian can use the "Mak'tar stealth haze" to evade capture. The Thermians have even learned from watching *Galaxy Quest* that they can document their own lives, and while we never see the documents they make, we can imagine that their texts resemble the dozens of fan-made *Star Trek* series now available on YouTube.

Or maybe they look more like *Rogue One: A Star Wars Story*? Working to publicize his film, the director Gareth

Edwards described how making *Rogue One* was more than a job for him, and instead the means of realizing his lifelong dream of actually visiting that galaxy long ago and far, far away. In making the film, he constructed a "360 degree" set at Pinewood Studios so that he and the actors and crew could film in what Edwards called a documentary manner. As he explained, he wanted everyone—himself, the crew, his actors, the viewers—to be able to fantasize "that this is a real historical event and George [Lucas] is on Tatooine with his camera crew, we're on our planets with our camera crew, and there's filmmakers on other planets with their camera crews." Edwards's promise to his viewers is that, instead of inventing a fiction, he is documenting truth.

That interview implies that Edwards is doing something novel, but George Lucas himself originally described the look of *Star Wars* as having the "strange graphics of fantasy combined with the feel of a documentary." Ever since, all geeks have shared this ambition. An *Empire* magazine article on Peter Jackson's second *Hobbit* movie, *The Desolation of Smaug*, promises readers firsthand access to the man's "approach to world-building," then extols the detail in the Lake-town set: "The specifics, right down to the nails, are stunning. A chess game lies idle on a nearby table . . . Jackson likes to imagine that he and his team have just landed in Middle-earth with their cameras and coffee trolleys and begun shooting." This fantasy permeates geek culture. In making his TV show *Firefly*, Joss Whedon constructed a life-size practical set of the series' spaceship, *Serenity*, which he showed off the first chance he got. In the pilot episode, the ship's captain, Malcolm "Mal" Reynolds, climbs up a ladder, moving from one deck to another. The camera travels before him, passing through a hole and recording his movement in one unbroken take. The shot is a promise: there's no trickery on display! The ship is real; Joss Whedon built it, just as George Lucas had engineers build the *Millennium Falcon*, and just as the Thermians, gaga for *Galaxy Quest*, built their own life-size version of the *Protector* (only their ship actually worked!). Later on, in the feature-length film sequel to *Firefly*, entitled *Serenity*, Whedon outdoes his earlier shot, again right at the beginning, presenting an intricate unbroken take that carries us through the entire ship, reintroducing us to the spacecraft's different sections, as well as to the people living aboard it. In fact, the two go hand in hand, since the characters have decorated their respective parts of the ship according to their personalities. Whedon describes his approach to the franchise as (you guessed it) "documentary," utilizing handheld camera work with loose framing and imprecise focus, an approach that extended to even the show's computer-generated shots of spaceships in flight, which were also made to look handheld, complete with blurs and sudden zooms.

Giving fantasies the look of history means creating the impression that they can be documented from dozens of different angles, which results not only in fiction pretending to be nonfiction, but in fictional nonfiction: faux encyclopedias and technical manuals, such as *The Star Trek Encyclopedia*, a reference volume first published in 1994, in which the TV show's designers not only documented all the alien planets and species that they'd invented, but reproduced engineering schematics of their starships and other devices. Paging through it, one discovers where Captain Picard's quarters are aboard the *Enterprise*, as well as everyone else's quarters, as well as how the Turbolift runs throughout the ship. This encyclopedia, which went through multiple editions, was eventually eclipsed by *Memory Alpha*, a wiki devoted to all things *Star Trek*. Other websites archive blueprints for all known Federation vessels, space stations, and weapons—even scans of faux documents, such as a "Star Fleet Medical Reference Manual" and a "U.S.S. *Enterprise* Officer's Manual." And while geeks are fond of describing how *Star Wars* differs from *Star Trek*—the former is science *fantasy*, as opposed to science *fiction*—LucasBooks has published its own books of this ilk, such as "Owner's Technical Manuals" for the *Millennium Falcon* and the Empire's monstrous Death Star, aka the "*Imperial DS-1 Orbital Battle Station*." Pick any modern-day geek franchise, and odds are someone has made, officially or unofficially (or both), technical schematics of its otherworldly vehicles, headquarters, tools, weapons, robots, and so on and so forth, each successive volume contributing more to the impression that these fictions are real, their wonderful gadgets and gizmos as solid and substantial as any trinkets or tools on Earth.

Also made to seem real are the lands that these wonders inhabit, the worlds themselves, which means they, too, can be documented—can be mapped. Indeed, it's unthinkable that one could publish a work of high fantasy today without including a map up front, a tradition undoubtedly popularized by Tolkien, who included a map of Middle-earth at the start of each volume of *The Hobbit* and *Lord of the Rings*. George R. R. Martin's *A Song of Ice and Fire* novels feature maps of Westeros, and each episode of the HBO adaptation, *Game of Thrones*, opens by taking its viewers on a 3-D tour of that fabulous continent, soaring over a mechanical map that brings each kingdom to life via whirling clockwork mechanisms that raise castles and other buildings. (The opening changes over the seasons of the show, reflecting shifts in power and other reversals of fortune.) For those who care to scrutinize the blood-soaked continent more closely, Random House has published *The Lands of Ice and Fire*, a collection of maps illustrated by Jonathan Roberts, an artist who specializes in fantastical cartography, and who produced the book from illustrations made by Martin himself.

J. K. ROWLING, MEANWHILE, has employed other means to give *Harry Potter* the look of history. In 2001, she fleshed out her series' Wizarding World with two supplemental volumes. The first, *Fantastic Beasts and Where to Find Them*, is a fake textbook supposedly written by the "magizoologist" Newt Scamander, with a foreword by the Hogwarts' headmaster, Albus Dumbledore. The textbook purports to be Harry's own copy, containing marginalia by him and Ron and Hermione. (Since then, the book has been adapted into a film series of its own, starring Eddie Redmayne as Scamander.) The second book, *Quidditch Through the Ages*, is supposedly written by one Kennilworthy Whisp, who recounts the rules and history of that fabulous high-flying game. This time the book is made to look as though it's been checked out from the library at Hogwarts. More recently, Rowling has used her Pottermore website to pen fictional articles for the *Daily Prophet* about the Wizarding World, such as reports from the 2014 Quidditch World Cup, written from the point of view of Harry Potter's love interest and eventual wife, Ginny.

This type of realism, the "found manuscript" approach, is a staple of geek culture, but it's hardly a new invention. Four hundred years ago, Miguel de Cervantes claimed he didn't write *Don Quixote* but rather assembled it from chapters that he found in the Archive of La Mancha plus a manuscript by the Moor Cide Hamete Benengeli, who had translated it into Spanish from the Arabic. Centuries later, Sir Arthur Conan Doyle told most of his Sherlock Holmes adventures from the perspective of Dr. John Watson, who didn't always get everything right, since he lacked Holmes's superhuman talent of perception, and wrote each story only after the fact, working from notes. Holmes sometimes scolded Watson for taking significant liberties with the facts. *The Sign of the Four* opens with the great detective claiming that the man's account of their previous case, *A Study in Scarlet*, had been needlessly romanticized, "which produces much the same effect as if you worked a love-story or an elopement into the fifth proposition of Euclid." Doyle's contemporary Bram Stoker, meanwhile, built *Dracula* out of fake diary entries, letters, and newspaper clippings, the Victorian equivalent of modern found-footage horror films like *The Blair Witch Project* and *Paranormal Activity*. Stoker even accounts for how those materials made their way into readers' hands: they're assembled during the course of the novel's events by the newlywed Mina Harker, who tells us she taught herself how to type in order to assist her husband, Jonathan. The novel ends with a note by Jonathan in which he despairs that readers, who lack access to the original documents, will never believe "so wild a story." His friend, the learned Dutch doctor turned vampire hunter Abraham Van Helsing, vehemently replies: "We want no proofs; we ask none to believe us!" History speaks for itself.

Sixty years later, the makers of Marvel Comics—Stan Lee, Jack Kirby, and others—maintained they were merely chronicling the adventures of the real-world Spider-Man, Fantastic Four, Incredible Hulk, etc., who really were battling aliens and monsters on the streets of New York City. *Fantastic Four* #10 (January 1963) sees Mr. Fantastic, Reed Richards, receive a phone call from Lee and Kirby, asking him to come over to the Marvel Comics office in order "to work out a plot." Richards muses: "Strange . . . We just finished discussing a new plot yesterday!" As he prepares to go, the Thing (who's lifting weights) tells Richards to give "those two goons" a warning: "Tell 'em if they don't stop makin' me look even uglier than I am, I'm liable to go up there and wrap this two-ton weight around their skinny necks!" Richards doesn't get the chance to deliver that message, however:

upon his showing up at the office, he's knocked unconscious by Doctor Doom. (The phone call, you see, was a trap.) A later issue, #176 (November 1976), revives the joke and carries it further. Stan Lee tries to reach the Fantastic Four, only for the artist George Pérez to report that "their answering service says they're out of town." Jack Kirby suggests that the Marvel crew "just make up some stories about the F.F." Roy Thomas and George Pérez recoil in horror. "What? Make up stories—?" asks Thomas. Pérez finishes the thought: "—instead of just drawing what really happened?" Stan Lee agrees: "Nice try, Jack. But it just isn't done."

This device, which has gone in and out of fashion at Marvel, was recently resurrected by the feature film *Logan*, in which the title character criticizes the younger mutant Laura for being "an X-Men fan." In particular, he's offended by the *Uncanny X-Men* comic books he discovers in her backpack, which depict him, the Wolverine, gallivanting about in the blue-and-yellow spandex costume he wore for years in the comics, but never in any of the films. "You do know they're all bullshit, right?" Logan asks Laura, also calling the magazines "ice cream for bedwetters," the same way the Thing complained to Reed Richards about his appearance, and Sherlock castigated poor Watson.

IN ALL OF these ways as well as many others, geeky fictions pretend to have the look of nonfiction, the look of history. In becoming fans of a franchise, then, geeks become like historians, specialists on a given world, masters of its flora and its fauna, as well as its languages and lineages and customs. They're like a person who keenly follows the current events in, say, Latvia, while others around them are only dimly aware that the country even exists. Those other people could, if they wanted, read about Latvia and its ways; they just prefer not to, choosing to occupy themselves with other pursuits, such as watching sports. (My sincerest apologies to Latvia. I do know that you're between Lithuania and Estonia, and that your capital is Riga.)

Replace Latvia with Latveria, the fictional country that Doctor Doom rules in Marvel Comics, and you have geekdom. Each artwork documents a bit more of the country, providing another delicious peek. Giving it all the appearance of history, of nonfiction, creates the impression the place is real and doesn't disappear whenever the artwork ends, the way that Narnia didn't disappear when the Pevensie children left it, returning to the Professor's house at the conclusion of *The Lion, the Witch and the Wardrobe*, or the same way that Oz didn't vanish when Dorothy made her way back to Kansas, toting Toto. Rather, the country keeps chugging along, existing behind and beyond the artworks that depict it, obeying its own rules, proceeding under its own power.

Being historians, being specialists, geeks feel compelled to keep up on the goings-on in that fictional land over yonder, even if they stop following a franchise. At *io9*, Charlie Jane Anders described how even after she quit watching

Star Trek: Voyager and *Enterprise*, she continued reading about each show. I myself do the same thing with *X-Men*, peeking in from time to time to see how the merry mutants are doing, catching up on their exploits via occasional stray issues and Wikipedia. (I wonder what Wolverine's doing *right now*.)

IN DEALING WITH these pretend historical documents, geeks remain ever vigilant, tirelessly patrolling artworks for any sign of artifice, anything that would violate their suspension of disbelief, and make the fantasy look unreal, reminding them that they're not Thermian, but human. Back in college, my friends and I delighted in Phil Farrand's *Nitpicker's Guides*, a series that scrutinized every episode of *Star Trek*, pointing out logical inconsistencies and continuity errors. (One of my dorm mates often boasted about having contributed a detail to one of the volumes.) Today, that practice survives in products like Mike Stoklasa's "Mr. Plinkett" reviews of the *Star Trek* and *Star Wars* movies, and *Empire* magazine's "spoiler special" podcasts, which give big blockbuster movies a thorough working over, zeroing in on plot holes and other contrivances. Discussing *The Dark Knight Rises*, the *Empire Podcast* team wondered: How did Bruce Wayne manage to make his way into Gotham after escaping from the Pit? How did Batman escape the humongous detonation at the end? How does Bane eat? They also pointed out how the opening of the film resembles the start of *Licence to Kill*, a nagging reminder that the movie is a fiction, Christopher Nolan being a tremendous James Bond fan. Those inconsistencies and reminders, the participant Nick de Semlyen confesses, "bring me out of the film a little." In other words, each time the pretense to documentation fails, de Semlyen, just like other geeks, is reminded that standing behind the film is Nolan, not history.

Which won't do. Marx famously said (after Hegel) that history repeats itself, "first as tragedy, then as farce," but geeks would prefer for artworks to not repeat at all. Not wanting one work to remind them of another, they agree with Peter Biskind that genre is something to be transcended, formula being the foe of art. They're therefore quick to note when artworks echo others, as when Nolan nods toward Bond, or as when a villain gets captured on purpose as part of his devious master plan, which happens not only in *The Dark Knight*, but in *The Avengers*, *Skyfall*, and *Star Trek Into Darkness*.

The geek desire to treat fiction like history also explains the community's marked aversion to spoilers. According to movie studios and their marketing teams, revelatory trailers and ads tend to attract filmgoers rather than alienate them, even when they spoil the final acts of films. This is less surprising than it might sound. In a *Film School Rejects* article, Scott Beggs points out several reasons why spoiler-laden trailers are now the norm. Studios are forced to distinguish their products in an overcrowded marketplace, as well as to reach different demographics, including viewers in foreign markets. There's no guarantee that more casual moviegoers will see any given trailer, since it's only the most enfranchised fans who watch every ad.

Geeks are those most enfranchised fans, and, perversely, many geeks are rabidly averse to prematurely finding out any details regarding an upcoming film or TV show's plot. At *io9*, for instance, articles that contain spoilers are heavily signposted as such, slapped with a bright purple band with a crossed-out eye to demarcate that the material below is potentially offensive. The lead designer of the card game *Magic: The Gathering*, Mark Rosewater, espouses a more extreme position, repeatedly stating that he refuses to watch trailers for films he knows he's going to watch, encouraging others to follow his lead. Rosewater's stance reminds me of a sports fan who's taped the big game because she had to go to work, and doesn't want others to tell her anything about it, especially not who won. She wants to go home and watch the tape and pretend she's watching the game live, which of course she can't do if someone accidentally or maliciously reveals the outcome. Part of what makes watching sports fun is not knowing what will happen, or who will win, and being forced to watch the match played out in (sometimes agonizing) real time, as well as being forced to accept whatever happens. (Our favorite team doesn't always win.) Geeks want the same thing from their artworks, at least the first time through: "Captain America is going to battle Iron Man? Gee, I wonder who will win? If you happen to know, don't tell me! I want to see the fight happen live!"

For similar reasons, geeks want their franchises to have "stakes," the sense that anything can happen. In the run-up to the release of *Captain America: Civil War*, several articles argued that the movie would need to kill off one of its many protagonists in order for the franchise to have "real stakes." As it turned out, none of the heroes died, although James Rhodes, War Machine, was seriously injured. Many geeks cried foul, complaining that "the fact that no one of tremendous importance died in *Civil War* speaks to what some fans consider an issue within the Marvel Cinematic Universe"— specifically, that viewers walk in knowing that central characters like Iron Man and Captain America aren't going to die. (They're wearing what geeks like to call "plot armor.") Another article echoed those concerns: "No one of importance dies in *Captain America: Civil War*, and someone should have . . . All the stakes-free punching and kicking has taken some of the juice out of these movies."

Why so much insistence on death? It's not that geeks are a bloodthirsty lot. Rather, they're decrying the appearance of contrivance, and demanding in its stead the look of history. In the real world, people suffer setbacks, reversals of fortune, injuries—and death. Peter Biskind celebrates films like *The French Connection* and *Mean Streets* for not proceeding by the numbers, and for daring to subvert audience expectations by ending unhappily. Geeks feel the same way, which is why they celebrate twists like the execution of Eddard Stark in *Game of Thrones*, and Han Solo's death at the hands of his son, Kylo Ren, in *Star Wars: The Force Awakens*. Anything less reminds them that the fiction is a fiction, being implausible and too much like superhero comics of yore—"ice cream for bedwetters," as Logan complained, in which the good guys always win, and the heroes all get to go home.

THAT SAID, DESPITE their aspiration to be like the Thermians, geeks don't want *actual* documentation—they don't want to see the actual reality of the artwork, or life itself. But neither does Peter Biskind, even though he might think that he does. Watching *Five Easy Pieces* or *The French Connection*, fans of realism want to see Robert Eroica Dupea and Detective Jimmy "Popeye" Doyle, not Jack Nicholson and Gene Hackman (respectively). Nor do they want to be alerted to the presence of the camera, or the crew members huddled behind it, or to the fact that the film was assembled out of thousands of smaller shots, with a soundtrack laid over that. Instead, they want a seamless whole, regardless of whether the artwork concerns class struggles on the West Coast, or political struggles in Westeros; NYC cops taking down a drug ring, or a wizard enlisting a Hobbit's help in destroying Sauron's One Ring.

What geeks want is (pretend) documentation of the secondary world, the thing being represented, not actual documentation of the people and props and sets that are doing the representing. When Peter Jackson shot and projected *The Hobbit: An Unexpected Journey* at forty-eight frames per second, geeks recoiled. Although Jackson had promised that the result would be more immersive, fans complained that the resulting imagery was precisely the opposite, perversely *too* realistic, laying bare the fact they were watching Ian McKellan and Martin Freeman walking about a set in makeup, not Gandalf and Bilbo Baggins striding Middle-earth. Some compared it to "behind-the-scenes footage" or the dreaded "soap opera effect" produced by HDTV's frame-interpolation, or "motion smoothing," feature. For the same reason, geeks have long rebelled against computer-generated imagery (CGI), which they decry for looking insubstantial and unreal, as opposed to practical special effects, which have a more convincing weight and solidity to them. To that end, they tend to rally around any movie that uses (or claims that it uses) practical effects. See, for instance, Katharine Trendacosta's *io9* article "The Model Spaceships That Made *Interstellar* Look as Real as Possible," which celebrates Nolan's insistence on using physical models that could be lit the same way that the sets and the actors were; see also Damon Lavrinc's *Jalopnik* post, "How the Man Behind the Machines of *Mad Max* Put a Hellscape on Wheels," which extols the fact that the vehicles in *Fury Road* are "functional, because the desert doesn't suffer mechanical fools lightly and CGI is bullshit." All in all, all geeks agree with the actor Oscar Isaac's statement, made while promoting *Star Wars: The Force Awakens*, that movies featuring actual puppets and sets have a "more ageless" quality to them, as opposed to those that rely "on the latest technology," which causes them to "date badly." (Here Isaac was clearly alluding to George Lucas's *Star Wars* prequel trilogy.) Appearing dated is, unsurprisingly, another cardinal sin for geeks, who now find the hairstyles in the original *Star Wars* distracting, since they make *Star Wars* look more like a movie shot on Earth in the 1970s (which it really is), and less like a fantastical adventure taking place a long time ago in a galaxy far, far away (which it really isn't).

Hence also my distress, when watching the first *X-Men* film, to see my beloved mutants wearing matching black leather outfits, rather than the colorful costumes they wore in the comic books, and careening about the screen in the wire-fu fashion made so popular by *The Matrix*. Not only was it a change, it was a sign of *X-Men* latching on to a trend. Similarly, when watching the sequel, *X2*, I couldn't help but note the emphasis placed on Xavier's School for Gifted Youngsters, an august campus with dozens of children running about, which seemed a concession to the success of *Harry Potter*. *X2* even prominently features a dark-haired young student with large rounded spectacles, although he lacks a lightning-bolt scar. What bothered me in both instances was how reality was imposing itself upon the secondary world, revealing that, rather than being internally coherent and consistent, the movies were susceptible to dominant commercial trends and other market forces.

Changes like these, even if they're practical, violate the look of history. When making *Spider-Man* in the early 2000s, Sam Raimi changed the character slightly, granting Peter Parker the power to spin webs from his wrists—so-called "organic web-shooters"—rather than having to rely on mechanical gadgets of his own invention, as he'd always done in the comics. Geeks lamented the decision, but not because it didn't make sense. They weren't opposed, per se, to Raimi's desire, like Frank Miller, to make Spidey more practical, sacrificing a smidgen of spectacle for plausibility's sake. But any change, no matter how minor, lays bare the artifice at the bottom of it all, the fact that in art, every decision is ultimately arbitrary. Why do spiders spin webs? Because they've evolved to; they don't have any choice in the matter. But why does Spider-Man have mechanical web-shooters instead of organic ones? Ah, because people—Stan Lee, Steve Ditko, others—made it all up out of whole cloth at the start of the 1960s.

In bringing *Galaxy Quest* to life, the Thermians preserved each aspect of the show, no matter how practical or impractical it was. Thus, Tommy Webber, the former child star who played the *Protector*'s pilot Lieutenant Laredo, finds he can navigate the new ship, since the Thermians based its operation on his hand movements back in the day, which were never random, but systematic. Confronted by a real set of controls, he recalls, "I remember I had it all worked out." Later, the ship's "digitizer" (its version of *Star Trek*'s transporter) similarly turns out to have been modeled on the performance of Fred Kwan. If anything, the Thermians are faithful to a fault. When stars Brian Nesmith and Gwen DeMarco are faced with a corridor filled with crashing metal devices, "the chompers," DeMarco momentarily breaks down, unable to comprehend why such a passageway would ever exist: "I mean, there's no useful purpose for there to be a bunch of chompy-crushy things in the middle of a hallway! . . . It makes no logical sense! Why is it here?" Nesmith responds, " 'Cause it's on the television show!"

The Protector was the Thermians' unabashed love letter to their idols, just as *Galaxy Quest* is an unabashed love letter to *Star Trek* and its fans. Trekkers in turn have come to embrace *Galaxy Quest* as a genuine *Star Trek* film. Patrick Stewart, Jonathan Frakes, Wil Wheaton, William Shatner, and George Takei have all professed their admiration for the movie, and attendees of the 2013 Creation *Star Trek* convention in Las Vegas voted it the seventh-best *Star Trek* film of all time. J. J. Abrams went even further, calling it one of the best *Star Trek* movies ever made.

But what's less obvious about *Galaxy Quest* is that it's also a film about *Star Wars*—or, more specifically, that it's a film about *Star Wars*' impact on *Star Trek*. The miracle wrought by the Thermians is the same one that George Lucas wrought as he labored to reinvent *Flash Gordon*, transforming a cheap and cheesy serial into a film with the look of reality itself—a historical document. Ever since then, all geeks have been Thermians, yearning not just for realist artworks but for the chance to step inside them and travel down their nooks and crannies, exploring regions only hinted at on-screen. As we've seen, realism provides the illusion that the artwork extends beyond the artwork's borders. In wanting to not only believe in that illusion but to enter it, live inside it, geeks keep pushing on those artificial boundaries, eager to travel beyond the limits of the frame.

six.

THE GREAT
GEEK GAME

O f all the wondrous devices aboard the Starship *Enterprise*, the most marvelous is the Holodeck, introduced in *Star Trek: The Next Generation*, a virtual-reality room that can be programmed to simulate any environment, from Paris to Victorian London to even fictional locations like the noirish office of the private investigator Dixon Hill. The Holodeck was just a room (actually, multiple rooms, on multiple decks—there were more than one), but in order for it to work, a user had to be able to touch the people and items that it contained, as well as to be able to walk in any direction without hitting one of the walls. To that end, the Holodeck employed technologies like "shaped forcefields" and "substrate treadmills," which created the impression that users were interacting with and moving through the simulated environment—or at least, that's what it says in my copy of *Star Trek: The Next Generation: Technical Manual*. Holodeck programs were just illusions, but to the people aboard the *Enterprise*, they seemed real, so much so that one episode of *TNG* dealt with Holodeck addiction.

In order to please geeks, artworks must function like Holodecks, creating the impression of a secondary world without any boundaries. Realism gnaws at apparent limits, making it look as though the fictional world extends beyond the borders of the artwork, endless both in time and space. Of course the artwork, like the Holodeck, *does* have limits; movies and novels have beginnings, middles, and ends, and don't let the audience choose where to look or where to go next. Geeks won't have that. *Star Wars* may have begun as a single movie recounting the adventure of a handful of plucky characters, but in the forty years since, it's become something else, a franchise and a universe unto itself, a historical account rapidly expanding into the past and into the future, as well as "horizontally," as artworks fill in further details about different moments. Of course, Lucas's original film encouraged this. He had the notion from the get-go of making a saga, carving the original flick from the middle of his lengthy initial draft because it seemed the most self-contained section. The resulting film's beginning in the middle of things, combined with its powerful realist approach, suggested that there was plenty more story both before and after, something Lucas confirmed when he released *The Empire Strikes Back* in 1980, supertitling it "Episode V," then renaming the first *Star Wars* "Episode IV: A New Hope" upon its rerelease in theaters in 1981.

However, back in 1987, George Lucas was walking away from *Star Wars*, putting the franchise on hiatus—he was switching the Holodeck off. But the geeks had other plans. That same year, West End Games secured the license to make a *Star Wars* role-playing game (RPG) in the spirit of *Dungeons & Dragons*. That game, first published in 1974, inspired a tabletop gaming fad that lasted until the late 1980s; recall how Elliott and his siblings and their friends are playing *D&D* at the start of *E.T. the Extra-Terrestrial.* West End, which specialized in military strategy games, decided to compete with *D&D* by making RPGs based on popular properties. (Their first one was based on *Ghostbusters.*) But in order for a *Star Wars* RPG to work, it needed to provide players with the sense that they were traversing that trilogy's landscapes, capable of traveling in any direction, all the while interacting with the inhabitants of Mos Eisley and the Death Star. To that end, West End had to create names and backstories for all the characters that players would encounter, as well as devise rules for how things like X-Wings and lightsabers worked.

In doing so, West End Games pushed *Star Wars*' boundaries farther out. As the company's then editor Bill Slavicsek recounted in 2012, "Suddenly Hammer Head was an Ithorian, Bib Fortuna was a Twi'lek, and Greedo was a Rodian." This information and much, much more went into *The Star Wars Sourcebook*, a "tome full of back story and world material" that wound up winning an Origins Award, the highest honor in gaming. *Star Wars: The Roleplaying Game* also sold well, resulting in hundreds of supplementary products and reprints that lasted through 1999.

The game's success undoubtedly caught George Lucas's attention, especially since other *Star Wars* revenue was in the process of drying up. Here was something other than a pop culture phenomenon, or children demanding the latest fad: here was a group of people eager not just to rewatch the movies that he'd made but to pretend they were living inside the *Star Wars* universe itself. They wanted more story, more characters, more settings, more strange inventions. Lucas had known of course that such people existed; he was a geek himself, and he'd advertised *Star Wars* at sci-fi conventions in the lead-up to its release. And geeks had been quick to embrace the film, seeing it dozens of times, publishing zines full of fan art and fan fiction about their favorite characters, and purchasing tons of *Star Wars* merchandise. But in the 1970s and '80s, such fans were still underground, a grassroots phenomenon, and Lucas hadn't been able to figure out how to manufacture products that specifically targeted them.

To be fair, no one had, not yet. During the 1980s, however, *Star Trek*, itself reinvigorated by *Star Wars*, suggested a possible path forward. In 1979, Paramount, which owned *Star Trek*, ended its licensing arrangement for that franchise with Bantam Books, awarding it to Pocket Books instead. (Paramount owned Pocket Books, and decided to pay itself.) Whereas Bantam had published *Star Trek* novels irregularly, Pocket ramped up production, publishing six books per year and effectively commercializing fan fiction. Instead of reading unofficial stories in underground zines, geeks could now enjoy a steady supply of the further adventures of Kirk, Spock, McCoy, and the rest of the *Enterprise* crew. When *The Next Generation* premiered in 1987, Pocket made novels for that show, too. (I read them all when I was younger.)

In 1989, Bantam Books, which was presumably looking to replace the lost *Star Trek* license, approached George Lucas with an offer to create a line of *Star Wars* novels. Lucas agreed, suggesting that they start with a sequel trilogy. He'd given up on his plan of ever filming one, preferring to focus on the prequel films. Bantam selected Timothy Zahn to write the sequels, finally giving fans the chance to learn what Luke and Leia and Han did after the Battle of Endor. According to Zahn, he was given mostly free rein in writing *Heir to the Empire* and its two sequels, and he quickly went to work devising a complex tale about a new Imperial Grand Admiral, a blue-skinned alien named Thrawn, and his tactically brilliant scheme to reverse the Empire's defeats and punish the Rebel forces. But while Zahn worked, someone at Lucasfilm sent him West End Games' sourcebooks, telling him he should use them to round out the corners of his adventure. Zahn did as asked, adding elements like Interdictor Cruisers and the dimensions of the two Death Stars. When his novels were published (between 1991 and 1993), they became bestsellers, thereby conveying West End's world-building to an even greater audience both in detail and in spirit. Now everyone, not just hobby gamers, could see that *Star Wars* didn't have to end.

Something new was starting to take shape: the *Star Wars Expanded Universe*, a wealth of additional content for fans who wanted more than just the original movies. Crucially, this new content could be sold in all sorts of ways. In 1994, Bill Slavicsek adapted West End's *Star Wars Sourcebook* into *A Guide to the Star Wars Universe*, a massive reference book that rivaled the *Star Trek* encyclopedias that were starting to go on sale. The guide allowed readers to revel in a bounty of extra details, learning that Greedo was a Rodian, that Bib Fortuna was a Twi'lek, and that Hammer Head was a . . . what was that species again? I understand if you've forgotten, or don't remember who Hammer Head is. That curious alien is on-screen for all of five seconds in *A New Hope*, a background character in the Mos Eisley Cantina, one of many extras intended to help give that seedy watering hole a crowded, otherworldly feel. Blink and you might miss him—although, to be fair, he also shows up in *The Star Wars Holiday Special*, where Bea Arthur pours him a drink from a red plastic pitcher, then pats his bent, elongated head (though geeks might want to forget that encounter). He also got a Kenner toy, released in 1978 and called simply "Hammerhead."

Well, obviously *Star Wars* role-players couldn't call him *that*. So the gamers at West End made up more information about the S-shaped fellow, including his real name and what he was doing before Mos Eisley, all laid out in *Galaxy Guide 1: A New Hope*, a 1989 supplement to the *Star Wars* role-playing game. In 1995, that information appeared in short story form in "The Sand Tender: The Hammerhead's Tale," one of sixteen pieces included in the Bantam collection *Tales from Mos Eisley Cantina*. Those books recount that Hammerhead is, in fact, an Ithorian named Momaw Nadon, high priest of a place called Tafanda Bay. He wound up on Tatooine, where he tended a secret garden, after being exiled by his people for treason; they thought he'd betrayed them when he handed over sacred agricultural lore to the Galactic Empire, when in fact he was trying to prevent the Imperial fleet from firing on his home planet's jungles. (You'll be relieved to learn that Nadon eventually reunited with his people, reclaimed his role as high priest, married, and fathered a son.)

By the mid-1990s, fans could do more than just rub elbows with Momaw Nadon in the RPG, or read about him. In 1995, Hasbro, which had acquired Kenner, began making new *Star Wars* figures. In 1996, they released an updated version of Hammerhead, who now bore his proper name, Momaw Nadon, and was far more elaborate than his 1970s counterpart, as befits his broadened backstory. Another version followed in 2006, in the *Star Wars* Saga Collection, even more detailed and with accessories like a staff and a pint glass. Yet another figure followed in 2010, this time twelve inches tall, and possessing more than thirty joints (or "points of articulation"), as well as different sets of replaceable hands, so he could more easily hold a variety of items. A promotional YouTube video released by Sideshow Collectibles extends the character's mythology even further, a staff artist observing that while the character comes with a Stormtrooper blaster rifle, "it's almost like he found it, customized it for himself." (The toy cost $110.)

And this is but one exceedingly minor character! For every alien creature in the cantina scene—for every alien, droid, or human in every scene in every *Star Wars* film— there is now some explanation as to who she or he or it is, how they arrived wherever they were, and what they did next. What was once mere background, the illusion necessary for a thrilling realist adventure, has become increasingly realized and increasingly embroidered. Such embroidery leads to new installments and new characters; the fictional world grows ever grander, leading to yet more installments, more characters, more stories and more backstories (as well as more merchandise).

Knowing that geeks like consistency, Lucasfilm developed a method for determining and communicating which elements of the *Expanded Universe* officially counted as *Star Wars*, ranking works according to a five-tiered system called "the Holocron," which ranged from "G-canon," or "Gospel," to "N-canon," or "Non-canonical." The company's onetime in-house continuity editor, Allan Kausch, called his work "a godlike undertaking," his duty being to "keep his finger on everything that came before" even as others kept "creating this universe." This endless expansiveness, paired with a stern eye toward maintaining continuity, has helped make *Star Wars* a pillar of geekdom, inviting its fans to revel in an extensive mythology that extends across a wide variety of products—something to suit everybody's taste. And revel they do. In the 2010 documentary *The People vs. George Lucas*, one fan exults: "The world he [Lucas] created is so much fun to play in!" Another fan, dressed as "Jedi Elvis," echoes that sentiment: "He gave us a huge, enormous sandbox to play in—and here we are, playing."

While endless embellishment characterizes *Star Wars*, it's hardly unique to that franchise, or even to fantasy. Recently there was talk of a *Die Hard* prequel film that would recount John McClane's "origin story," telling what the cop did before he took on Hans Gruber and his band of thieves at Nakatomi Plaza. Critics largely pooh-poohed the idea as unnecessary. Typical was Noah Berlatsky's *Guardian* article "We Don't Need a *Die Hard* Origin Story." Maybe the film will get made, and maybe it won't. But with geeky franchises, prequels and sequels are taken for granted. The Marvel Cinematic Universe could never be a single film, or even a single film series. Already, it's spilled out beyond the boundaries of the movies into various TV shows, such as *Agents of S.H.I.E.L.D.*, starring fan favorite Agent Coulson, as well as other programs on Netflix—*Daredevil, Jessica Jones, Luke Cage*, and *Iron Fist*—that depict what happened in Manhattan after the fight between the Avengers and the alien Chitauri. And still this doesn't suffice, doesn't tell enough of the story, so there are several "One-Shots," short films that further illuminate deeper nooks and crannies of the Marvel-verse. *Item 47* sees a young couple stumble across a Chitauri laser gun unaccounted for after *The Avengers*, which they use to rob banks before being apprehended by Agent Coulson's compatriot Agent Jasper Sitwell, who winds up recruiting them for S.H.I.E.L.D. For his own part, Sitwell appears in another One-Shot, *The Consultant*, as well as in *Thor* and *The Avengers*, before *Captain America: The Winter Soldier* reveals him to be a Hydra double agent. (The Winter Soldier throws him from a speeding car, presumably to his death.) Another short, *All Hail the King*, reveals what happened to the villainous Trevor Slattery after *Iron Man 3*, while another, *Agent Carter*, tells an adventure caper starring Peggy Carter, Captain America's love interest in *Captain America: The First Avenger*. The Peggy Carter short proved so popular with fans that it spawned a short-lived TV show of the same name. And while the One-Shots seem to have ended (for the time being), Marvel is currently planning a half-dozen further TV shows that will feature established characters like the Punisher and the members of the Defenders, as well as heroes yet to be seen on-screen, like the Inhumans, Cloak and Dagger, the New Warriors, and the Runaways.

SO MUCH GEEKY embroidery doesn't always go so smoothly. Sprawling serial narratives offer multiple opportunities for their creators to make mistakes. Sir Arthur Conan Doyle spent forty years, 1887 to 1927, producing the novels and stories starring Sherlock Holmes, a tangle of tales told out of chronological order and featuring numerous inconsistencies. Watson reports in *A Study in Scarlet* that he was injured in the shoulder in Afghanistan, where a "Jezail bullet shattered the bone and grazed the subclavian artery." Later on, though, in *The Sign of the Four*, he tells us that the wound is in his leg, and even later he says, much more vaguely, that the bullet's "in one of my limbs." (No wonder Sherlock scolded his writing.) In reality, Doyle either forgot or didn't care what he'd previously written, or just changed his mind. But to admit that is to admit that the work is fiction, and some fans of Sherlock Holmes were geeks, and wanted an in-world explanation—inner consistency. So they invented the "Great Game," in which they attempted to reconcile all the events of the Sherlock Holmes novels and stories into a coherent whole, a consistent timeline, as well as to rationalize the apparent breaks in logic. Put another way, they tried transforming a body of work produced in piecemeal fashion over forty years into something that looked not like fiction but unvarnished truth—a historical document, a timeline.

Decades later, in the 1960s, Marvel Comics created its own version of the Great Game, known as the No-Prize. This concept developed in the letters column of *Fantastic Four* circa 1963, where the writer and editor Stan Lee often ran contests to reward the company's loyal fans. The contests, however, lacked prizes because (as Lee explained it) "we're cheapskates," and because he wanted to have lots of winners. By *Fantastic Four* #33 (December 1964), the No-Prize had evolved into a reward for readers who could explain how apparent mistakes weren't really mistakes. None other than George R. R. Martin, then a fan all of sixteen years old, wrote in to complain about how *Fantastic Four* #29, despite possessing many exceptional qualities, nonetheless erred by bringing back the villainous Red Ghost without explaining how that evil fellow had escaped his fate back in *FF* #13, when "he was stuck on the moon being chased around by three super-powered apes livid with hatred and waving Mr. Fantastic's paralyzer ray." Lee confessed to "Georgie" that he'd forgotten all about this due to publishing deadlines, then offered "another generous no-prize to the reader who can come up with the best explanation of how he saved himself." Two issues later, Lee awarded that No-Prize to a fan whose letter explained how the Red Ghost must have "raced to the outer edge of the Blue Area, where there is no air, and held his breath while the apes, not knowing the danger, would rapidly lose their breath, thus falling unconscious." Lee praised this "simple, sincere, straightforward answer" (!), then awarded six additional No-Prizes to the other fans who'd written in to offer their own explanations. A few years later, in the summer of 1967, Marvel began making physical No-Prizes, mailing winners empty envelopes upon which was stamped: "Congratulations! This envelope contains a genuine Marvel Comics' No-Prize which you have just won! Handle with care!"

Today, geeks are playing a new Great Game, the Great Geek Game, inventing logic and continuity where none as of yet exists. They call this activity "retconning," short for "retroactive continuity," and through it, they restore the impression that the fictional secondary world exhibits Tolkien's vaunted inner consistency. On the original *Star Trek* series, aired in the mid- to late 1960s, budgetary limitations led to the Klingons being depicted as bronze-skinned humanoids with angled eyebrows (kind of like Spock's) as well as goatees (on the males), and a penchant for green-and-black costumes that wouldn't have looked out of place on the campy *Batman* television show. A decade later, the Klingons who appeared in *Star Trek: The Motion Picture* looked vastly different, with ridged foreheads, prominent fangs, long braided black hair, and samurai-like armor. No longer simple savages, they began evolving into a more sophisticated species, a warrior culture with a complex code of honor.

Which was awesome, but geeks naturally wondered why the 1960s Klingons had looked anomalous—and never mind the fact that it had been due to a smaller budget. They wanted an in-world, historical answer. Eventually the TV show *Deep Space Nine* took a cheeky stab at addressing the inconsistency, in the 1996 episode "Trials and Tribble-ations," a celebration of thirty years of *Trek*. In it, our heroes travel back in time to the events portrayed in the classic *Original Series* episode "The Trouble with Tribbles," where they encounter old-style Klingons. Amusingly, the Deep Space Niners at first don't even recognize those bronze aliens as Klingons. When a waitress alerts them to the error of their ways, they turn to Worf, their Klingon companion, who assures them, "They *are* Klingons." (He takes a lengthy pause.) "And it is a long story." His crewmates, standing in for *Star Trek* fans, wonder whether the change in appearance was caused by "genetic engineering" or "a viral mutation." Worf puts an end to their speculation, curtly responding: "We do *not* discuss it with outsiders!"

Viewing that episode when it aired, I was delighted by the non-answer, which seemed a clever way of saying that no further explanation would be forthcoming. But I was wrong. Nine years later, a pair of episodes of the series *Enterprise*, "Affliction" and "Divergence," addressed the change in a far more plausible fashion. As it turned out, original Klingons—the ones in the 1960s *Star Trek*—were suffering from a virus that resulted when Klingon scientists experimented with crossing humans with Klingons, in a failed supersoldier program. In time, the virus's effects faded, returning Klingons to their wrinkled-brow appearance. (Still, this doesn't explain those chintzy green-and-black costumes . . .)

In this way, geek franchises are constantly expanding, pushing against boundaries both outer and inner—the limits of the Holodeck—even as their creators and fans patrol them, retconning them, playing the Great Geek Game to rein them back in. This push-pull relationship drives the development of geek franchises, creating the illusion of purposeful continuity and consistency, the sense that the whole thing is unfolding according to a plan, which of course doesn't look like a plan but like history. Some authors, like Alan Moore and Peter David, excel at this kind of work, regularly penning installments that neatly redefine what's gone before, tying up loose ends. But then additional works get made, and the franchise resumes spiraling out of control, and the Great Geek Game is once again afoot.

BUT THERE REMAINS yet another aspect of this game, another way in which geeks rail against fiction's inherent artifice, another way in which they reach out and probe the limits of the Holodeck, hoping to not meet with any walls. To have multiple Holodeck programs, multiple secondary worlds, is to have multiple fictions, each one pointing out the fictiveness of the whole, as well as the spatial and temporal boundaries of the worlds depicted therein. And so geeks aspire time and again to dissolve the boundaries *between* disparate artworks and franchises.

Once again, Marvel Comics is instructive. In the 1960s, Stan Lee and his compatriots worked hard to sell their readers not just a single comic, but an entire fictional shared universe, in which the Fantastic Four hung out with the Avengers, and in which Spider-Man, by swinging around a corner, could run into Thor or Wolverine. Over time, every Marvel character has encountered every other, a practice that in the mid-1980s culminated in massive company-wide crossovers that are by now an annual tradition. In these crossovers, epic story lines play out across multiple titles, roping in every character, major and minor.

Today, we see that same logic at work in the Marvel Cinematic Universe, where characters freely come and go, joking and bickering and fighting and forging alliances, all in real time. *The Avengers* assembled six characters from previous Marvel films (Iron Man, Hulk, Thor, Captain America, Black Widow, and Hawkeye), bringing them together in a single work, even putting them all on-screen in a single shot, as they prepared to do battle with an invading alien horde. Geeks waxed ecstatic about this image, which they called "the money shot," and likened it to a comic book "splash panel" (a single illustration spread across one or even two pages for dramatic impact). They loved it because it demonstrated that all their heroes were really there, all at the same time, sharing the same space. How could that be, unless it actually happened? Look, Ma, no faking! Unsurprisingly, the sequel, *Age of Ultron*, featured a similar shot, showing the six Avengers leaping into the fray during an assault on a Hydra base—in slow motion, no less, giving viewers more time to savor the splashy moment. Toward the end of the film, another unbroken shot depicts the same six Avengers battling a massive army of Ultrons, this time joined by three new recruits: Scarlet Witch, Quicksilver, and Vision.

But geeks craved more. *Captain America: Civil War* upped the ante in a fight scene at the Flughafen Leipzig/Halle airport, which saw fourteen different superheroes square off against one another—and this in a film that featured twenty important characters, and a plot that sprawled across a half-dozen countries. And still that wasn't enough. The next two *Avengers* films, *Avengers: Infinity War* and its as-yet-untitled sequel (to be released in May 2018 and May 2019, respectively), promise to feature not only the Avengers, but the Guardians of the Galaxy, as well as characters from the recent *Doctor Strange*. No doubt those films' directors, Anthony and Joe Russo, are planning at least one shot that shows off over a dozen heroes at once.

This desire, like the other geek desires that we've encountered, is endless, and unwilling to tolerate arbitrary limits. Geeks are painfully aware that while *The Avengers* assembled the Avengers, Sony owns Spider-Man, and Fox owns the Fantastic Four and the X-Men, meaning that what should be a single Marvel Cinematic Universe remains fractured, split into at least three separate secondary worlds. This conflict came to a head in 2014 and 2015, when *X-Men: Days of Future Past* and *Avengers: Age of Ultron* each featured their own version of the character Quicksilver, one played by Evan Peters, the other by Aaron Taylor-Johnson. The geek mind rankles at such an incongruity, leading fans to fervently wish that all Marvel titles could be collected under one roof. Hence their joy when Sony and Marvel announced in early 2015 that they'd worked out a deal wherein Spider-Man could appear in MCU films "on loan," like actors in the days of the studio system, leading to Ol' Webhead's debut in *Captain America: Civil War*, showing up at that crowded Flughafen Leipzig/Halle airport fight. In return, Iron Man guest-starred in the aptly named *Spider-Man: Homecoming.*

Once this sort of thing gets going, it's impossible to stop. Geeks love merging different properties, devising theories about how various works and franchises can be integrated, using accidents and coincidences to argue that multiple artworks are in fact taking place in the same continuity. *Empire* magazine's Chris Hewitt has jokingly suggested that Dean Norris's SWAT Team Leader in *Gremlins 2: The New Batch* is the same SWAT Team Leader the man went on to play in *Terminator 2: Judgment Day*, implying that (and this is the important part) we could someday see the Terminator plagued by the mischievous, vicious Gremlins. (Me, I'm still waiting to see the Terminator take on the Predator as well as the Aliens, as well as, why not, Robo-Cop, and the dinosaurs from *Jurassic Park*, as well as the Gremlins.) Another more popular fan theory posits that *Indiana Jones*, *Star Wars*, and *E.T. the Extra-Terrestrial* all take place in continuity with one another, never mind that *Star Wars* was set in a different galaxy, and in the past. Other theories attempt to resolve all the Pixar films and even the films and TV shows starring Kyle MacLachlan.

This impulse is evident throughout geek culture, where artists have built whole new artworks by combining characters and worlds. Neil Gaiman's *Sandman* comics drew on mythology and folklore to tell stories in which Thor and Loki cavort with Titania and Puck, while Alan Moore and Kevin O'Neill's comic *The League of Extraordinary Gentlemen* features characters derived from preexisting works of fiction: the Invisible Man, Dr. Jekyll, Mina Harker, even Winnie-the-Pooh and the Martian tripods from *War of the Worlds*.

Other artists have taken a much narrower focus. In the first issue of *Teenage Mutant Ninja Turtles*, the artists Kevin Eastman and Peter Laird piggybacked their characters' origin story onto that of *Daredevil*. (They were, like many, big fans of Frank Miller.) Heroic Matt Murdock saves a blind man from a speeding truck, but in the process gets struck by a falling radioactive canister that blinds him, even as it heightens his remaining senses to a superhuman degree. That much is in the Marvel Comics. In Eastman and Laird's version of the story, however, the canister continues tumbling onward, striking a bowl of four turtles held by a child onlooker. The bowl shatters, pitching the reptiles and the canister into a sewer, where they are gathered up by a rat who happened to observe the entire incident. The radioactive goo mutates all five animals into humanoid form, and the rat, named Splinter, proceeds to train the Turtles as ninjas so they can avenge his dead master's murder at the hand of the evil Foot Clan. (These details pay further homage to *Daredevil*: Matt Murdock's mentor's name is Stick, and he battles the Hand.) Thus, in theory, the Turtles could climb up out of the sewers and run into Daredevil, as well as any other inhabitant of the Marvel Universe. While that hasn't happened yet, they have encountered other comics characters, including Batman, which means of course that the Caped Crusader could someday team up with the Man Without Fear.

As it happens, the Turtles became a hit (that's putting it mildly), and in 1986, their grim and gritty black-and-white comic got revamped as a children's cartoon and matching toy line. This involved many concessions on Laird and Eastman's part. The Turtles lost their tails, and were given different-colored masks so kids could more easily tell them apart. The swearing and sibling rivalry disappeared, and the human Foot Clan ninjas all became robots so the Turtles could bash and smash them without drawing blood. Their arch-foe, the Shredder, got toned down, becoming a much more comical villain who bickered with a pink blob of an alien named Krang. The Turtles' human friend April O'Neil was also transmogrified, changing from a somber, complex brunette with a mideighties perm into a chipper redhead decked out in a banana-yellow jumpsuit. This version of the Turtles proved fantastically popular, spawning three live-action films, several video games, and countless more comics. For most people who grew up in the 1980s, this is the definitive version of the Turtles. I didn't discover the black-and-white comics until I'd become a fan of the cartoon and movies. (I'm still rather fond of the first film, which among other things boasts beautiful animatronic Turtle costumes, created by Jim Henson's Creature Shop.)

Since that time, there have been more versions of the Turtles, such as the animated Nickelodeon series that ran from 2003 to 2010, being a somewhat more serious take on the teenage ninjas, though it still fell short of the violence and adult themes of the original comics. That Nickelodeon series led to an animated feature, *Turtles Forever*, which didn't shy away from the different versions of the characters, but addressed that discrepancy head-on. The film begins with the Nickelodeon Turtles encountering their 1980s counterparts, via some nonsense involving travel between dimensions. Hijinks ensue, much of it stemming from the dated nature of the 1980s Turtles, who of course spout their catchphrases ("Cowabunga!" "Pizza!") and speak directly to the camera, which bewilders the newer Turtles. Cleverer still, the octet eventually winds up in a third dimension where it's eternally the eighties and New York City is black-and-white and violent and gritty. Of course they encounter there the four original Turtles, who quickly prove the superior ninjas, before all twelve Turtles band together to defeat a common foe.

What's so brilliant about this film, made in 2009 to celebrate the twenty-fifth anniversary of the franchise, is how handsomely it rewards all Turtles fans, no matter which version of the franchise they prefer (and for fans of all three versions, the film must be their holy grail). It allows the three different eras of Turtles to shine in their own ways, getting along and taking digs at one another (even if it does privilege the Nicktoons Turtles, I observe only slightly bitterly). Fittingly, it concludes by cutting to live action, to find Laird and Eastman putting the finishing touches on the first Turtles comic in 1984, wondering whether their endeavor will succeed.

Would that all problems were solved so easily! Why can't the Avengers meet the Justice League? Who would win in a fight, the Incredible Hulk or Superman? Which is faster, the *Millennium Falcon* or the Starship *Enterprise*? While the original *Star Trek* crew has, to date, encountered the X-Men,

DC's Legion of Superheroes, and the casts of *Doctor Who* and *Planet of the Apes* (in various comics), and while Chewie and Han have rubbed shoulders with Indiana Jones—also in comics—and crossed paths, oddly enough, with the animated television series *Phineas and Ferb*, there hasn't yet been an official *Star Trek–Star Wars* crossover. So it's been up to fans to bring that magnificent meeting to life.

Geeks have long used fan fiction to mash properties together, sharing their stories first in zines, then on the Internet. Now, they can realize these alternate fantasies via fan films. The first one I saw was the 2003 short *Batman: Dead End*, a labor of love directed by Sandy Collora, who'd worked in the special effects departments on *Men in Black*, *The Crow*, and *Predator 2*. His film featured a wonderful version of the Batsuit, and scored extra points by casting Walter Koenig's son Andrew as the Joker. The film's first twist comes when the Joker is murdered mid-cackle by a Predator, who then pits his deadly gadgets against the contents of Batman's utility belt. But then both warriors realize they're surrounded by Xenomorphs from the *Alien* franchise. Collora's next fan film was a fake trailer for a live-action team-up between Superman and Batman, *World's Finest*, which appeared in 2004, over a decade before Warner Bros. got around to making *Batman v Superman: Dawn of Justice*.

The proliferation of home video, Internet access, and film editing software has made it easier than ever to recycle old footage into new mash-ups. In one short film on YouTube, Captain Picard and his fellow officers on the *Enterprise* receive the stolen plans for the Death Star, only to be confronted by Darth Vader on an Imperial Star Destroyer. (Spoiler: Vader wins by Force-choking the *Enterprise*'s crew, although Data manages to escape in a shuttlecraft.) In another, the *Next Generation* crew stumbles upon the Death Star and the rest of the Imperial fleet. The encounter rapidly devolves into a frenzied exchange of proton torpedoes and laser blasts before the Death Star fires on the *Enterprise*, which beats a hasty retreat. Yet another video imagines what would happen if the *Star Trek* villains the Borg tried to assimilate the Death Star. Meanwhile, other geeks have used Flash animation to combine franchises. The Web series *How It Should Have Ended* ends its episodes with Batman and Superman having coffee in a diner, often joined by other heroes, like Mario or the Avengers. These coda crossovers, the "Super Café" segments, have become so popular that they were compiled into their own videos, so viewers can watch them by themselves.

The ultimate logic, the ultimate geek fantasy, is to combine all geek properties and franchises ever made, collapsing the many different worlds and continuities into a single, believable world, akin to a child mashing his or her toys together. Which is what Guillermo del Toro did when directing the opening credits sequence for the 2013 installment of the annual *Simpsons* Halloween episode, which he crammed with dozens of allusions to works of fantasy and horror. The director claimed as his inspiration *Mad Magazine*, which he spent hours scrutinizing as a child, trying to catch every reference the artists stuffed into their panels. Geeks gave the same attention to del Toro, combing through the 165-second-long clip and posting their findings in forums and videos. (Some of the references turned out to be pretty obscure, to films like Brian De Palma's *Phantom of the Paradise* and John Carpenter's *In the Mouth of Madness*.) More recently, *The Lego Movie* delighted in combining characters from *Star Wars*, *The Lord of the Rings*, DC Comics, *Teenage Mutant Ninja Turtles*, and more, before revealing its world to be, quite fittingly, the product of a little boy mashing his toys together (or his father's toys together).

But even were all the fantastical secondary worlds to suddenly dissolve into one, there would still remain another boundary, one more artificial limit that geeks would yearn to overcome.

seven

GEEKING OUT

hile introducing Howard Hawks's classic Western *Rio Bravo* at the 2007
Cannes Film Festival, Quentin Taran-
tino called it "one of the great hang-out movies," his idea
being that you spend so much of the film's 141 minutes
cooped up with John Wayne's John T. Chance and his allies

in the town jail as they wait for their foes to attack, that Chance and the others "actually become your friends." Even better, Tarantino continued, is that when you watch the movie again, "they already are your friends, and you're just hanging out with John T. Chance, and Dude, and Feathers." Howard Hawks himself might have agreed with Tarantino: he all but remade *Rio Bravo* seven years later, as *El Dorado*, then again, albeit more loosely, as *Rio Lobo*.

Tarantino claimed that hang-out movies are rare, but geeks beg to differ—or maybe they're just better at making imaginary friends? Time and again, geeks return to beloved TV shows, movies, comics, and novels in order to hang out with their favorite fictional characters, drinking in the slow middle section of *The Empire Strikes Back*, in which Princess Leia and Han Solo hide in an asteroid from the Empire, their bickering giving way to smooching, or rewatching *Star Trek: The Next Generation* start to finish, once again vicariously walking the halls of the *Enterprise*, and sitting down to play poker with Data and Worf and Troi and Geordie and Dr. Crusher. Geeks will even rewatch bad entries in a franchise, films like *Star Trek III: The Search for Spock* and *Star Trek V: The Final Frontier*, just to be able to pass time with cherished friends like Kirk and his crew.

But geeks have long thought of artworks as places where one can hang out. Right at the start of his 1939 lecture on world-building, "On Fairy-Stories," J.R.R. Tolkien describes himself not as a *reader* of *stories*, but as a visitor of other places, "a wandering explorer (or trespasser)" in a fantastical other realm that's full of peril, containing "pitfalls for the unwary and dungeons for the overbold." For Tolkien, for geeks, stories are opportunities to escape to another place, which is why Lucas labored so mightily to make the planets in *Star Wars* seem real, why the gamers at West End invented so much backstory for the regulars at the Mos Eisley Cantina, and why Neill Blomkamp said he wouldn't want to make films that didn't involve "creating a world for people to go to." When geeks buy tickets to see movies, in their minds they're purchasing tickets to travel elsewhere—on a spaceship, or in a TARDIS, or through a magical portal akin to the wardrobe in *The Lion, the Witch and the Wardrobe*, through which the Pevensie children passed from war-torn England into Narnia.

The final barrier to overcome in geek storytelling is, therefore, the one between the fictional world and ours: it is fiction itself. This is why geeks favor realism and world-building, which impart to fiction the look of nonfiction, and the weight of historical fact. It's also why so many geek art-works craft the illusion that our reality is being overwritten by another, that a fantastical other world is spilling into ours, or colliding with ours, its inhabitants invading, crashing through in spectacular fashion. Countless posters and T-shirts depict, say, every hero in the Marvel Universe or DC Universe rushing dramatically toward the viewer, who stands in risk of being trampled. One comic book artist, George Pérez, even specializes in drawing these images. Similarly, the poster for the movie *The Muppets* shows its lead stars Jason Segel and Amy Adams standing with their arms and legs outspread in front of a host of unruly Mup-pets, desperately trying to hold them back. That image, coupled with the taglines "Muppet Domination" and "They're closer than you think" suggests that Henson's fuzzy horde is about to (re-)invade our world. (Geeks, being geeks, created a message board at the bottom of the film's IMDb page where they bemoaned how all the Muppets weren't in fact there.)

These images partake of the aesthetic of the sublime, which the British philosopher Edmund Burke described as "the strongest emotion which the mind is capable of feeling," an involuntary response provoked by the perception of something terrible, but at a sufficient enough distance to render the experience pleasurable. Burke's concept was famously revised by Immanuel Kant, who specified that we experience the sublime when we find ourselves at the limit of our mental ability to comprehend either quantity or speed—for example, hundreds of Muppets rushing at us. Another instance of the sublime is on display in the scenes in *Return of the Jedi* when the Rebels attack the Death Star, which include dizzying shots in which so many spaceships are moving at the same time—quantity, speed—that viewers can barely process what's happening, no matter how many times they've delighted in the film. Two decades later, Lucas pushed this aesthetic further in his prequel trilogy, leading his producer, Rick McCallum, to boast that "every single image" in *The Phantom Menace* was "so dense," with "so many things going on." The long, unbroken shot that opens *Revenge of the Sith* outdoes *Return of the Jedi* in terms of complexity, repeatedly filling the screen with more speeding spaceships than the mind can comprehend.

For the Romantics, the greatest source of the sublime was nature, a force too large and powerful to be comprehended, let alone adequately represented. One simply had to go see the Matterhorn, and stand in its terrifying presence (close, but not too close), enjoying a dreadful frisson—and even then, one couldn't quite believe that the mountain was real. Geeks are Romantics, too, but instead of the majesty of this world—the Matterhorn, Niagara Falls—they want the majesty of another. This is why geek artworks must represent *universes*, with too many places and peoples and things to take in at any given moment. There must be hundreds and hundreds of Muppets or DC superheroes or Pokémon. A recent article at *Gizmodo*, "Computer Analysis Reveals the Stunning Complexity of the *Star Wars Expanded Universe*," proudly reports on how Swiss researchers found that all the *Star Wars* movies, novels, comics, TV shows, and video games, when taken as a whole, chronicled "36,000 years" of story, featuring "a whopping 21,647 characters"—7,563 of them major—"dispersed among 640 distinct communities on 294 planets."

That's an ideal geek artwork, one so vast that it can't be processed in one viewing, or any number of viewings. Nothing less is sufficiently geeky, or worthy of obsessive analysis. Tolkien claimed that faerie is "a realm that is wide and deep and high," being home to "all manner of beasts and birds," plus "shoreless seas and stars uncounted." In the days leading up to the release of *Guardians of the Galaxy*, the writer-director James Gunn teased fans with the promise that one setting in particular, the Collector's Museum, would contain too much background detail for viewers to process in the theater, requiring instead that they pause their eventual Blu-ray copies in order to fully absorb it all. Zack Snyder similarly promised that *Man of Steel* would be crammed to overflowing with delightful elements that viewers would be able to catch only on subsequent viewings—what geeks call "Easter eggs" or "Blu-ray stuff." His screenwriter, David S. Goyer, echoed this claim, asserting that fans would need to see the film "three or four times" to take it all in. As was the case with Guillermo del Toro's *Simpsons* opening, geeks were keen to accept the challenge, documenting all the Easter eggs online, then speculating as to their portent, whether a satellite that we glimpse, or a billboard on-screen for all of two seconds, implies that Bruce Wayne and Lex Luthor and other DC Comics characters might show up in the following film. (Surprise, they did.)

This kind of "fan service" goes right over the heads of general moviegoers, even as geeks eat it up. (They like their Easter eggs.) Whooping and hollering and waving plastic lightsabers, decked out in robes and bearing magic wands, they barrel into the theater, giddy beyond belief to watch the latest entry in a franchise. They even shriek with delight just to see a *trailer* for it (assuming it doesn't give too much away). No wonder people dismiss them as fan*girls* and fan*boys*, don't consider them real adults. For their part, geeks don't deny or resist those labels, remaining embarrassingly sincere in their enthusiasms. Above all else, they want to forget that they are watching a work of art, to believe they're en route to another world. And once they're there, they want to have the experience that Tolkien laid out in his essay, to have their tongues tied by the place's exotic nature. I'm reminded of the disorientation I felt when I moved to Bangkok, Thailand, in my late twenties, as my mind and body struggled to process sights and sounds that the Thai found ordinary, commonplace, but that were new and overwhelming for me.

I wound up spending two years in Thailand, during which time I acclimated to life there, so much so that when I returned to America, it was the United States, the land of my birth, that now seemed strange to me, dizzying and foreign. I was like the Pevensie children in *The Lion, the Witch and the Wardrobe*, who spend fifteen years in Narnia, growing accustomed to that other country's foods and customs and speech. Only one day, while out hunting a magical stag, do they stumble upon the lamppost that marks the portal back to England, and thereby return, pushing through tree branches that transform into winter coats as they themselves transform back into children, remembering in the process who they were.

Geeks want a similar experience as they shuttle back and forth between this world and the secondary one, to which end their love of the sublime is practical, instrumental. They know, as Tolkien wrote, that visitors to faerie shouldn't "ask too many questions, lest the gates should be shut and the keys be lost." The sublime is their means of bypassing self-consciousness and surrendering to pure feeling, to the sensation of "geeking out." When the lights go down on the latest Marvel movie, and the newest episode begins, geeks want to be confronted with awesome spectacle beyond their ability to absorb. They wear this desire openly, keeping it ever on display. The fan site *Making Star Wars* declares, "In this current age of *Star Wars*, with several new films on the way, our heads are about to explode with excitement." At the now-defunct geek blog *Topless Robot*, two of the top-ten tags were "Insanity" and "Awesomeness." All that excitement and insanity and awesomeness overwhelms the mind and body, rendering the geek unable to do anything other than experience a delightful mixture of ecstasy and terror. The conscious mind is forced to take a backseat as one undergoes the experience, as when riding on a roller coaster (those things again) or when caught in the throes of orgasm, which is precisely why geeks call such moments "geek-gasms" or "fangasms."

Geeks like art because it provides them with these experiences, and they like realist artworks because they prove the most immersive. As such, they tend to favor any feature that makes art more immersive, such as 3-D and IMAX films. Of course they'd love to have actual Holo-decks. But geeks will use anything that works, whether it's books, TV shows, movies, video games—or something else altogether. Hence all the extracurricular activities that they get up to, from Renaissance Faires to live-action role-playing ("larping") to good old-fashioned *Dungeons & Dragons*, and so much more. The *Enterprise D Construction Project* is a virtual-reality tour of the famous starship setting of *Star Trek* (the version seen in *The Next Generation*), and it promises fans the chance to "walk the entire length of the ship" in a "seamless" virtual experience that makes them feel as if they're "actually on board," able to visit "every room." Part of the pleasure is hearing all of the ship's sounds just the way one remembers, including the constant thrum of the *Enterprise*'s warp engines. That sound is so comforting to me that I've fallen asleep to it, thanks to the person who posted a twenty-four-hour-long loop of it on YouTube. (That user, crysknife007, specializes in "ambient geek sleep aids," and has posted dozens of such videos, including ones made from *Star Wars*' TIE Fighter engines and *Doctor Who*'s TARDIS.) Other geeks, meanwhile, are busy creating officially licensed virtual-reality experiences, such as Industrial Light & Magic's *Star Wars* program, *Trials on Tatooine*. And in nonvirtual space (also known as the real world), the "*Star Trek* megafan" James Cawley has reconstructed the sets of the original *Star Trek* in Ticonderoga, New York, where he offers fellow Trekkers the chance to pretend they're really standing on the *Enterprise*'s bridge.

Meanwhile, conventions like the San Diego Comic-Con have become havens for cosplay, short for "costume play," a practice that can be traced back generations but that exploded in popularity in the 1990s. Roaming the Con's halls, one sees geeks dressed up as Mario and Luigi kidding around right next to Stormtroopers straight out of *Star Wars*, behind whom stands a Dalek from *Doctor Who*, as well as Sergeant Nick Fury and Black Widow. Everyone's there, just like in the poster for *The Muppets*, from the best-known characters to the most obscure, alive and well and posing for photos. It's the *Star Wars* cantina scene made flesh, a motley crew speaking not only languages native to Earth but fictional tongues like *Star Trek*'s Klingon or J.R.R. Tolkien's Dwarvish and Elvish. Out back, other geeks are running around with brooms, playing Quidditch for real—or as real as it can be played so far removed from the grounds of Harry Potter's Hogwarts, in a world without any wizards. Since its creation in 2005 at Vermont's Middlebury College, "Muggle Quidditch" has seen the development of league play, and a governing body in the form of the International Quidditch Association, which organizes a world cup. The common ideal uniting all of these hobbies is the dream of crossing the threshold between reality and fiction, and setting foot inside the fantasy itself.

ONCE YOU UNDERSTAND what geeks are looking for, the type of experience that they're in the market to buy, you get why so many fantasy artworks are being transformed into franchises, which are especially well suited to delivering ongoing serial narratives across a wide variety of media. Another contributing factor is the way in which many marketing departments have recently shifted their philosophy and approach. Whereas traditionally companies were in the business of manufacturing and selling products, some have increasingly come to think of themselves more as purveyors of experiences, their reasoning being that people aren't looking to purchase a product per se, but rather a positive experience that they associate with a given product.

That's why, in the late 1990s, Warner Bros. advertised

their forthcoming film *The Matrix* via cryptic posters and TV spots that directed viewers to visit WhatIsTheMatrix.com, where they could pretend to be hackers like Neo, playing games and discovering codes to unlock content such as concept art and behind-the-scenes videos. Since then, other marketing teams have produced analogous campaigns, so-called Alternate Reality Games (ARGs) that offer tantalizing make-believe conspiracies in which something is amiss, our world not being what it seems. Intrigued consumers then spend hours branding themselves, visiting websites, and calling phone numbers in scavenger-hunt fashion in order to unlock yet more content, which is really more advertising, but delivered such that participants associate a grand sense of mystery with the franchise underneath. ARGs, which have been used to promote *The Blair Witch Project*, *Lost*, *Cloverfield*, *Prometheus*, and more, hold a special appeal for geeks, who remain ever-eager to trade in the real world for a more fantastical version.

Marketers have similarly zeroed in on the geek love of fictional nonfiction. One ad for *Prometheus* was designed to resemble a TED Talk being given in the year 2023 by the founder of that franchise's fictional Weyland Corporation, Peter Weyland (played by Guy Pearce). Like so many real TED speakers, Weyland begins by telling a charming anecdote, recounting how T. E. Lawrence's secret to pinching out matches with his fingers was supposedly "not minding it hurts." Weyland then pivots to recounting the Prometheus myth, explaining how by stealing fire from the gods, that Titan gave humans "our first true piece of technology." A litany of other tech milestones follows: stone tools, the wheel, gunpowder—"a bit of a game-changer, that one"—continuing into the present day and then beyond, encompassing fictional technologies like "cybernetic individuals" that, Weyland promises, "in just a few short years, will be completely indistinguishable from us." This, Weyland claims, makes us humans the gods now, a line that causes the unseen audience to titter. But Weyland assures them (and us) that his goal is perfectly noble, being only "to change the world," a pat conclusion that meets with rapturous applause. A follow-up video introduces one of Weyland's cybernetic creations, an individual known as David (played by Michael Fassbender), who regales us with his capabilities: "I can assist your employees. I can make your organization more efficient. I can carry out directives that my human counterparts might find . . . distressing or unethical."

These types of ads are so commonly used to promote geek franchises nowadays, they are almost rote. The marketing campaign for *X-Men: Days of Future Past* included a website for the fictional Trask Industries, which advertises their supposed goals of "preserving humanity through technology" and "responding to the genetic threat," and includes its own fake industrial videos that promote the company's Sentinel robots. Another website, TheBent Bullet.com, insinuates that various famous historical figures were secretly mutants, and features a video in which an authoritative male narrator gravely recounts the role played by the villainous Magneto (Michael Fassbender again) in

John F. Kennedy's assassination. The text below that video links to more ads for the film, and invites viewers to answer the question: "Do you think Magneto is guilty or innocent? Tell us why in the comments." All of these ads pay off in *Days of Future Past* itself, which depicts a future in which mutants have been hunted to near extinction by runaway Sentinel robots, and reveals that Magneto was in fact trying to *save* JFK from assassination (because the president was a mutant). (Three years after the film's release, those viral YouTube videos are still doing good work, offering viewers the chance to rent or purchase *Days of Future Past* online with just the click of a button.)

Geeks gleefully play along with such ad campaigns. Part of what makes the past two decades the Golden Age of Geekdom is that we're getting not just so many wonderful movies and TV shows, but elaborate role-playing experiences—and all given away for free! Not that there aren't also products that one can buy, to thereby relive the fun. Such products need not bear any obvious relationship with the franchise. Recently while waiting in line at a department store, I noticed a bag of chocolate-chip cookies adorned with the familiar *Transformers* logo, and the smiling faces of Bumblebee and Optimus Prime. What do those "robots in disguise" have to do with cookies of any kind? Your guess is as good as mine! (Maybe they're secretly made of metal?) But the company making the cookies, Primary Colors, which manufactures a variety of snacks sold in packaging sporting different Hasbro brands, was clearly hoping that my love for those heroic robots, whom I've known since childhood, would compel me to purchase the cookies. (I declined.)

Meanwhile, Hasbro, known to most as a maker of toys and games, has spent the past decade itself transforming, becoming a multimedia entertainment company. In 2014, Hasbro even tried to purchase DreamWorks Animation, before the deal was scuttled by Disney. The company's current CEO, Brian Goldner, ascended to that position between 2000 and 2008 by reinventing the *Transformers* action figure line as a blockbuster Hollywood film series, his thinking being that toy sales buoy movie ticket sales, and vice versa. He learned this strategy in the 1990s while working for Haim Saban, whose Saban Entertainment successfully rebranded the Japanese TV show *Super Sentai* as *Mighty Morphin Power Rangers*, which it then sold through what Goldner has called an "'immersive' strategy in which one sales and marketing platform is used to reinforce another." Fans could not only watch *Power Rangers* on TV, but buy all kinds of merchandise. As Goldner explained, "As [Saban Entertainment] introduced the brand on television, they also surrounded the audience, which became excited about the brand, with all kinds of other experiences. You went to Universal Studios and saw a stage show of *Power Rangers*. You could buy books about *Power Rangers*. You could buy bedding or T-shirts, so a young person could experience *Power Rangers* in any format they wanted."

Including theme parks that bring the brand to life all around you. Walt Disney pioneered this approach over sixty years ago with Disneyland, which opened in 1955, and was followed in 1971 by Walt Disney World Resort. At those wondrous parks, visitors can interact with employees dressed as Mickey Mouse and Minnie and Donald and Daisy and Snow White—commercial cosplay—and can also experience rides (or experience standing in line for hours for rides) in different-themed lands: Main Street USA and New Orleans Square, as well as the more fantastical Frontierland and Tomorrowland.

More recently, media companies have taken to designing new lands around popular brands and their internally consistent secondary worlds. In 2010, the Universal Orlando Resort opened the Wizarding World of Harry Potter, an attraction that features replicas of the Hogwarts Express, Ollivander's Wand Shop, Hogwarts School of Witchcraft and Wizardry, and Hogsmeade, all designed to help fans pretend that they're wizards following in the footsteps of Harry Potter and his friends. Visitors select wands (or pretend the wands are selecting them), come face-to-face with a hippogriff (i.e., ride Flight of the Hippogriff, a roller coaster), then retire to a tavern to down glasses of Butterbeer. (Said Butterbeer, which is vanilla soda with butterscotch topping, costs seven dollars a glass. The cheapest wands, meanwhile, sell for twenty-five dollars, while the more interactive models will set you back forty-eight.) A second section of the attraction opened in 2014 at Universal Studios Florida, boasting an elaborate re-creation of Diagon Alley. The success of these theme parks has not been lost on Disney, which is constructing two *Star Wars* lands, one in Anaheim, California, the other in Bay Lake, Florida.

Those attractions, scheduled to open in 2019, promise to faithfully re-create the worlds and characters of *Star Wars*, allowing patrons the chance to not only step aboard the *Millennium Falcon*, but to fly it into battle against the Empire, then swing by (wait for it) the Mos Eisley Cantina for a refreshing glass of blue milk. (No doubt Momaw Nadon will be there, bobbing his great twisted head.) What's more, apparently visitors will be able to pledge their allegiance to either the First Order or the Resistance, a decision that will affect their experience of the attractions, which will be presented as episodes in an overarching narrative. In this way, visitors won't just be riding rides, but participating in something akin to a live-action role-playing game.

Never one to be outdone, especially by *Star Wars*, James Cameron has built his own theme park at Walt Disney World Resort's Animal Kingdom: "Pandora: The World of *Avatar*," which opened in late May 2017. There, fans can imagine they're walking the surface of that planet via attractions like the Satu'li Canteen (a restaurant) and rides like the Na'vi River Journey. Describing his visit to the park at *io9*, Germain Lussier enthused about how everything inside the park's twelve-acre confines creates the illusion that one has actually journeyed to Pandora: the employees (who are pretending to be native Na'vi aliens) "greet you in the native language" and "refer to James Cameron's *Avatar* as a documentary" while recounting trivia and tales about the planet's flora, fauna, and history. Visitors will also be able to pay $75 to have their faces scanned, and personalized avatars made of them.

All of these parks are selling immersive virtual experiences; the more one spends, the more immersive the experience is. They are also designed to tie in with the ongoing larger franchises. No doubt the trivia recounted by the "Na'vi inhabitants" of Pandora syncs up with the world that will be on display in the forthcoming *Avatar* films: in addition to the park, Cameron has been planning not one, not two, not three, but *four* sequels to *Avatar*, all to better show off the elaborate world-building he's spent the past ten years devising, "1500 pages of notes on the world and the cultures and the different clans and different animals and different biomes and so on." His plan, he explained to the *Los Angeles Times*, has been to create a "bible" that later writers (and theme-park designers) can consult for consistency's sake while bringing the franchise to life, so he can give his fans the world fully formed up front, minus inconsistencies. In doing so he intends "to compete head on with . . . the Tolkiens and the *Star Wars* and the *Star Treks*," whose fans, Cameron's observed, "want to live somewhere else," losing themselves in "a persistent alternate reality" that's been wholly realized, richly detailed, "and worth their time." (James Cameron gets it.) Accordingly, Cameron's business partner Jon Landau has claimed that the material being developed, that gargantuan bible, would fuel projects for "20 years or more in various media, some of which have yet to be invented." These two men have learned George Lucas's lesson well, and are already hard at work on *Avatar*'s own expanded universe.

This approach to marketing—promoting a product

through emotionally resonant, immersive, fun-oriented activities—is not unique to geek culture. Red Bull routinely sponsors memorable sporting events, ranging from the spectacular, like Felix Baumgartner's "Red Bull Stratos" skydive, to the farcical, such as the touring Red Bull Flugtag (German for "air show"), in which participants sit inside makeshift flying machines as they're pushed off a pier and into water. But for geeks, these marketing efforts are heaven on earth, their fantasies come true.

Geeks are also of special interest to marketers because in addition to being loyal, lifelong customers, they tend to serve as brand ambassadors. Not only do they spend their time devouring the brand, consuming it and seeking out news about where it's headed, they enthuse about the brand on social media, making blog posts, podcasts, fan videos— gladly and for free. They also labor to convert friends and family members into fans. At a brunch I recently attended, a man roughly my age proudly told me how he'd just shown his young son, who was wearing a Lego *Star Wars* T-shirt, the original *Star Wars* for the first time. This situation is playing itself out right now in homes across America and beyond, as geeks conspire to groom a whole new generation of nerds.

But success breeds its own problems, and the best-laid plans often go awry—or as the Man in Black advised Inigo Montoya in *The Princess Bride*, "Get used to disappointment." Because while we're living in the Golden Age of Geekdom, which might last another twenty years, if not even longer, there's no guarantee that geeks will see their dearest dreams come true.

TO BE
CONTIN-
UED . . . .

PART III

eight

I'VE GOT A BAD FEELING ABOUT THIS

The Importance of Being Geeky

Before I went to college, I wouldn't have dreamed of being caught dead reading *X-Men* comic books in public—but how times change. By the turn of the millennium, I was able to watch a popular *X-Men* movie in a mainstream multiplex in my hometown. In the decades since, geek culture has only become more popular, more mainstream. Today, many are happy to wear a Chewbacca T-shirt while going to see the new *Star Wars* film, or unwind after school or work playing *Pokémon GO*. But that having been said, not everyone is a hardcore geek, staying up nights to finish their homemade Wookie costume so they can cosplay at the San Diego Comic-Con, or breed a complete Smogon OU-tier Pokémon team with perfect IVs, natures, and Hidden Powers—hobbies that require significant investments of time and often money.

Having spent lots of time among geeks, being a geek, I know how easy it is to forget that not everybody shares our passions, that not everyone wants to devote each waking moment to SF and fantasy, or to the minutiae of *Buffy the Vampire Slayer* or *Magic: The Gathering*. On YouTube, I subscribe to a channel, "*Star Wars* Explained," whose owner combs through that franchise's extensive offerings, new and old, in order to answer esoteric questions about its lore. No topic is too obscure; typical are videos like "The Ancient Secret of the Massassi Temples on Yavin 4" and "The Tragic Story of Mas Amedda after the Battle of Endor and the End of the Galactic Civil War." At present, I'm one of nearly three hundred thousand subscribers, and the least-watched videos draw at least thirty thousand views, so obviously some people want to know these kinds of things. But a channel like this is too much for most folk, who regard *Star Wars* as a bunch of enjoyable movies to kick back with now and again. Even I can't honestly say I much care what Mas Amedda did in the heady days after *Return of the Jedi*. I didn't even know who Mas Amedda was until I watched that video.

This situation creates a dilemma for any company with a franchise. As Peter Jackson's *Lord of the Rings* trilogy went into production in the late 1990s, its financer, New Line Cinema, estimated that "serious Tolkien fans" would account for only 25 percent of ticket sales. The series of novels was forty years old and not exactly summer beach reading. Neither did New Line know that the Golden Age of Geekdom was dawning, or that *Harry Potter* was going to make fantasy lit cool again. As such, they decided that in order for the films to be financially successful, they would have to be accessible to moviegoers at large. In the days leading up to the release of *The Fellowship of the Ring*, I definitely didn't grasp that. Having been a fan of Middle-earth since middle school, I was daydreaming about how I'd finally get to see every last detail of Tolkien's saga up onscreen. So I was stunned, when I saw the movies, to find I was watching action flicks with CGI cave trolls and scenes like the one where Legolas surfs down stairs on a shield. And what was this beefed-up romantic subplot between Aragorn and Arwen? Where was Tom Bombadil? Where was Glorfindel? Where were all the poems and songs?

I was alone in my dismay, since the films were wildly successful, raking in the cash and winning Oscars. Even hardcore geeks seemed to like them well enough. But the legions of new *LOTR* fans for the most part haven't wanted to hear folks like me prattle on about Ainulindalë and

Valaquenta, or how Ar-Pharazôn is imprisoned in the Caves of the Forgotten until the Last Battle and Day of Doom. Instead, they'd rather make funny Boromir memes based on his famous line about not simply walking into Mordor. ("One does not simply / pass linear algebra.")

One does not simply / cater to the geeks. For starters, there aren't that many of them. And no matter how many hardcore fans a franchise has, it will lose them over time, as fans pass away (sad, but true), or are drawn away by other things, including the rigors of everyday life. I can no longer while away whole days playing *Magic: The Gathering* like I did when I was living in the Geek Dorm—or, at least, it's harder to. For a franchise to survive, just to stay the same size, it must always be attracting new fans to replace the ones it's losing. The more it caters to its most entrenched fans, making products only they can understand, the harder it is for new fans to jump in. Not too long ago, I showed my parents *Captain America: Civil War*, despite their not having watched any previous MCU films, partly because I wanted to see what they'd make of it. They were totally at sea, recognizing only Captain America and Spider-Man. While I, a die-hard Marvel fan, reveled in what I think is one of the greatest superhero films ever made, my parents fell asleep. (Sorry, Mom and Dad.)

Yet at the same time, a franchise can't afford to alienate existing fans. New Line knew that the *Lord of the Rings* films had to appeal to Tolkien geeks: 25 percent is still 25 percent, and if those fans decided the movies were evil incarnate, worse than Sauron's One Ring itself, they could cause a lot of harm, generating significant negative publicity. So New Line sought them out online and assuaged their fears, wooing them, even while it courted general viewers as well, folks who couldn't tell a Hobbit hole from a hole in the ground. New Line ran one set of ads during reruns of *Star Trek: The Next Generation*, aimed at geeks, plus another set during *Angel*, aimed at convincing young women the movies would make for good dates.

This dilemma, of needing to appeal to both geeks and non-geeks, has played out repeatedly over the past twenty years. What's more, as long as there are franchises (effectively forever), this problem will persist. Different companies, different franchises, have attempted different solutions. Marvel Comics launched its Marvel Cinematic Universe by making a host of stand-alone films, each one focused on a different character: Iron Man, the Incredible Hulk, Thor, and Captain America. Some fans (like me) saw every movie, but some saw only the ones that most appealed to them, such as *Iron Man*, which proved the biggest hit. But those four films also laid the groundwork for a larger film to come that would draw all the fans together: *The Avengers*, which upon its arrival in 2012 became Marvel's most profitable movie to date.

But this created a new problem, the one that caused my parents to conk out. The next *Avengers* film would have to feature those six characters, plus more, rewarding existing fans but making it harder for new viewers (like my parents) to come aboard. Marvel compensated by making sequels to each stand-alone film except *The Incredible Hulk*, which had underperformed. More important, it made different stand-alone films: *Guardians of the Galaxy*, *Ant-Man*, *Doctor Strange*. Those films released pressure, so to speak, allowing fans to catch their breath, as well as providing a point of entry for newer fans. Someone born in 2008, when *Iron Man* was first released, is ten today, and perhaps just getting into Doctor Strange. She hasn't seen the older films and might never see them. But she can follow Doctor Strange into the new films, like *Avengers: Infinity War*. If she likes what she sees, the other characters she finds there, she can go back and watch their old films, or watch the sequels starring them. Meanwhile, Marvel keeps lining up new stand-alone films, spotlighting new characters like Black Panther and Captain Marvel.

That's one solution to the dilemma. Here's another. Since purchasing Lucasfilm, Disney has made two very different *Star Wars* films that play like polar opposites. *The Force Awakens* catered to a general audience by not only bringing back the principal characters, but by portraying them in the most familiar way possible. The Rebellion won in *Return of the Jedi*, blowing up the second Death Star and defeating the Empire—except not really, since *The Force Awakens* effectively resets the timeline back to the start of *A New Hope*. Han and Chewie are once again flying around the galaxy, working as smugglers. Leia has gone back to leading a Rebellion that's still a Rebellion, even though it's called the Resistance for some reason, and she's a general now, not a princess. The Empire, meanwhile, has rechristened itself as well, as the First Order, and still seems to be running the galaxy. And just like before, it's building a secret superweapon, Starkiller Base, which is for all intents and purposes a new Death Star. (The Empire hasn't learned very much.) In the midst of this we meet a young woman who, like Luke, has great potential as a Jedi, but who's stuck on a desert planet that looks like but isn't Tatooine. She encounters a cute little robot, BB-8, who contains stolen data that must be delivered to the Rebellion. Han and Chewie help her do that, stopping by a bar that isn't Mos Eisley Cantina. And all the while they're chased by an ominous man in black and wearing a mask, but who isn't Darth Vader.

None of these parallels were by accident, but by design; they were Disney's means of tapping into the general populace's love of *Star Wars*. Geeks, predictably, grumbled about the similarities. They liked the movie overall, but that didn't stop them from complaining about how history was repeating itself, and how *Force Awakens* was essentially a remake of *A New Hope*. One fan even made a video that compared the two films side by side. But Disney wasn't making *The Force Awakens* for the geeks—at least, not primarily for them.

Geeks got more excited about Disney's follow-up film, *Rogue One*, which promised not to retread well-worn ground but to tell how the Rebels stole the plans for the original Death Star. Geeks salivated at the thought of seeing this section of the timeline illustrated, having spent decades wondering exactly how Princess Leia came by those plans before stashing them away inside Artoo. But for non-geeks, *Rogue One* was a much harder sell. How many people who have seen *Star Wars* remember that little Artoo was carrying "stolen data tapes," and not just a recording of Princess Leia? Those plans are really just a means of getting the movie going, bringing the good guys and bad guys into conflict. What's more, most of the characters in *Rogue One* were unfamiliar, and there wouldn't be any Skywalkers or Jedi Knights or lightsaber duels. Instead, the film was selling the world of *Star Wars* itself, a chance to visit that galaxy again, and see AT-ATs and Stormtroopers in action, and hear familiar sounds, like those distinctive blaster effects. It was the *Expanded Universe* on-screen.

Geeks intuited that *Rogue One* entailed risks, was Disney's means of testing the waters to see how far they could push their new purchase. How much of the Holodeck could they sell? As Rob Bricken succinctly (and sibilantly) put it at *io9*, "Are audiences ready for *Star Wars* sans Skywalkers?" If not, he fretted, Disney would retreat to more familiar parts of the franchise, "perennially [sticking] to the same dozen or so characters, when there's literally an entire galaxy to explore." Like all geeks, Bricken wants to strike out for virgin territory, to explore a *Star Wars* galaxy that feels like an actual galaxy. Indeed, the rest of the article gives the impression that Bricken believes that the *Star Wars* galaxy *actually exists*, and is just waiting to be documented: "There could be countless heroes and villains out there, who are just as cool as Han Solo or as terrifying as Darth Vader, but we'll never know, unless someone gets to tell their stories." I doubt that Bricken sincerely believes those things are "out there"; rather, he wants to maintain the illusion that *Star*

Wars films are historical documents, a point he more or less acknowledges when he states that the challenge for *Rogue One* is to demonstrate that "the depth that has always seemed a part of the franchise is in fact real," rather than "merely an illusion." Of course any sense of depth in the franchise *is* "merely an illusion" (confidential to Mr. Bricken in Eternia: *Star Wars* is and has always been totally made-up), but in order for *Star Wars* to work its magic on the geeks, in order for it to deliver the experience that they crave, its illusion must appear indistinguishable from reality.

Less enfranchised viewers don't feel that way, and they didn't attach such existential significance to *Rogue One*. Instead, they wondered why Rey and Finn and Kylo Ren weren't in the trailers for the film—wasn't this the sequel to *Force Awakens*? Confronted with that confusion and other marketing concerns, Disney wound up conducting reshoots in the summer of 2016. Those additions apparently expanded Darth Vader's presence in the film, adding among other things the sequence at the end where he chases the Rebels as they trade off the Death Star plans like relay runners, his crimson lightsaber flashing in the darkness, mowing them down. Accordingly, the trailers and posters released in the second half of that year made sure to prominently feature Vader. Obviously, Disney did lack faith in filmgoers' willingness to see a movie not about Skywalkers, so they brought in the biggest, baddest Skywalker of all. In the end, the Mouse House was right to worry: *Rogue One* grossed only one billion dollars to *The Force Awakens*' two.

This dilemma is what we might call the "homework

problem." As we know, geeks love doing homework, freely choosing to do things like memorize the periodic table of the elements, and π to a hundred decimal places. They're excited by big, sprawling franchises with lots of character names to learn. It's a way for them to show off: "I can name every single person on *Game of Thrones*!" But most people don't want to do any homework, especially if that homework requires first consuming dozens of other movies or TV shows or novels or comics, an overwhelming obligation that ruins the fun. This is why a film like *Logan* gets promoted as "a superhero movie for people who don't like superhero movies": a person doesn't have to watch the previous ten *X-Men* films, or read any of the comics, in order to get what's going on, and enjoy what's on-screen. People appreciate that. Most people are not nerds. They don't want to study. They want to party!

Even I, a lifelong *Star Wars* fan, balked at the initial posters and cast photos for *Rogue One*. Who were all these people I didn't know? Did I want to learn their names, their life stories, just to watch the movie? The news that Forest Whitaker would also be in the film, playing Saw Gerrera, a military leader from the *Clone Wars* TV show, didn't provide further encouragement, since I'd never seen that show. Would I need to watch it first? I didn't want to watch it. In the end, I went to see *Rogue One* (of course), but I would have preferred to watch a stand-alone Darth Vader movie. (I think most people would agree.)

Geeky artworks routinely encounter the homework problem. The more the artwork caters to geeks, the more daunting it comes across to non-geeks. In effect, the artwork produces two separate audiences, each one looking for different things. That's why the film critic Roger Ebert alerted his readers when he knew nothing about a franchise except what was on-screen. He ends his review of the first *X-Men* film with the suggestion that fans who "understand subtle allusions . . . linger in the lobby after each screening to answer questions." Reviewing the 2005 adaptation of *The Hitchhiker's Guide to the Galaxy*, Ebert went even further, musing that the film "should only be reviewed by, and perhaps only be seen by, people who are familiar with the original material to the point of obsession," since they alone would understand "its in-jokes" and its "references." He stresses throughout that review his unfamiliarity with Douglas Adams's work, asking that fans "stop reading right now before I disappoint or even anger you," since he was writing for "others like myself, who will be arriving at the movie innocent of *Hitchhiker* knowledge." As it turned out, that film didn't do well, making its budget back but not warranting a sequel. It was too geeky for casual fans, but also alienated geeks, who resented the liberties it took with its source material. (I kinda like it, myself.)

The next stand-alone *Star Wars* film will focus on Han Solo, recounting his charmingly roguish ways from the days before he joined the Rebellion. That strikes me as smart, smarter than *Rogue One*. Non-geeks will be drawn in by Han and Chewie and Lando Calrissian, characters they already know, while geeks will be eager to see an earlier part of the *Star Wars* timeline get filled in. (Meanwhile, you know Disney has to be trying to figure out a way to make *Star Wars* films set between *Return of the Jedi* and *Force Awakens*.)

THE HOMEWORK PROBLEM points out a pitfall in the Golden Age of Geekdom, its inherent perversity. Geeks can't believe they're getting these movies and comics and TV series, and much more besides that. But the entertainment industry's loyalty isn't what geeks care most about: realist depictions of internally consistent fantastical worlds. In loving that, geeks remain about as alone as they've always been. Rather, entertainment companies like making money off geek concerns—and non-geek concerns. If people like a given artwork, whether it's geeky or non-geeky, then those companies will make more, as long as people pony up.

The more successful a franchise is, therefore, the more it's at risk of losing its geeky nature. That's why geeks loathe Michael Bay, under whose baseball-capped auspices *Transformers* went from being geeky cartoons and comic books to a series of live-action films that bear little resemblance to what had gone before. Rather than making what geeks wanted to see—realism, world-building—Bay vandalized the characters, painting bright red flames on Optimus Prime's sides, and having Bumblebee take a leak on John Turturro. The geeks are not amused, but Bay doesn't care; nor does he care if his plots don't make sense, or whether the action's incoherent, nothing more than a colorful blur. Geeks, jaded, now seize on anything that Bay does, thinking he's trolling them, purposefully trying to spite them. He probably doesn't know that geeks exist.

And why should he know, or care? Bay's been making the *Transformers* films for viewers at large, people who casually enjoyed the cartoon and toys in the 1980s, not the die-hard *Transformers* fans, geeks who read the gritty *Generation 2* comic books in the 1990s, or watched the *Unicron Trilogy* in the mid-2000s. To like Bay's movies, one need not know anything about the robots except that they're giant and they transform. His strategy's worked: each *Transformers* film has been a blockbuster, the third and fourth installments each grossing a billion dollars worldwide. (In comparison, the 1986 feature-length animated *Transformers: The Movie* made under $6 million.) Geeks are dumbfounded. Why do people reward these movies, which don't make any rational sense, and don't dwell on *Transformers* lore, regaling us with detailed depictions of the alien robots' home planet, Cybertron? The answer, quite simply, is that there are more non-geeks than geeks, and non-geeks are happy with *Transformers* as it is. They're entertained.

As such, a sense of insecurity haunts each geek franchise. If this could happen to *Transformers*, it could happen to anything. When Michael Bay announced he was planning to make a live-action adaptation of *Teenage Mutant Ninja Turtles*, fans feared the worst. Bay didn't help by suggesting he might make the Turtles aliens. One popular YouTube video revised the lyrics of the 1980s cartoon's theme to speculate on what other changes might lie in store: Donatello being a homeboy from the hood, Raphael "a robot clone." As it happened, Bay, who only produced the film, left the Turtles teenage mutants, although many fans complained about their appearance, as well as the movie's juvenile tone.

Geeks know, even if only subconsciously, that corporations get to play in the sandbox, too, except their playing is official—they *own* the sandbox, and they'll make whatever sells. To that end, it doesn't matter what any single person thinks, even if that person happens to be the artist. More than a hundred years ago, Sir Arthur Conan Doyle tried to kill Sherlock Holmes by throwing him over the Reichenbach Falls while he grappled with his arch-foe, Moriarty. That was in 1893, a mere six years after Doyle created the fabled sleuth. But his readers demanded more Holmes. Finally, in 1901, Doyle gave in, resurrecting the detective in *The Hound of the Baskervilles*, a novel set prior to the incident at the falls. And in 1903, in "The Adventure of the Empty House," Doyle retconned Holmes's demise: the detective reappears and explains to an incredulous Watson how he managed to throw Moriarty over the waterfall thanks to his mastery of "baritsu," Doyle's take on Japanese wrestling. Many more Holmes adventures followed until 1927, then beyond Doyle's passing in 1930.

Frank Miller learned a similar lesson decades later, when he tried killing off Elektra in *Daredevil* #181. She gets stabbed in the stomach by the villainous assassin Bullseye, then crawls to Matt Murdock's apartment only to expire in his arms. As far as Miller was concerned, that was the end: Elektra was dead and gone for good. But his ninja assassin, like Holmes, was much too popular to stay dead, though

Miller tried his best to prevent her resurrection. Nine issues later, the Hand ninja clan unearths her coffin and attempts to revive her corpse in a mystical ceremony, but her body disappears. She's last seen climbing a mountainside, accompanied by the enigmatic caption "He must never know." Miller's intention was to remove her from the comic, warning future authors to leave Elektra in peace—that Daredevil should never encounter her again. But after Miller departed Marvel, the company brought Elektra back in *Daredevil* #324 (January 1994). Since then, she's appeared not only there, but in her own comics series, the 2003 *Daredevil* film, the 2005 stand-alone film *Elektra*, and season two of Netflix's *Daredevil* TV show.

Popular characters never stay dead. They can't really die, since they aren't really alive. Any character can be resurrected; any artwork can be retconned. *X-Men*'s Jean Grey has come back from the dead so many times it's practically become one of her mutant powers (in addition to her telekinesis). Even whole fictional universes can be destroyed and re-created, repeatedly. We've already noted that Batman's sales were poor in 1985. But all of DC's comics were struggling. The company's editors concluded that their decades of continuity were too complex for newer readers—the homework problem. So they decided to reset everything, starting their comics over from scratch. Of course, to placate older readers, they whipped up a story line that explained why, inside the fictional world of the comics, things were changing, some geeky mumbo jumbo entitled "Crisis on Infinite Earths."

Disney did something similar when they purchased Lucasfilm, quietly announcing that they didn't feel obliged to abide by the *Star Wars Expanded Universe*. They rebranded it "*Star Wars Legends*," no longer canon but instead now a resource they can draw on if desired. All those marvelous, intricate details invented by West End Games and Timothy Zahn, and the hundreds of artists who followed them—it's as though they suddenly cried out in terror before being suddenly silenced. (Whither Momaw Nadon, gentle tender of all that's green?)

Franchises—successful ones, at least—are malleable, going wherever the money is. After Bryan Singer's *X-Men* became a hit, the comic books changed, its characters shedding their colorful spandex for black leather outfits. Professor X was drawn to look more like Patrick Stewart, Wolverine more like Hugh Jackman. Marvel was trying to accommodate new readers who'd been attracted by the movies. Of course, not everything changed. It wasn't as though the past forty years of the title vanished, disappearing like the team's resident teleporter, Nightcrawler, in a flash of brimstone and purple smoke. But more people were watching the movie than reading the comic, so . . . The most that fans can hope for is that if a given change is unpopular enough, then the powers that be will walk it back—but that still means following the money. And if there's a sudden influx of new fans, then they're the ones who will get what they want.

This is why geeks are so concerned that the artists making comics and films are also geeks. If so, there is hope, however tenuous and fragile, that someone will be there fighting to keep the artwork geeky, and consistent with the past. Any necessary changes will be respectful, not arbitrary. Geeky artists, for their part, often go to great lengths to insist on the genuineness of their fandom. Peter Jackson's enthusiasm for *The Lord of the Rings* was reported on endlessly, as was Ian McKellan's. Marvel has similarly portrayed directors like Jon Favreau and Joss Whedon as lifelong fans of the company's comics and characters. And Simon Pegg and Edgar Wright are venerated as saints by geeks, a fact Pegg celebrated by entitling his autobiography *Nerd Do Well*. This need to flaunt one's geek cred extends to critics as well, being the flipside of Roger Ebert's disclaimers. In writing this book, I've felt obliged to demonstrate my own geeky background and bona fides, even as I imagine that some readers out there will doubt the sincerity of my commitment.

Geeks are quick to pounce whenever they sense someone isn't a fellow traveler. While on *The Daily Show* in 2013, J. J. Abrams confessed he didn't like *Star Trek* as a kid, finding the series "too philosophical." He was trying to sell his upcoming *Star Trek Into Darkness*, explaining why he made the film for everyone, not just nerds—he was appealing to non-geeks. Jon Stewart cut him off, saying, "I stopped listening to you when you said you didn't like *Star Trek*," then added, "I saw your mouth was moving after that, so I'm assuming you apologized." Abrams reiterated his point: "We tried to make it work for people like me, and people like you." Guess what? Geeks didn't want to hear that. Later, aware that geeks were fuming in their lairs, Abrams made a bid for redemption, claiming he'd fallen in love with the show in the process of making the film. I didn't and still don't believe him. As an article at *The Daily Dot* expressed it, "The publicity for *Into Darkness* has been solidly high school: don't worry—it may be *Star Trek*, but it's not for nerds anymore!" Geeks catalogued the many offenses: Abrams had made the film too much for general audiences, watering down the world-building and the characters to the point of caricature, replacing them with frenetic action scenes. There were too many white men—a YouTube video set footage to the *Flight of the Conchords* song "Too Many Dicks on the Dance Floor"—while the few female characters were treated as sex objects. What's more, *Into Darkness* dared remake the most beloved *Star Trek* movie of them all, *The Wrath of Khan*, reworking its most familiar scenes. This time around, Kirk, not Spock, sacrifices his life to save the ship—only to get resurrected by Khan's blood, of all things. Geeks felt betrayed. *Star Trek* was turning into *Transformers*.

So they rejected it. At the 2013 Creation *Star Trek* convention in Las Vegas, a group of hardcore Trekkers ranked the franchise's feature-length films first to last. Number one was *The Wrath of Khan*, which is hardly surprising. Number six was Abrams's first *Star Trek* film, the one from 2009. But *Into Darkness* wound up last, in thirteenth place, and "was met with boos when it was mentioned." Some argued that Abrams's films shouldn't even be considered, especially since they were set in an alternative universe; as far as those fans were concerned, that universe doesn't exist. An argument like this is an example of "fanon," short for "fan canon," when geeks take matters into their own hands and decide what's official and what isn't. In this case, it's also the ultimate form of retconning: to declare an installment in a franchise beyond the pale, unredeemable, nonexistent. It was no more than a bad dream.

Abrams later apologized to fans for the way he'd handled *Into Darkness*, in particular admitting that he should have let viewers know that Benedict Cumberbatch was playing Khan Noonien Singh, instead of engaging in the deception and rigmarole that the character's name was "John Harrison." The reason that happened, Abrams explained, was because Paramount didn't want moviegoers to feel they needed to know who Khan was in order to watch the film—once again, the homework problem. But this apology still annoyed fans, since it confirmed that *Star Trek* was no longer just for them, and that the needs of the many nongeeks outweighed the needs of the geeky few.

That point was further driven home in 2016, which saw the fiftieth anniversary of *Star Trek*. *Star Trek Beyond*, released on July 8 of that year, is a simplistic action flick that includes, among other things, a scene in which the *Enterprise* crew sabotages an alien terrorist's swarm of ships by blasting the Beastie Boys' song "Sabotage," a callback not to Trek's expansive mythos but the first J. J. Abrams film. One year prior, the writer/actor Simon Pegg revealed that Paramount was instructing him to make *Beyond* "more inclusive," more palatable to an even wider audience. Abrams's two films, while successful, grossed under half a billion bucks each, while Marvel's two *Avengers* films brought well over a billion each. According to Pegg, Paramount wanted *Star Trek Beyond* to be "fun, brightly coloured," more a "Saturday night entertainment," maybe "a Western or a thriller or a heist movie" starring Kirk, Spock, and McCoy. In the end, they settled for a *Fast and Furious* knockoff, which does make sense: *Furious 7*, like the *Avengers* films, grossed $1.5 billion worldwide. Watching *Beyond*, I was forced to grimly conclude as I gritted my teeth that the *Star Trek* I love—progressive, cerebral, philosophical, and psychologically complex—is no more.

BUT EVEN WHEN a single nerdy creator remains at the helm of a given franchise, that doesn't ensure things will go swimmingly for fans—and here, as with all things geeky, it comes back to *Star Wars*. Ever since 1997, geeks have had a love-hate relationship with their god, George Lucas himself, because of the ways in which he's been altering the deal. As early as 1981, fans started noticing he was fiddling around with *Star Wars*, making minor changes. For instance, he added the words "Episode IV / A NEW HOPE" to the opening crawl. That didn't annoy fans, but some criticized the addition's inelegance. In the 1977 version, after the crawl finishes scrolling upward, the camera pans down, revealing Tatooine and its moon. All is still, quiet, only for the Rebel Blockade Runner to burst into view, being followed and fired upon by the Imperial Star Destroyer. According to geeks, when Lucas changed the length of the crawl, he threw off the timing of the intricate interplay between the imagery and the score.

Which is annoying, but presumably most folks can live with that. More egregious were the changes that Lucas made when he rereleased the film in 1997 as the *Special Edition*. Most notoriously, Lucas altered the scene where Han Solo gets held up by Greedo, a green-skinned alien bounty hunter (a Rodian!). In the original, Han coolly stalls for time while unholstering his blaster under the table, then blasts Greedo to smithereens. But in the *Special Edition*, Greedo first fires at Han, missing him somehow, despite his being at point-blank range, only after which Han fires back. Fans were outraged, claiming that not only did the edit make no sense—how could Greedo miss?—it ruined the integrity of the scene, as well as Han's character. "Han Shot First" became a rallying cry among geeks, never mind the fact that, originally, Greedo was planning to take Han to Jabba, and didn't shoot at all. (I guess "Only Han Fired" doesn't have the same ring to it?) Geeks were further incensed when Lucas was photographed wearing a "Han Shot First" shirt. Just like Michael Bay, George Lucas—*George Lucas!*—appeared to be trolling them.

Their outrage was commemorated in a 2002 episode of *South Park*, in which the juvenile heroes break into Lucas's Skywalker Ranch to steal the negatives of *Star Wars* and thereby save them from any further desecration. Would that this had actually happened. Since then, Lucas has tinkered further with his movie, and not for the better as far as most geeks are concerned. Some fans created a Google Plus photo album documenting 350 differences between the 1977, 1997, and 2004 editions, accompanied by detailed commentary. Others made the 2010 documentary *The People vs. George Lucas*, which lists its own litany of changes. Still others circulated petitions online, demanding the release of the original theatrical versions on Blu-ray. Lucas did release those cuts on DVD in 2006, but they were taken from the 1993 Laser-Disc editions, and not remastered; they were also letterboxed, and not anamorphic widescreen. Thus, in a perverse state of affairs, the original theatrical release of *Star Wars*, arguably the most famous film ever made, is nearly impossible to see today, at least in high definition. So some geeks have taken it upon themselves to re-create it, producing the so-called Despecialized editions, made using different film releases and cels and production stills. Other fans have restored a thirty-five-millimeter print of the original 1977 theatrical release.

But what drove die-hard fans truly crazy was Lucas's prequel trilogy, released from 1999 to 2005: a master class in how to piss geeks off. The original *Star Wars* trilogy is grandiloquent and operatic, replete with powerful moments: Luke watching Tatooine's twin suns set, Han being frozen in carbonite, Darth Vader solemnly telling Luke, "I am your father." There's also humor, comic relief, but the movies aren't goofy, except for (admittedly) when the Ewoks beat up the Stormtroopers using rocks and sticks toward the end of *Return of the Jedi* (which most geeks don't like). But *The Phan-*

tom Menace effectively switched genres, being cartoonish and absurd, and more squarely aimed at kids. The biggest offender by far is Jar Jar Binks, a cartoon character more in the spirit of Roger Rabbit than Chewbacca—precisely what James Gunn was trying to avoid when he put Rocket in *Guardians of the Galaxy*. (No doubt Gunn had a few sleepless nights when he feared he was making another Jar Jar.) Every aspect of the Gungan known as Binks strains credulity, from his appearance to his antics to his accent (regarding which, why do the aliens in the prequels mostly speak English, rather than otherworldly languages that are subtitled, like in the original trilogy?). As one fan put it in *The People vs. George Lucas*, "My heart sank when [Jar Jar] started talking. I was like, 'Oh, it's that kind of movie'"—a cartoon for kids.

These changes in tone confront the viewer at every turn, in every scene, making it impossible to reconcile the prequels with their predecessors. Is *Star Wars* supposed to be a space opera, or more juvenile fare with poop jokes and crude attempts at slapstick? Compounding the problem is the shift in the series' aesthetic. Gone is the gritty, lived-in quality, the realist sci-fi approach that distinguished the original films. Instead, the artifice of the prequels is apparent—flaunted, even—the spotless sets and costumes and props looking as if they were manufactured just before they appeared in the film (which they were). This, and not *Star Wars*, was a return to a pre–New Hollywood aesthetic, a shiny retread of *Flash Gordon*. Rather than shoot on actual locations, Lucas mostly worked in soundstages, using green screens and CGI to fill in elaborate digital backgrounds, while in the foreground, characters traded lines while walking or sitting around. Their stilted deliveries didn't help the films feel less fake, though I have sympathy for the actors, who had to utter some terrible prose, including immortal lines like Anakin's limpid attempt at seducing Padme in *Attack of the Clones*, "I don't like sand. It's coarse and rough and irritating, and it gets everywhere. Not like here. Here everything's soft . . . and smooth." And while the prequels added new characters, and dramatized more of the timeline, they wound up making the *Star Wars* galaxy feel smaller, not more expansive. As it turns out, Anakin built C-3PO; he was "the Maker." Greedo was Anakin's childhood playmate. Jabba the Hutt presided over the podrace where Anakin won his freedom. Obi-Wan knew, and fought with, Boba Fett's dad, who was also the source of all the clones in the Clone Wars. Everyone turned out to know everyone else. This raised new questions that the movies, infuriatingly, didn't answer. Why didn't Obi-Wan and Darth Vader later recognize C-3PO and R2-D2? Are the Stormtroopers really all clones? Why did Obi-Wan speak so glowingly about Anakin to Luke? ("He wanted you to have his lightsaber, which he used to murder children. He was a good friend.")

What's more, the prequels frequently echoed the original trilogy, apparently by design. In *Attack of the Clones*, when Obi-Wan travels to the ocean planet Kamino, the building he lands on looks like Cloud City, in *The Empire Strikes Back*. After that, he battles Jango Fett in an asteroid field, another nod toward *Empire*. Anakin loses an arm to Count Dooku, just as Luke later loses a hand. These and other contrivances—*the many other contrivances*—stick out, precluding any suspension of disbelief, preventing us viewers from thinking we're watching history in the making.

Since fans couldn't lose themselves in the work, didn't feel they were back out in space again, they rejected the films, railed against them. In the British sitcom *Spaced*, Simon Pegg's nerdy character Tim burned his "*Star Wars* stuff" in a parody of the Darth Vader pyre scene at the end of *Return of the Jedi*. The next episode opens with him ranting at a child for daring to like *The Phantom Menace*, which Tim dismisses as a "jumped-up firework display of a toy advert!" then continues: "You are so blind! You so do not understand! . . . People like you make me sick!" When others tell him it's been eighteen months since the movie came out, and that he should swallow his disappointment, Tim responds with the lament, "It still hurts!"

Fans felt shattered, violated. Not only were the prequels crap, their obvious artifice made the original trilogy look fake, too. How could a person watch *A New Hope* without recalling *The Phantom Menace*? As Mike Stoklasa, another burned fan, put it in his "Mr. Plinkett" *Phantom Menace* critique, that movie ruins the whole of *Star Wars*, doing damage that is "totally beyond repair." As he moans: "The unfortunate reality of the *Star Wars* prequels is that they'll be around forever. They will never go away. They can never be undone." Everything has been ruined—*everything*.

That is why, just as with other offending fantasy artworks, geeks had to wish away the prequels, negate them, obliterate them, retcon them right out of existence. It's not uncommon to hear fans declare that, as far as they're concerned, the prequel trilogy—what? Sorry, never heard of them. In *The People vs. George Lucas*, one panel participant states, "In my *Star Wars* universe"—in his fanon—"the numbers 1, 2, and 3 don't exist." Another fan goes to even more desperate lengths to imagine an alternate, prequels-free present: "George Lucas talked about making prequels, but they never made it past screenplays before he died on the Van Wyck Expressway in a fiery car crash in 1989, right after making *The Last Crusade*."

Which was, in case you didn't know, the final Indiana Jones film. Although there were rumors that Lucas and Spielberg planned to reteam to shoot a fourth one, involving crystal skulls (I think?), they never got around to it. It's just as well. Imagine what a disaster that would have been! Why, it might have been worse than the prequels!

nine.

WHY SO SERIOUS?

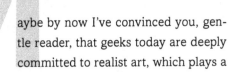aybe by now I've convinced you, gentle reader, that geeks today are deeply committed to realist art, which plays a crucial role in their fantastical game of pretend. But I imagine that some of you are still shaking your heads, and muttering that all I've managed to do is to miss the point: the

fact remains that geek art has little to do with *reality itself*, and that obsessing over robots and mutants and aliens and so on is itself unsettling and unhealthy. According to this line of reasoning, the basic problem with the geeks is their obsession with the unreal. Or, as Simon Pegg put it to *Radio Times* magazine, the problem is that so many people now are "walking out of the cinema really not thinking about anything, other than the fact that the Hulk just had a fight with a robot." (It seems that Pegg didn't care for *Avengers: Age of Ultron*.) The result, for Pegg, has been a "dumbing down" of the culture, an infantilizing that's taken "our focus away from real-world issues." Movies like *Ultron* are "very childish," unlike the New Hollywood classics (Peter Biskind's ears prick up): "*The Godfather, Taxi Driver, Bonnie and Clyde* and *The French Connection*, gritty, amoral art movies." Since we've seen that the difference between those films and the geek films isn't grit, isn't realism, then in order for Pegg to be right, and for Biskind to be right, the missing ingredient has to be something else, namely subject matter.

Pegg later walked back his comments, claiming he'd been misunderstood. But it's worth addressing his complaints because they're hardly remarkable, having been made in one form or another by critics like Peter Biskind, Alejandro G. Iñárritu, Kay Hymowitz, and Gary Cross, as well as countless others, and having been echoed by numerous geeks. Subject matter is why so many people dismiss geek culture out of hand as pointless, childish, stupid, unserious, inartistic, and, in a word, *bad*. So what if the artworks are realist? That might make them even worse! If the Incredible Hulk is just a cartoon, then fine. The problem sets in whenever anyone—let alone a grown adult!—starts taking Ol' Green Genes seriously. Geeky stuff is kiddy fare, and growing up requires its abandonment. If the artwork features the Hulk, then the artwork is for kids, and that is that. Any adult who buys a copy of the comic, or a ticket to the movie, is a forty-year-old virgin to be pitied.

At its core, this argument claims that the only good artworks, the only redeeming ones, the only ones suitable for adults, are those about actual things—"real-world issues," artworks whose subject matter actually exists. Cops and robbers are real, while talking cyborg raccoons and Incredible Hulks are unreal, imaginary, as insubstantial as phlogiston. By such logic, it's somehow wrong for art's subject matter to be supernatural. The more unreal the subject is, the worse it is, while the more real it is, the better. A variation on this argument can be found in the idea that geek culture is somehow inferior, stunted and immature, because its artworks often exclude certain real-world content, such as discussion of present-day politics, or families struggling with poverty, or sex scenes. Since the characters in the *Harry Potter* franchise go on dates but never get any further than snogging, those novels and movies are incomplete, lacking essential adult-world elements, which makes them okay for children, perhaps, but inappropriate for adults.

We've already seen this type of thinking on display in *Easy Riders, Raging Bulls*, where Biskind argues that art gets better the more it mirrors reality. But sometimes geeks trade in this kind of reasoning, too. Self-professed "Geek

Queen" Helen O'Hara, writing in *GQ*, praised the movies of the Marvel Cinematic Universe for providing "a new chance for superheroes to develop like, you know, people," by having the characters continue across multiple films and TV shows, where they're depicted dealing with trauma and the consequences of their actions. O'Hara contrasts this with previous superhero movies, from *Blade* through Christopher Nolan's *Dark Knight* films, which followed (she claims) a 1-2-3 pattern: first an origin story, then a sequel where the hero considers quitting, then a third installment where the hero turns bad for a while before redeeming himself, followed by a reboot. This O'Hara considers "an immature way of storytelling . . . stuck in perpetual childhood where there is no real change or consequence beyond a set point." On the one hand, we see O'Hara's geeky allergy to formula and reboots, signs of artifice that give the game away. But on the other, she is arguing that the films of the MCU are more mature than older superhero fare because they better imitate real life.

There are multiple problems with this line of thinking and with the idea that being about or more like "the real world" somehow makes an artwork more serious, more mature, and more artistic. But let's not kid ourselves. While the classic New Hollywood pictures—canonical works like *Five Easy Pieces*, *The French Connection*, *The Godfather* parts one and two, and *Taxi Driver*—were all realist, more or less, they weren't documentaries. They were artworks, fictional films, fictional *genre* films, and what's more, they hardly represented the 1970s as a whole. Mind you, I don't think that makes those movies somehow not great; they're all great films. But if one's argument is that those films are great *because* they were somehow realer than other artworks, closer to life, then surely it has to be a problem they still left so many real things out. I think the New Hollywood was great, but it was also, by and large, a white male movement, cis and straight, and (except for some notable exceptions) blithely unconcerned with women, or people of color, or other ethnic minorities, or gays or those who are transgendered.

But even if the New Hollywood didn't go far enough, perhaps it still stepped in the right direction, and maybe Biskind's point still stands? Certainly many agree that in order for art to be good, to be adult and sophisticated, it must be a drama that addresses a real-world issue. Time and again we see this argument made, both explicitly and implicitly, by prestige critics, who condemn works of fantasy as juvenile and frivolous, daring to endorse them only when they tackle real-world matters head-on. The film critic Dave Kehr, tasked in 1982 with reviewing *Raiders of the Lost Ark*, grumbled that the adventure was nothing more than a "giggly pastiche of a Republic serial"—a bad copy, then, of something already bad to begin with. He compared it unfavorably with George Romero's *Dawn of the Dead*, accusing Spielberg and Lucas of lacking "Romero's underlying moral seriousness." The seams may show more in *Dawn*, which of course was made with one-thirtieth of the budget that

Raiders had, but for Kehr, Romero succeeds artistically, because while his movie may contain zombies, they come with an anticonsumerist message, stumbling about as they do inside a shopping mall. Lucas and Spielberg, by contrast, despite being at the height of their combined powers and fame, acted irresponsibly by playing Indy straight, rendering all the raiding realistically, and avoiding moral instruction. Nothing to be had here, folks, but giggles and thrills, fistfights with Nazis and daring escapes from basements full of snakes. This mentality persists. Kehr's fellow critic J. R. Jones lambasted *Avengers: Age of Ultron* for lacking anything that would "dignify the gaping-idiot spectacle," such as "social commentary or serious drama."

The *New York Times* critic A. O. Scott makes the same point but backward in his review of *Revenge of the Sith*, which, it will help to remember, came out in 2005. Writing about it, Scott applauds George Lucas for "clearly jabbing his light saber [*sic*] in the direction of some real-world political leaders." In particular, Scott likes the moment where Anakin Skywalker turns and glowers at Obi-Wan Kenobi, then whiningly intones in his angst-ridden voice, "If you're not with me, you're my enemy." Just in case you didn't get it, Scott makes the subtext text: the villain is "echoing the words of George W. Bush." Scott likes even better Kenobi's reply, that "only a Sith thinks in absolutes." (That sure showed the Bush administration!) Scott admits that this exchange might strike some viewers as "overwrought," barely even subtext, but he gives Lucas kudos nonetheless for injecting that galaxy far, far away with dialogue hitting closer to home. "For decades," Scott writes, Lucas "has been blamed (unjustly) for helping to lead American movies away from their early-'70s engagement with political matters, and he deserves credit for trying to bring them back." Arguments like these litter the critical scene, sharing in common the agreement that if a movie jabs its lightsaber at the proper real-world leaders, then it's okay; it gets a pass. But if it doesn't, then it's drivel, mindless spectacle, the new opiate of the masses, the product of a culture industry unconcerned with art.

For what it's worth, I agree that Hollywood, and the entertainment industry at large, isn't in the business of making art. But neither is it in the business of *not* making art. Better to say that it's an industry that's largely *indifferent* to art. If people want to buy tickets to movies because they think they're art, then great! The movies are art! Buy away! But if art isn't selling this month, don't worry, because the movies are all art-free! *Hollywood makes whatever people buy.* It's an industry, not entirely dissimilar from other industries, such as the manufacture and marketing of toothpaste and automobiles. And what's more, that is how it's always been. Martin Scorsese and William Friedkin didn't get to direct motion pictures because they were *artists*. Rather, because their movies made money, Hollywood turned a blind eye to the fact they were making art, the same way it turned a blind eye to the fact that Tim Burton and Christopher Nolan, in making their lucrative *Batman* movies, were making art.

So the problem isn't the fact that one type of movie is more commercial, more industrial than another: they're *all* commercial, all commodities, all products of the same industry. Rather, the problem is whether some movies are more *edifying* than others. And what we have here, when all is said and done, is a deep anxiety about the escapist nature of fantasy, the concern that it takes us away from the real world, even if only temporarily, thereby distracting us from the problems at our door. It's an old prejudice: geeks are immature losers who can't hack it in the real world, so they immerse themselves in artworks about unreal things, rather than—I don't know—taking their cars in for oil changes, then sitting in the lobby, scanning Twitter for headlines about Zika and global warming. Or watching Real Art, which confronts us with Real World Issues: biopics and movies about the Holocaust and war and disease and racism, movies that educate us, the way that *12 Years a Slave* and *Spotlight* and *Moonlight* do. Why, one should get college credit just for watching them! But what does a person learn when the Hulk throws down with Ultron? Absolutely nothing! It's all empty calories, both the movie and the popcorn that the viewer crams in his mouth in between guffaws. How despicable and moronic!

Perhaps it's due to my own geeky immaturity, but I have to guffaw myself when I hear these kinds of arguments. I won't deny that geek art is escapist. How could I, after I've just spent chapters documenting geek culture's commitment to constructing elaborate secondary worlds, then surrendering to the fantasies they depict? But I will disagree with the argument, which is really more like an assumption, that escapism is a problem.

Before I explain why, let me address an obvious objection, and state for the record that anybody who mistakes fiction for reality has a problem. If a geek believes that Harry Potter is a real person, or that Klingons exist, or that zombies might soon attack, then, by all means, that person's in dire need of help, and we should stage an intervention. But this is true of anyone who believes in any fiction, fantastical or not. I know Democrats who watched *The West Wing* and now think that what the United States needs is a president just like Jed Bartlet, if not Martin Sheen. And the United States recently elected a very different president, Donald Trump, who seems deeply confused about what's true and what is a lie, repeatedly claiming that his inauguration was attended by millions more people than were actually there, and that other millions illegally voted for Hillary Clinton (although, curiously, they did so only in places like New York and California, driving up the popular vote but not affecting the Electoral College). And in the aftermath of Trump's victory, much has been written and retweeted about "fake news" and the censorship of scientific research on topics like climate change, issues where the fundamental problem is a failure to agree on what constitutes our shared reality.

Are geeks at greater risk for this affliction than other people? Are they more prone to live in worlds of their own making than the real one? Certainly that's a common stereotype—that geeks would rather retreat to made-up, simpler places, safe spaces, inhabited by imaginary friends, than deal with the hard complexities of the actual world.

The ensuing insults write themselves: grow up, take a shower, go on a date, join the human race—as William Shatner famously put it on *Saturday Night Live*, "Get a life!" Step out of your parents' basement, explore that strange land that surrounds you. Peter Biskind indulges in this stereotype in his chapter on Steven Spielberg and *Jaws*, entitled "Revenge of the Nerd," where he writes that, even when Spielberg was making *Jaws*, he was "emotionally still a teenager [who] subsisted on Twinkies and Oreo cookies [and] slept in white crew socks and white T-shirts." (God forbid.) On the following page, Biskind highlights how as a twentysomething, Spielberg "had little experience with women, and was extremely awkward and uncomfortable around them." Spielberg may have been a late bloomer, not having had a serious girlfriend until he was thirty—Amy Irving, who later became his first wife—but Biskind is taking a very cheap shot. Who cares whether Spielberg was getting laid if he was a great artist, making important movies? Furthermore, lots of New Hollywood movies weren't illustrations of life, but fantasies. In exchange for revising *Dirty Harry*, John Milius requested "a $2000 gun." Writing *Magnum Force*, this time with Michael Cimino, earned him yet another gun: Clint Eastwood gave him one of Dirty Harry's .44 Magnums. Meanwhile, Martin Scorsese's films, while certainly gritty, also revel in artifice. *Mean Streets* ends with a man crying, "Good night, good luck, and god bless you!" as people applaud and a woman pulls down a window shade as if it were a curtain. *Taxi Driver* features flamboyant camera work and editing, being a fever dream whipped up by

Paul Schrader, who also wrote the outlandish revenge fantasies *Rolling Thunder* and *Hardcore*. No matter what people might claim now, those movies weren't documentaries.

But sure: many people gravitate to SF and fantasy and superhero comics because they're socially isolated. The director Edgar Wright has described how he turned to fantasy while growing up in "a very small town which was kind of boring." Encouraged by his artist parents, he daydreamed in order to make his life more interesting and exciting. (He later filmed *Hot Fuzz* in his hometown, in an attempt to realize his childhood imaginings.) Frank Miller, speaking with *The Comics Journal* in 1981, expressed something similar: "I grew up as a comic-book junkie. I think that came from being miserable in Vermont, from being a maladjusted child." He also admitted that his desire to make comics about vigilantes like Daredevil and Batman stemmed from his own frustrations with living in New York City in the early 1980s. (That said, he took pains to distinguish those impulses from reality, confessing "the one time where I actually got punched in the mouth—hard—was one of the ugliest experiences in my life. It certainly generated the ugliest emotion I've ever had.") For my own part, while my childhood was far from miserable, I was never very popular, and most of my friends were make-believe. I'll freely admit that one of the reasons why I fell in love with *Star Trek: The Next Generation* and *Uncanny X-Men* was because they provided me with solace from grade school and high school, places I disliked. *Star Trek* was more than just a TV show, *X-Men* more than just a comic. They were my means of dreaming of a better life, and I invested a great deal of myself in them from the age of ten through eighteen.

But wasn't that exactly what the movies were for a young, asthmatic Martin Scorsese, who obsessively rewatched the films of Michael Powell and Emeric Pressburger? Wasn't that what bodybuilding was for Arnold Schwarzenegger, whose father abused him, and who dreamed of moving to America, to become like his idol Steve Reeves? Escapism comes in many forms, being a means of coping with *alienation*, dissatisfaction with the current state of things. And in escapism can be found the motivation to change one's life. One of the reasons why I went away to college was because I was enamored with *X-Men* comics, and Professor Xavier's School for Gifted Children. I wanted to see what else was out there, beyond the valley where I grew up, meet different people. Perhaps that was shallow of me, but it's how I summoned the courage to leave my home, and later take a job in Thailand.

Meanwhile, *Star Trek: The Next Generation* remains the single most compelling vision of the future that I know. The inhabitants of the Starship *Enterprise* have replicators and access to a sickbay, free housing and education and food and health care. They live without scarcity, money, or crime. They treat one another with respect, regardless of gender or ethnicity or sexual orientation. They're all equals. Transporters have erased distance, while universal translators have eliminated language barriers, making the sum knowledge of numerous societies available to all. As such, everybody is free to do whatever they want, whether it's study engineering or medicine, or become an artist. What's more, this vision of the future is self-critical, committed to over-coming its own deficiencies, which is why later incarnations of *Star Trek* featured a black captain and a female captain.

Star Trek's willingness to envision a better future is why it's appealed for so long to so many. I'm not embarrassed to admit I'd rather live in the world that *Star Trek* depicts, in terms of its morals and freedom from scarcity, than the world I currently live in, and that isn't just escapism—it's aspiration. (Beam me up, Scotty.) As a friend of mine once said, "*Star Trek* is our religion." Exactly right. That's why I'm still passionate about the franchise and its characters, like Data and Picard, who embody its principles, and serve as role models, made-up though they may be. And that's why I hated, hated, hated the past three *Star Trek* films, and felt so betrayed by them. It wasn't because they featured different actors, or different *Enterprise* set designs. It was because the moral values that I associate with *Star Trek* were discarded.

For similar reasons, I walked into *Logan* not only feeling hopeful, but with a great sense of trepidation. I wasn't just looking to be entertained; I was looking to see a great film, one that respected the investments I've made in that charac-ter and his world. Even as an adult, I retain a strong senti-mental attraction to Wolverine, a loner whose gruff exterior hides his lack of self-worth. That struck a nerve with me as a kid. If nothing else, *Logan* provided me with a chance for self-reflection; I can't watch the film without remembering my past. But for non-geeks, it's just a movie, cool or not cool, good or bad. They either like it or they don't, and then they go on to something else. I understand that. When the Chicago Cubs won the World Series in October 2016, it didn't mean much to me, because although I live in Chicago, I am not and never have been a Cubs fan. But I have friends who were overjoyed, because they've been Cubs fans since they were children, and have spent their lives rooting for the team. This seems very healthy to me, not to mention very human; I understood why they were happy, and didn't insult them as stunted degenerates who couldn't handle adult-world responsibilities. (Okay, I did, but only a little, and all in good fun.)

No less an adult than Barack Obama, when asked by *Rolling Stone* about the contents of his iPod, confessed that its "2000 songs" were "more heavily weighted toward the music of my childhood" than toward "new stuff": "a lot of Stevie Wonder, a lot of Bob Dylan, a lot of Rolling Stones, a lot of R&B, a lot of Miles Davis and John Coltrane." Obama even admitted that music served, while he was president, as a welcome means of escape: "Music is still a great source of joy and occasional solace in the midst of what can be some difficult days." My parents still listen to the Beatles and the Beach Boys, music that they enjoyed when young; indeed, they sometimes still listen to the same vinyl LPs my mother bought as a teen. This isn't uncommon. The Rolling Stones are still on tour, and plenty of baby boomers are happy to tell you how much better things were back in the days of their youth. In Steven Soderbergh's 1999 movie *The Limey*, Peter Fonda's character, Terry Valentine, describes the sixties (to his much younger lover) in terms that geeks can readily understand, comparing that decade to a dream of a faraway place "that maybe only exists in your imagination." Upon waking up, you can't entirely remember what you saw, the lay of the land. But "when you were there, though, you knew the language. You knew your way around." Reading Peter Biskind's *Easy Riders, Raging Bulls*, I'm often touched by how much his book resembles Terry Valentine's speech, expressing Biskind's own dream of returning to a glorious time, now lost.

SO MAYBE ESCAPISM has its place. But to caricature geeks as dweebs who want nothing more than to run away from reality is to overlook geek culture's numerous political commitments. Scratch the surface of a geek artwork, and you'll find serious concerns. As it turns out, fantasy is still always about the real world—what else is there for art to be about? The resident *New Yorker* film critic Anthony Lane found *Scott Pilgrim vs. the World* underwhelming: "no more than a skit," as you'll recall, "padded out with visual fluff" but lacking depth or substance, its fights "all painless panic" rendered in a "zippy update on old *Batman* shows." (*Not* a compliment.) But his fellow critic Richard Brody disagreed, seeing the film as "an exemplary portrait" of the anxieties of today's "middle-class, technologically connected teens." In his view, the movie represents how young people construct their senses of self from what they see in "graphic novels and video games," then perform those selves on social media, which requires "the constant maintenance of a self-aware guardedness." In this regard, Brody considers the film a modern update to the classic French New Wave movie *Breathless*, in which Jean-Luc Godard and Jean-Paul Belmondo portrayed how the youth of their generation modeled their behavior on movie stars. Brody concludes by declaring, "*Scott Pilgrim vs. the World* presents a richer blend of the contemporary adolescent experience than any teen comedy I've seen." (I agree.)

Even big dumb summer blockbusters like *Avengers: Age of Ultron* are still "about" the real world, after a fashion. I'll admit I didn't think the movie great; nor did most geeks. But even when watching a mediocre action film, there's no real getting away from real life. When the Hulk kicks and punches a robot (actually, robots), isn't the underlying motivation behind the scene an anxiety over modernity made manifest? The Hulk, like Godzilla, is a by-product of the nuclear age, and he reflects (by way of Robert Louis Stevenson's Mr. Hyde) our deep-seated fears about nuclear warfare and radiation. Not for nothing do his fellow Avengers describe him as an out-of-control "rage monster." Ultron, meanwhile, is the latest in a long line of automata—dating back to Mary Shelley's Frankenstein's monster, if not further—that wriggle free from human control to run amok. When we watch those two grotesqueries fight, we're watching our id slug it out with our ego, both having been weaponized by the Industrial Revolution. The fact that *Avengers: Age of Ultron* isn't a particularly good artwork— that it doesn't tell as good a story as *Frankenstein* or *The*

Terminator—reflects badly on its creators, to be sure, but its badness isn't due to it's not being about "something real."

The same year that *Age of Ultron* came out, Simon Pegg starred in *The World's End*, a movie about a grown-up yet out-of-control alcoholic who winds up battling not one, not two, but a whole horde of evil robots. (They're also alien invaders. Take that, Hulk!) Pegg swore to *Radio Times* that he planned to "retire from geekdom," to "go off and do some serious acting." But *The World's End* is deeply moving, a powerful portrait of alcoholism and the way aging tests one's friendships. It would be terrible if Pegg did not consider his acting in it "serious."

If anything, I think we don't take geek culture seriously enough, being too quick to dismiss its artworks as stupid and frivolous, instead of taking the time to read them, to try interpreting them before we criticize them. Part of the problem is that many people, especially older people, remain allergic to geekdom, still holding the prejudices they associate with nerds. This seems especially true of prestige critics, who, in their desire to not be perceived as geeks themselves, staunchly protest that they don't understand a lick of the geeky movies they're watching, popular fare that the culture is forcing them to view. Geeks signal to one another that they're members of the same club, initiates of the same secret guild. Prestige critics do the opposite; they signal to their readers that they have *nothing to do* with that guild, or with the geeks. To them, being able to distinguish Wolverine from his nemesis Sabretooth, or even *Star*

Wars from *Star Trek*, is a point of pride, which is what leads so many to claim that superhero movies both make sense only to comic book fans and lack any complexity or nuance, a difficult circle to square.

This bias persists because geek culture was once underground, alternative, part of its own counterculture that's right now in the process of going mainstream. And like all countercultures—alienation incarnate—geek culture embodies a particular set of politics. Geeks tend to be secular, as well as proscience and protechnology, and they like artworks that endorse those values. Geeks think of artworks as places to speculate about technologies and social structures, ways of living, that today are only imaginary. That's why the geek blog *io9* publishes articles on geek artworks side by side with reports on scientific discoveries and technological advancements. The editors, writers, and readers of *io9* don't distinguish between the two. Visiting *io9* recently, I came across posts about the novels of the *Star Wars Expanded Universe*, Elon Musk's ongoing plans to send humans to Mars, and an article about costumes on *Game of Thrones*. As the site's tagline puts it, "We come from the future."

In this way, geek culture retains its origin in philosophy and science, and the practice of using artworks as thought experiments, the means for modeling outcomes. Utopian artworks like *Star Trek* model our aspirations by projecting a better world, while dystopian artworks like *Blade Runner* and *The Terminator* model our fears. By projecting alternate visions of what *could* be, geeks are trying to come to grips with the present moment, and where it might lead.

I've already laid out why I think *Star Trek* is pretty much the greatest thing ever, at least when it comes to proposing a vision of the future. But obviously *Star Trek* is also very much concerned with the here and now, as are most geek artworks. Only someone unfamiliar with geek culture could accuse it of being indifferent to politics and moral struggles. Instead, geeks have long used their hobbies to express their views on such issues. Cosplayers, for instance, routinely assert their right to dress up as whatever characters they admire, regardless of ethnicity and sex. And creators of fan fiction and fan art have long made "slash" works that depict characters of the same sex—say, Kirk and Spock—in romantic, even erotic entanglements. Today, one favorite pairing is "Stucky," which pairs Captain America with his childhood best friend, Bucky, who grew up to become the Winter Soldier. This led to a fan campaign, #GiveCaptainAmericaABoyfriend, requesting that Marvel officially make Captain America bisexual. On June 4, 2016, a cosplayer who goes by TheRoaringGirlCosplay posted to her Tumblr account an image, taken at a convention, of her playing as Captain America while kissing a fellow cosplayer who's dressed as the Winter Soldier. Behind the pair stand Chris Evans and Sebastian Stan, the actors who officially portray Cap and Bucky in the Marvel Cinematic Universe. Underneath the photograph, TheRoaringGirlCosplay wrote, "They thought we were fabulous! #GiveCaptainAmericaABoyfriend." Later, she edited the post to add, "They were totally cool with it! Seb said, 'Ohh! Hahaha, nice!' And Chris started giggling. The guy behind us said they high fived after we left!"

This kind of political advocacy can be found throughout geek culture, becoming both more common and more visible as geek culture becomes more mainstream. Many geeks oppose gender discrimination, criticizing, say, how it's taken Wonder Woman seventy years to get her own movie, or how slow Marvel has been to make a superhero film with a female lead. Or that there are so few female directors. Or that franchise toy lines often omit female characters, resulting in a dearth of Black Widow merchandise, for example, or Rey merchandise. In the case of *Star Wars*, the most common female action figure—at times the *only* such action figure—has been "Slave Leia," a depiction of Leia's capture by Jabba the Hutt in *Return of the Jedi*, where he forces her to wear her notorious golden bikini. Toy companies claim that's the only female action figure that sells, because their customers are all boys; similarly, Hollywood studios have claimed that people don't want to watch action movies with female leads. But geeks have never been ones to accept the way things have been for the way things have to be.

The prestige critics want artworks depicting the world the way it *is*. They regard anything other than that as apolitical distraction. But geeks want artworks depicting the world *the way it could be*. Which means their conflict isn't over whether art should be political; both sides agree that it should. They both think art instrumental. Instead, their disagreement is merely over *tactics*. Which works better? Depicting what is, or what might be? I have to confess, I don't really know. Maybe both ways are perfectly fine? (It's nice having choices.) What's more, the geek approach only makes sense, and only works, if one understands how things currently are. How else could one tell that the artwork's depicting something different? So if you ask me, I don't think there's any real disagreement between the two sides, and that the critics and the geeks should kiss and make up.

What a beautiful note to end on. But as it happens, we're still not done, because art is more than politics by other means. Art is *art*, with values all its own, and a politics all its own. To understand the meaning of that, and the significance of that, we must examine art on its own terms, taking it seriously as art, which involves reading it and interpreting it, trying to figure out what the people who made it are up to. So in the final chapter, let's do precisely that. Let's take a closer look at geek art, asking whether it's any good for anything other than escapism.

ten.

BACK OUT IN SPACE AGAIN

The Beauty of *Star Wars*

n 1997, Roger Ebert reviewed the crime thriller *Freeway*, which stars Reese Witherspoon and Kiefer Sutherland. He loved the film, which he described as a retelling of a "Grimm fairy tale in a world of poor white trash, sexual abuse, drug addiction and the 'I-5 Killer,' who prowls the freeways in search of victims." (That's Kiefer Sutherland's character, in case you couldn't guess.) Then, knowing that some of his readers wouldn't believe that the movie was actually good, purely due to its subject matter, Ebert warded off their complaints about his celebrating "such trash" by formulating "Ebert's Law, which reads: A movie is not about what it is about. It is about how it is about it."

Ebert was right. In order to understand and objectively analyze a film, or any artwork, one needs to examine what the filmmaker is saying about the subject matter, the content. That's why the measure of an artwork is more than just content, its subject matter, and can never be reduced to how closely the artwork resembles the real world. Realism is merely a means to an end, and only one way of making art. Artworks can be realist or nonrealist, dramatic or comedic, sincere or ironic, figurative or abstract, as well as different combinations of those approaches. Put another way, artworks are more than just mirrors held up to the world. Through them, artists respond to the real world, yes, but they respond also to other artworks. That's why learning to read an artwork, to interpret it and evaluate it, requires study and practice, learning how to untangle the web of allusions, of conventions and associations, through which artists encode and transmit meaning. Whatever else it happens to be, an artwork is also always a text, a representation of the world after a fashion, but never the world itself. As the philosopher Alfred Korzybski famously put it, "The map is not the territory." No artwork, not even a realist one, is any closer to the real world than any other.

Instead, all artworks are equally close, and equally distant, being entirely artificial.

Of course some desire to pretend otherwise, aspiring to make the map and the territory one, and artworks synonymous with the world. Peter Biskind regards the New Hollywood not only as direct documentation of the counterculture, but as *being part* of the counterculture, the two inextricably bound up with each other. His view is ultimately a Romantic one, I think, in which the movies made by the New Hollywood served as the counterculture's soul. As long as the counterculture was healthy, its soul was healthy, and the movies turned out good. But when the counterculture floundered, then failed, its soul sickened, and the movies went all to pieces. That's why Biskind has so little regard for the later New Hollywood films, "megabuck" flops like Martin Scorsese's *New York, New York*, Steven Spielberg's *1941*, Michael Cimino's *Heaven's Gate*, Paul Schrader's *Cat People*, William Friedkin's *Sorcerer* and *Cruising*, and Francis Ford Coppola's *One from the Heart*, all of which he decries as decadent works, made by men who'd lost touch with the muse, with the activity on the ground. After those failures came the dark time, the reign of the Emperor (Ronald Reagan), during which the New Hollywood directors went into exile from the studios, and few, if any, good pictures were made. How could one make them? The counterculture had been lost. If the movies got good again, then that would mean the culture was healthy once again, and vice versa. (It's like the White Tree of Gondor!)

But that's impossible now, because sellouts like Lucas and Spielberg poisoned the soil, leaving the truer artists, Scorsese and Altman and Friedkin, bereft, doomed to wander, homeless in an era of corporate franchises, in a land of unchecked corruption and consumption.

Geeks also wish to transform art into reality, but for reasons other than Biskind's. We've already seen their own unique Romantic urges, their fierce desire to have art not be art, but foreign lands that they can enter and therein lose themselves, and experience the sublime. To that end, they want art to document some stable other world. In March 1990, members of the rec.arts.comics newsgroup fell to discussing the quote "Metropolis is NYC by day, Gotham City is NYC by night." (Its source is unknown.) One user chimed in to complain about how different artists at different times have portrayed those two different cities in different ways—that some have "set them across a bay from each other," while others have located them elsewhere, sometimes a continent apart. As a result, "there are more than enough references to place them just about anywhere along the northern half of the east coast, if not somewhere inland." For instance, John Byrne located "Metropolis in the Midwest." The user then concludes that "it would be nice if DC actually came out with a definitive map of the DC universe and would then stick to it."

This is the geek desire par excellence. Of course Metropolis and Gotham are *fictional* cities, and as such don't have to be portrayed any single way, or represent any single thing. They are instead open-ended means for repre-

I FIND YOUR LACK OF FAITH DISTURBING

senting whatever it is artists want to represent. Whoever said that Metropolis is NYC by day, and Gotham NYC by night, understood that, and was making a metaphorical point. And a metaphor can't be mapped, not in any conventional way.

That discrepancy troubles the geek mind-set, with its preference for realism. Representations, which include metaphors and allegories and other types of meaning, undermine the illusion that Gotham City is a real place, somewhere out there. The geeks don't want Gotham City to mean multiple things; the geeks don't want Gotham City to mean *anything.* Instead, the geeks want Gotham City to function the same way that real cities do. Real cities don't represent, either metaphorically or in any other way; rather, real cities simply *are.* New York City *is* New York City, nothing more and nothing less. The geeks want Gotham City, similarly, to be only Gotham City, and not look as though it's representing another thing. To that end, they want a definitive map that identifies where Gotham City is, and where Metropolis is in relationship to that, an extra-artistic model set down in stone, a frozen past that later artists should inherit and be forced to abide by, re-creating that layout on every page, in every frame, in every scene.

This way of thinking and working is fine if one is making, say, a TV show, or a comic book miniseries, which requires consistency across episodes—unity inside the artwork's boundaries, between its beginning and its end. But it isn't fine if one is proposing that this apply to *all* artworks made with a given character or premise, because what's lost with that approach is the ability of later artists to use Gotham City in their own ways, to tell different stories about that imaginary place. In making his classic graphic novel *Batman: The Dark Knight Returns*, Frank Miller devised the Gotham City that he needed, a realist city that looked a lot like NYC, caught in the grip of a killer heat wave. He gave it twin towers for Harvey Dent, Two-Face, to attack; he gave it an amusement park for the Joker to terrorize. He gave it the places and features he needed to tell the story he wanted to tell, which in many ways continued his work on *Daredevil*, and put his work in conversation with vigilante films like *Dirty Harry*, *Death Wish*, and *Taxi Driver*. Soon after that, Tim Burton revised Gotham City to make his desired films, as did Joel Schumacher after that, and then Christopher Nolan.

That's how it should be. Artists should always be free to rework characters and other fictional concepts. Of course, new Batman artists are obliged to engage with the character's long history, and the city the man calls home. But they are also free to act *against* that history, which is to a large extent already contradictory. Some of those artists might choose to tell realist stories; others might choose to take less realist approaches, preferring expressionism and caricature. And others might combine realism and nonrealism. But being able to choose Gotham's placement and appearance is essential. More is at stake than artistic freedom. Franchises and long-running serial artworks must remain open-ended and malleable to survive, lest obsessive obedience to the past make them inaccessible to newer audiences—due to the homework problem, as well as the danger of becoming stale, old-fashioned, out-of-date. Just imagine if DC Comics had decided back in the 1940s that Bob Kane and Bill Finger's approach to Batman was gospel, and that all artists after them had to slavishly write and draw the strip the same way those two men had. It's hard to believe there'd be any *Batman* fans around today.

Being wholly imaginary, fictional characters neither live nor die; nor do their cities ever crumble into ruin. The only demise that fictions face is if people lose interest in them, and forget them. In this regard, characters are like concepts, not unlike "democracy" and "free will," intangible things one can't discover in the real world, not directly. Instead, they're principles that we've devised and then embodied, enshrined, in institutions like government, schools, the law. Such concepts always remain works in progress; we keep refining them, redefining them according to the spirit of the times.

Characters work in much the same way. Consider Luke Skywalker. Lucas created him so that *Star Wars* would have a hero. In the first film, Luke is a wide-eyed youngster dreaming of escape from his home planet, the remote desert world of Tatooine. He has courage and skill as a pilot, but he's also naïve and impulsive, driven by his emotions. He falls under the tutelage of Jedi Master Obi-Wan Kenobi and, as the older man says, thereby takes his first step into a larger world. By the movie's end, he's managed to trust his feelings and use the Force to blow up the Empire's Death Star, becoming a hero of the Rebellion. Along the way, he makes friends, finding a big brother in Han Solo, and a love interest in Princess Leia. Yes, a love interest: it's clear from *Star Wars* that Lucas intended Luke and Han to be rivals for Leia's affections. In *Skywalking*, Lucas's biographer Dale Pollock quotes his subject as saying in regard to the three heroes, "It was the classic triangle plot . . . One good guy, one bad guy. Who is the girl attracted to?" And when Harrison Ford demanded that Han Solo be further developed in *The Empire Strikes Back*, Lucas decided that "fit [his] plan to duplicate the love triangle in *Gone With the Wind*: Han as Rhett Butler, Leia as Scarlett O'Hara, and Luke as Ashley Wilkes. 'It has to be a real triangle with real emotions and at the same time, it has to end up with goodwill,' Lucas said."

As *Star Wars* was nearing completion, Lucas hired Alan Dean Foster, who had ghostwritten the *Star Wars* novelization, to write a sequel, *Splinter of the Mind's Eye*. Remember, Lucas was worried that *Star Wars* would be a flop, and figured the novel could form the basis for a cheaper follow-up film, to help recoup losses. *Splinter* is thus a much simpler affair. Luke and Leia crash-land on a jungle planet, where they get caught up in a race against Darth Vader for the Kaiburr Crystal, a mystical gem capable of amplifying Force powers. Setting the tale in a single environment was a means of keeping costs down (plus Lucas seems to be fond of jungles). Luke and Leia appear because Mark Hamill and Carrie Fisher were contractually obligated for two sequels; Han is AWOL because Harrison Ford had signed on for only a single film.

Splinter of the Mind's Eye is not a particularly good novel, but it remains interesting today because it reveals an alternative path for *Star Wars*, what might have been. Luke spends a fair amount of the story lusting after Leia. As early as page 3 we're reading about how "whenever he looked at her, the other"—that's Leia—"caused emotions to boil within him like soup too long on the fire, no matter if she was separated by near vacuum as at present or by only an arm's length in a conference room." (It's not clear how Luke looks at Leia across the "near vacuum" of space. He uses the Force?) Throughout, Luke is riddled with anxiety as to whether the aloof princess might reciprocate his feelings, given he's just a simple farm boy. Clearly Lucas hadn't decided yet that Luke and Leia were brother and sister, and the Luke-Leia-Han love triangle would persist into *The Empire Strikes Back*. There is also no evidence in *Splinter* that Darth Vader is related to Leia or Luke, Lucas not deciding on the "I am your father" business until he made *Empire*.

This is how characters develop, sometimes with as many false steps and dead ends as there are strides forward. Lucas didn't fully figure out who Luke Skywalker was until he made *Return of the Jedi*. (All's well that ends well.) And now that the Jedi Master is appearing in a new trilogy of films, the time has come for others to figure out what remains to be done with the fellow. Indeed, J. J. Abrams has claimed that Lucasfilm president Kathleen Kennedy convinced him to write and direct *The Force Awakens* by asking him, "Who is Luke Skywalker?"

As long as they appear in artworks, characters remain works in progress, necessarily so. Like philosophical concepts, how they develop, and what they go on to be, have to make sense in relation to the past. One can't throw out the values comprising democracy and start over. In the same way, an artist can't remake Princess Leia as a wisecracking robot determined to eat all the chocolate in the world, or transform Wolverine into an alien graffiti artist who dreams of someday owning a gold-plated pair of dentures. (Well, they could, but they'd probably confuse and alienate people.) There are core features defining any popular character that it would be difficult for any artist to jettison. Batman originally used a gun, until someone decided that the character should eschew such weaponry, since his parents were murdered with one. That change made sense; it made Batman better, more refined. So when Zack Snyder had Batman use guns in *Batman v Superman: Dawn of Justice*, his creative decision didn't make logical sense, and didn't move the character forward.

But that isn't to say that Batman can't change, or can't use a gun, provided that use is justified. Rather, he's all change, so much so that over the years, he's split into incompatible versions, as often happens with concepts. He started out as a gentleman crime-fighter, only to be forced by the Comics Code Authority to become more cartoonish, the kid-friendly Caped Crusader, head of the Bat Family (which included a costumed dog, because dogs were popular in the 1950s, thanks to *Lassie*). That take on Batman culminated in Adam West's Batusi-ing television portrayal, "the campy Batman," which fit the spirit of the zany and irreverent mid- to late sixties. The following decade saw a renewed emphasis on gothic elements and detective work, resulting in Dennis O'Neil and Neal Adams's Batman, which influenced Tim Burton and the 1990s cartoons. Around the same time, in the mid-1980s, Frank Miller created the brooding Dark Knight, which was evolved by Christopher Nolan. That version of Batman is dominant now, and Zack Snyder and Ben Affleck didn't stray too far from it when making *Batman v Superman*. But the grimmer, grittier, darker Batman hasn't eliminated the more gothic Batman, or even the campy, silly Batman, who resurfaced briefly in Joel Schumacher's two 1990s films. And who can say? Maybe in ten years' time, people will grow bored of Batman being so grim and so dark, and will yearn for a lighter take on the character. There are already signs that might be the case. Will Arnett's *Lego Movie* Batman gently parodies Christian Bale's grittier, gravel-voiced performance: "Darkness / No parents / Continued darkness / More darkness . . ." Or maybe a new variation on Batman will emerge? As always, creators and fans will embrace what they think best, rejecting the rest.

TO INSIST ON one version of Batman—solely a realist one— would mean to lose all of that, and whatever may come. Of course, having multiple versions of Batman and Gotham City reveals the inherent artifice of them all. Perhaps that would trouble Peter Biskind; for him, any sign of contrivance weakens an artwork, makes it less authentic, less genuine, less expressive. For geeks, signs of artifice also ruin the artwork—they ruin the fantasy, make them remember they're looking at art, not a foreign place. But whatever it is that Biskind wants, and whatever it is that geeks want, art *is* artifice, through and through. It is contrivance all the way down. That is why contrivance and artifice aren't, in the end, enemies of art. Even realism, in which the artist labors to conceal his or her hand, remains contrivance. *Realism is just another way of doing artifice.*

Artifice and contrivance are in fact the foundations of art, its basis, as are formula and conventions. To love art as art means to love those things, because that's all art ever is: something artificial that someone made. Rather than being a limitation, artifice *is* the nature of art, which isn't weakened by how it differs from the world. Instead, its differences from the world define what art is. In the case of film, each shot is only ever so big, the frame leaving out much more than it lets in. A shot is also only so long, having a beginning and an end. (Art's always bounded.) Those restrictions are the basis of film artistry. *Citizen Kane* would not be better if its images were expanded, taking in more of the title character's surroundings. Nor would it be better if they were in color, or in 3-D. And it wouldn't be better if viewers could hijack the camera and move it around, left or right, up or down, choosing to see different angles, different points of view, different scenes. Nor would it be better if we could wander Kane's mansion, Xanadu, smelling its smells, sitting down beside visitors and sharing with them meals and conversations, feeding the unruly cockatoo, or assisting Susan with her many jigsaw puzzles. *Citizen Kane* is defined by the restrictions of each shot; it is composed of what those shots exclude in addition to what they admit, as well as the order in which they were placed. Each shot—each composition, each edit—is the result of a series of choices, and the movie called *Citizen Kane* is the sum of those choices, the sum of the shots.

To love *Citizen Kane* is to love precisely that. And to love art is to love its limits, its boundaries, which are the nature of the medium itself. It's to love the thing the artist made given those constraints, and to wonder why he or she made it that way—why Welles chose to place the camera *here*, and to cut *there*, to wonder why he joined this strip of film to that one, in that way. To love an art form is to wonder what other artists have done given the same materials, the same medium, regardless of subject matter. To love art is to love the medium, which is never life itself, but something smaller, a stage representing a field in England, instead of an actual field in England. The beauty of art is finite; it is the beauty of the frame, and how the artist worked inside it, employing their given set of materials, and organizing the whole.

If one is truly devoted to art, then one wants to study these things, know these things. But if one is devoted to geekdom, then one might not want to study them or the history of an art form, learning how artists do what they do. Knowing the practice—how the sausage gets made, so to speak—will reveal the artifice, making it harder to surrender to the spell. When I watch a movie, I see the cuts because

I have trained myself to see them; I can't not see them. I see each shot as a composition, observing its boundaries, like depth of field. I see the film as a production; I see its design, its organization. None of this ruins the movie for me, because I love seeing these things. (I love film.)

But at the same time, none of this stops me from being a geek, up to a point. While I like watching films from all different times and places, my favorite movies remain fantasy films. I still remember the awe I felt watching *Return of the Jedi* for the first time, and Tim Burton's *Batman* for the first time. My love for those movies led me to want to watch other films, to take film classes while at college, where I first read books about film history and film style. That led to my interest in film aesthetics, the different approaches that people could take to the medium. I started watching French New Wave films, surrealist films, classic Hollywood films, independent films, silent films, experimental films. I started attending film clubs and film festivals, then writing about films, which led to my teaching film, and blogging about film, and eventually projects like this book.

To recoil from artifice, to despise it, is to love something else, to want something else, something other than art. It is to want to live on the Starship *Enterprise*, rather than watch a *Star Trek* movie or TV show. The more one wants the movies and shows, the more one cares about what makes them good in relation to other movies and other shows. But the more one wants the *Enterprise* itself, the less one cares about the art. That person still watches the movies and shows, but only because they can't go live on the *Enterprise*.

But if they could, then they would no longer need the art-works. That's why so many geeks don't want there to be any boundaries, any limits, in their art. They don't want the artwork, but what the artwork represents. And they don't want the artwork to ever end, because they don't want their experience of its subject to ever end. But art always ends. It has to; that's what makes it art.

As for the artwork known as *Star Wars*, that touchstone of geekdom, its guiding star—what was it, exactly? In the beginning, Lucas didn't set out to build another galaxy, a sandbox for other people to play in. Nor did he set out to make a franchise that he would oversee and revise until he was old. Nor did he set out to destroy the New Hollywood, or to infantilize the culture. He wanted simply to make a film, complete in itself, with a beginning, middle, and end, a single movie that would delight and enthrall those who saw it. Did Lucas succeed? Is *Star Wars* good? Or is it merely a means to a fantasy? Is it serious, even adult? Is it a work of art? What exactly did Lucas make?

Let's find out.

AT ITS HEART, *Star Wars* is a coming-of-age story. In this it recalls Lucas's previous film, *American Graffiti*, which fol-lows a group of teens as they spend a long night cruising around Petaluma, California, in their cars. The start of *Graffiti* sees two of its male leads, Steve and Curt, contem-plating their futures. Steve is getting ready to leave for college, while Curt is thinking of staying in town, despite having been offered a scholarship. In the end, the two men trade places, each one having changed his mind: Curt leaves while Steve stays. The final title cards tell us that Curt became a writer, while Steve wound up an insurance agent in Modesto, California, Lucas's hometown. Through this, Lucas was reflecting on his own decision to leave home to study film at USC. Already, becoming an artist is linked with leaving home.

In *Star Wars*, Lucas created a different surrogate, whom he this time named after himself. Luke Skywalker is an orphan, working on his aunt and uncle's moisture farm but yearning to travel elsewhere. (Lucas was raised on a walnut ranch.) Luke has talent as a pilot, but it's wasted on Tatooine, where the only fun to be had is hanging out at Tosche Station and shooting "womp rats" in his speeder, the *Star Wars* equivalent of tinkering with cars and cruising while listening to rock 'n' roll. That's how Lucas spent his teenage years, dreaming of becoming a race car driver. Fate intervenes, though, and Luke gets swept up in the larger current of history, leaving home with Ben Kenobi, a mysterious, mystical warrior. Under his tutelage, Luke learns the ways of the Jedi Knights, a lost order whose ranks included Ben and Luke's dead father. Together, they travel to a city, Mos Eisley, then to an even bigger city, the Death Star, which is the size of a small moon. Luke finds decadence and corruption in the former, soulless sterility in the latter.

Lucas depicts these proceedings with a realism that he learned, like his colleagues in the New Hollywood, from the French New Wave, Italian neorealism, and cinema verité. But *Star Wars* still kept one foot planted in previous science fiction, the "big message" allegorical films of the late 1960s and early '70s—*Planet of the Apes* and *Soylent Green*—plus novels like *Brave New World* and *Nineteen Eighty-Four*. Lucas had already responded to these works in his first feature, *THX 1138*, a portrait of a man who flees a society rendered docile by drugs, TV, and consumerism elevated to the level of religion. Lucas continued his allegorical storytelling in *Star Wars*, which tells how a lowly farmer rises up to take down an oppressive, mechanical Empire. Along the way, the farmer rejects his own dependence on technology: only by switching off his computer does Luke manage to blow up the Death Star.

Allegorical realism, then, or realist allegory. Lucas also threw in ideas he'd gleaned from German Expressionism. John Williams's score is highly expressive, assigning Wagnerian leitmotifs to the major characters. From Fritz Lang, Lucas borrowed the design of C-3PO, modeled on the robot in *Metropolis*, Maria. (The look of the city planet of Coruscant in the prequel trilogy was also inspired by that film.) More important, Lucas adopted the German Expressionist conceit of using landscapes to communicate information about the characters and the plot. Some geeks have decried the "mono-biome" aspect of *Star Wars*—of the entire trilogy—calling it unrealistic for all the planets to be reduced to just one climate. But Lucas's interest here wasn't strictly realist, but blending expressionism with realism. The desert planet of Tatooine reflects and amplifies Luke's frustrations and his desire to get away. A child of the frontier, Luke yearns for the tempting city lights. But once he arrives on the Death Star, he finds the place cold and industrial, immiserating and intolerable. Aided by a ragtag band of companions, he winds up rejecting that metropolis, escaping and joining a Rebellion headquartered in an Edenic jungle. Their temple home is tropical, lush, the exact opposite of where Luke started, and the "new hope" of the movie's eventual subtitle.

The Rebellion is Lucas's take on the counterculture. While researching and writing *Star Wars*, Lucas read Carlos Castaneda's 1974 book *Tales of Power*, an account of the Yaqui "man of power" Don Juan Matus, who spoke of a "life force." Matus became Obi-Wan Kenobi, and many of the wise sayings that Ben tells Luke are revised Castaneda. Early drafts of *Star Wars* also had characters searching for "Kyber crystals" so they could harness the power of the Force, a bit of New Age mysticism. (Those crystals resurfaced in *Splinter of the Mind's Eye*, then became the key component in Jedi lightsabers, and were recently resurrected as a plot point in *Rogue One*.) In the end, the hippie-like Rebellion triumphs because of its alliance with men like Kenobi, who passes his power on to Luke, his chosen heir.

But the Rebellion is more than just the counterculture; it's Lucas's metaphor for the New Hollywood itself. Many have observed that Han Solo was modeled on Francis Ford Coppola, the cocksure older brother whose fortunes rise and fall at the drop of a hat. Lucas met Coppola when Lucas was in his early twenties, roughly the same age that we find Luke. Han's a smuggler eking out a living under the nose of the Empire, pursuing adventure by the seat of his pants. He always needs money to pay off some debt, and although he wins massive fortunes through gambling, he can never hold on to the prize. This is what keeps him in thrall to slimy crime lords like Jabba, gangsters who thrive under the Empire, with their nightclubs and their dancers. Han Solo abandons this life to side with the goodhearted Luke, and join the Rebellion.

In this view, the Empire stands in for Hollywood, a stifling enterprise always interfering with people, changing the terms of the deals that it makes. Lucas hated having his films cut, hated having to compromise his artistic vision. After Warner Bros. cut four minutes from *THX 1138*, Lucas refused to speak to the studio's chairman, Ted Ashley, for a decade. He was similarly outraged when Universal cut four minutes from *American Graffiti*, an experience that led him to vow he would never again surrender creative control on any of his pictures. That's why he refused to move to L.A., the corrupt big city, and instead insisted on producing his own films in San Francisco. He expressed his frustrations with Hollywood to Dale Pollock at the dawn of the 1980s: "The studio system is dead . . . The power is with the people now. The workers control the means of production." That wasn't quite true, but Lucas wanted the same thing as Peter Biskind: for the counterculture-fueled New Hollywood to supplant the moribund studio system of the past. Lucas and Coppola dreamed of becoming successful independent filmmakers, and establishing an artists' commune in San Fran: American Zoetrope, Skywalker

Ranch. What drove and enabled this dream was the Force, Lucas's metaphor for art, the thing one leaves home to pursue, an invigorating power with which one can oppose the soulless Empire. The Force surrounds us, but only a gifted few can sense it and grow attuned to it, becoming shamans, leaders. Fittingly, Ben Burtt created the sound of the Jedi's weapon, the lightsaber, by combining the sound of a movie projector with a television set.

The tragedy of Darth Vader, then, is that he's a fellow artist, after a fashion. But he was seduced and twisted long ago by Hollywood, the big-city entertainment industry, having taken the quick and selfish path of easy reward, the path that leads only to the Dark Side. But Vader remembers the power of art, and knows it's more powerful than the Death Star. At the end of *Star Wars*, when Luke destroys the Death Star—when Lucas blows up Hollywood—Darth Vader isn't killed but is sent spiraling away, free to pursue his own fate.

In making *Star Wars*, Lucas was doing more than indulging in his nostalgia for *Flash Gordon*. Like Luke, he was searching for something. You can see it if you look. He'd graduated from USC feeling ambivalent about Hollywood. On the one hand, he loved movies. On the other, he could see how hard it was to make art in Hollywood. But his dream of becoming an artist had taken him this far, had gotten him out of Modesto. He resigned himself to becoming an editor, or maybe making documentaries and small experimental films. The risk was becoming like Darth Vader, doomed to know what art was but surrounded by an Empire that didn't care. The generals Vader deals with are working stiffs who put all their trust in their machines, and who speak of the Jedi, when they speak of them at all, as feeble sorcerers devoted to a religion whose "fire has gone out of the universe." That fire is both the Force and art. Both animate life. In becoming a Jedi, Luke rekindles that fire, but the danger always remains of succumbing to the Dark Side, of becoming the Empire's next servant.

Star Wars was Lucas's means of remaining independent, of making a movie he wanted to see. It's a deeply personal picture, combining his autobiography with elements taken from all the older movies he loved, the films that inspired him to become a movie director. Hollywood and the film industry as a whole was a soulless machine, wicked and corrupt, in love with making money, not art. But it had managed nonetheless to produce some great movies, which Lucas had absorbed while at USC. Besides *Flash Gordon* and *Buck Rogers*, besides *Metropolis*, *Star Wars* alludes to *Alphaville*, *Forbidden Planet*, *The Hidden Fortress*, *The Searchers*, *Triumph of the Will*, and *Yojimbo*, plus World War II fighter pilot films, and Arthur Lipsett's obscure 1964 experimental short *21-87* (which was another source for the term "the Force"). Lucas synthesized those disparate influences into a single fantastical epic, a testament to film artistry.

When *Star Wars* took off, becoming a runaway hit, a financial juggernaut, Lucas tried to harness its energy, its fire. He wanted to use its profits to create his own jungle temple, a private film studio, Skywalker Ranch, an alternative to Hollywood, a lush and verdant place outside the city. There on the outskirts, he'd retain full control, offering the other New Hollywood artists a place to work, a safe haven from the Empire. One can doubt whether Lucas succeeded in this task, whether he didn't become a slave to his own creation, which over time even he began to second-guess, and tinker with. The fire dimmed, went out. But there can be no doubt that *Star Wars*, the original *Star Wars*, wholly succeeded. It's Lucas's portrait not just of himself, but of his ambitions, and the New Hollywood's ambitions. It is a portrait of the New Hollywood itself. That old lost order was never exclusively devoted to realism. Rather, those actors and writers and directors fought to get out from under studio contracts and censorship, to make their way in the world at large, where they could make whatever pictures they wanted to make. So, too, did Lucas. By synthesizing realism and expressionism, pop culture and counterculture, the avant-garde and the geeky, he made a film embodying their commitment to art as rebellion and iconoclastic force. The New Hollywood's masterpiece, George Lucas's masterpiece, *Star Wars* is a movie about freedom.

NOTES

INTRODUCTION: THE GOLDEN AGE OF GEEKDOM

8 *In 2002, the top four films*: Brandon Gray, "*Spider-Man* Takes Box Office on the Ultimate Spin: $114.8 Million," *Box Office Mojo,* May 6, 2002.

10 *In a recent article in* Bloomberg Businessweek: Devin Leonard, "The Pow! Bang! Bam! Plan to Save Marvel, Starring B-List Heroes," *Bloomberg Businessweek*, April 3, 2014.

10 *Alicia Keys won praise*: Aaron Couch, "Alicia Keys Covers *Gummi Bears* Theme on *Late Night* (Video)," *Hollywood Reporter*, November 21, 2012.

13 *While making* Return of the Jedi: Dale Pollock, *Skywalking: The Life and Films of George Lucas* (1983; Da Capo Press, Updated Edition 1999), 273.

14 *"it'll be a big movie"*: Miriam Bale, "Jeremy Irons Wanted to Join the Circus but Was Too 'Middle Class,'" *Indiewire*, December 12, 2014.

14 *"a bloated sequel"*: Drew Hunt, "*Thor: The Dark World* (review)," *Chicago Reader*, November 6, 2013.

14 *"eminently missable"*: J. R. Jones, "*Thor: An IMAX 3D Experience* (review)," *Chicago Review*, May 4, 2011.

14 *"costliest"* . . . *"simple-minded"*: Ben Sachs, "*The Avengers* (review)," *Chicago Reader*, May 3, 2012.

15 *"Take away the toys"*: Anthony Lane, "Battle Weary," *New Yorker*, May 6, 2013, 88–89.

15 *"a film of ideas"*: David Denby, "Drifting," *New Yorker*, October 7, 2013, 88–89.

15 *"no more than a skit"*: Anthony Lane, "The Current Cinema: Tough Guys," *New Yorker*, August 6, 2010.

15 *"restless graphic wit"*: Anthony Lane, "The Film File: *Scott Pilgrim vs. the World*," *New Yorker*, August 13, 2010.

16 *"Popcorn pictures have always ruled"*: Peter Biskind, *Easy Riders, Raging Bulls* (Touchstone, 1998), 344.

16 *"childish"* . . . "The French Connection": Huw Fullerton, "Simon Pegg Criticises Science-Fiction and Genre Films for 'Dumbing Down' Cinema," *Radio Times*, May 19, 2015.

17 *he and his cohost, Jay Bauman, routinely complain*: See for instance RedLetterMedia, "*Half in the Bag*: Cheap Thrills and *The Grand Budapest Hotel*," March 29, 2014, and "RLM's 2014 Summer Movie Round-up," April 3, 2014.

17 *"poison"* . . . *"not growing up"*: Mike Fleming, "Alejandro G. Iñárritu and *Birdman* Scribes on Hollywood's Superhero Fixation: 'Poison, Cultural Genocide'—Q&A," *Deadline Hollywood*, October 15, 2014.

17 *Kay Hymowitz opens her book*: Kay S. Hymowitz, *Manning Up: How the Rise of Women Has Turned Men into Boys* (Basic Books, 2011), 1–2.

18 *"for cultivated and complex pleasures" [and following]*: Gary Cross, *Men to Boys: The Making of Modern Immaturity* (Columbia University Press, 2008), 233.

19 *"boy-man" [and following]*: Cross, *Men to Boys*, 3.

1. "OH, I'M BACK OUT IN SPACE AGAIN": THE REALISM OF *STAR WARS*

25 *"character- or theme-driven" [and following]*: Biskind, *Easy Riders, Raging Bulls*, 343.

25 "Star Wars *was the film"*: Biskind, *Easy Riders, Raging Bulls*, 316.

25 *"the mirror opposite"* . . . *"I feel badly about that"*: Biskind, *Easy Riders, Raging Bulls*, 343–45.

27 *the code, which had prohibited*: "The Hays Code," BFI Screenonline, n.d.

29 *"a new generation"*: Biskind, *Easy Riders, Raging Bulls*, 125.

29 *"one of a kind"*: Biskind, *Easy Riders, Raging Bulls*, 250.

29 *"to make films about their own lives"*: Biskind, *Easy Riders, Raging Bulls*, 227–28.

29 *"a gangster film"* . . . *"life as he knew it"*: Biskind, *Easy Riders, Raging Bulls*, 250.

30 *"art imitating life imitating art"*: Biskind, *Easy Riders, Raging Bulls*, 271.

32 *Supposedly, Elba really punched Pine*: Scott Huver, "How Chris Pine Got a Real-Life Shiner from Idris Elba While Filming *Star Trek Beyond*," *People*, July 22, 2016.

33 *"crude and badly done"* . . . *"done really well"*: Alan Arnold, *Once Upon a Galaxy: A Journal of the Making of* The Empire Strikes Back (Ballantine Books, 1980), 220.

33 *Lucas couldn't secure*: "A Long Time Ago: The Story of *Star Wars*," *Omnibus*, July 7, 1999, YouTube, uploaded by Black-

dog TV—Cinema on October 27, 2015, youtube/G2kWQ oL7pKs.

34 *"Lucas has created"*: Michael Kaminski, "The Early Drafts of the *Star Wars Trilogy*: The Reviews," *The Secret History of Star Wars*, April 2, 2013.

35 Forbidden Planet, *a clear influence on Lucas*: Arnold, *Once Upon a Galaxy*, 221.

35 *"spaceships that were operated like cars"*: Pollock, *Skywalking*, 154.

36 *"sleek"* . . . *"quasi-military feel"*: Pollock, *Skywalking*, 171.

37 *Lucas had maritime engineers*: Pollock, *Skywalking*, 160, 214.

37 *The other starships*: Pollock, *Skywalking*, 172.

37 *"was rolled in the dirt"*: Pollock, *Skywalking*, 160.

38 *"The sounds of the real world" [and the following description of Chewbacca's mask]*: Pollock, *Skywalking*, 178–79.

38 *"was hell bent" [and following]*: Biskind, *Easy Riders, Raging Bulls*, 263.

40 *when Martin Scorsese shot* Taxi Driver: Gregg Kilday, "*Taxi Driver* Oral History: De Niro, Scorsese, Foster, Schrader Spill All on 40th Anniversary," *Hollywood Reporter*, April 7, 2016.

40 *The president of 20th Century Fox, Alan Ladd, Jr.*: Pollock, *Skywalking*, 176.

41 *"banished"* . . . *"ethnicity"*: Biskind, *Easy Riders, Raging Bulls*, 16.

41 *But the director did understand*: Pollock, *Skywalking*, 150.

42 "Star Wars *was about*": Biskind, *Easy Riders, Raging Bulls*, 327.

42 *The cantina scene*: Pollock, *Skywalking*, 175.

42 *"The illusion was there"*: Pollock, *Skywalking*, 182.

2. THE CHILDREN OF SPIELBERG AND LUCAS

44 *In the days leading up*: Pollock, *Skywalking*, 180–85.

44 *"raw and painful" [and following]*: Roger Ebert, "*The Exorcist* (review)," rogerebert.com, December 26, 1973.

46 *The word* geek *first appeared . . . Brooklyn College*: *OED Online*, Oxford University Press, March 2014.

47 *That word,* fantasy *. . . making the imagined visible*: *OED Online*, Oxford University Press, March 2014.

47 *Helen O'Hara more than once insisted*: "Empire Podcast #236: Derek Cianfrance," *Empire Online*, November 4, 2016.

48 *"a technical marvel [without] much else going on"*: "*Half in the Bag* Episode 102: *The Revenant*," YouTube, uploaded by RedLetterMedia on January 25, 2016, youtube/cwJTnUkyvVg.

48 *the duo derided* Boyhood: "*Half in the Bag*: The 2016 Oscars," YouTube, uploaded by RedLetterMedia on February 24, 2016, youtube/kX50REHezPY.

48 *geek blog* Topless Robot: *Topless Robot* shut down on December 17, 2015, three months after rebranding itself (on September 14, 2015) as *The Robot's Voice*. See www.therobotsvoice.com/2015/09/topless-robot-has-become-the-robots-voice.php & www.therobotsvoice.com/2015/12/so-long-and-thanks-for-all-the-whose-responsible-this.php.

48 *"[we] never really came to a consensus"*: Luke Y. Thompson, "Breaking Bad Spoiler Discussion Thread," *Topless Robot*, September 29, 2013.

48 *"a nerdy movie or not"*: Rob Bricken, "I Have No Idea If *The Lone Ranger* Is a Nerdy Movie or Not, but Here's the Trailer," *Topless Robot*, October 3, 2012.

51 *"Will someone tell me"*: Roger Ebert, "The Great Movies: *2001: A Space Odyssey*," rogerebert.com, March 27, 1997.

51 *"too obscure and downbeat"*: Pollock, *Skywalking*, 142.

53 *In his 1920 volume* Space, Time and Gravitation: Sir Arthur Stanley Eddington, *Space, Time and Gravitation: An Outline of the General Relativity Theory* (Cambridge, U.K.: Cambridge University Press, 1920). Accessed via Archive.org on February 10, 2017.

53 *"faerie" [and following]*: J.R.R. Tolkien, "On Fairy-Stories," 1939. Accessed via excellence-in-literature.com on February

10, 2017. www.excellence-in-literature.com/wp-content/uploads/2013/10/fairystoriesbytolkien.pdf.

56 *Edgar Rice Burroughs's* John Carter of Mars: Pollock, *Skywalking*, 142.

56 *every "person, beast"*: Pollock, *Skywalking*, 134.

56 *Lucas worked out detailed histories*: Pollock, *Skywalking*, 166–68.

56 *This wealth of material*: Pollock, *Skywalking*, 146. See also Michael Kaminski, "The Complete History of the Sequel Trilogy: Episodes VII, VIII and IX." *The Secret History of Star Wars*, March 14, 2013.

58 *Its designer, Matt Jefferies*: "BBC Online-Cult-*Star Trek*-Matt Jefferies-Why NCC-1701?" *BBC Online*, February 7, 2011.

58 *When Kirk and the others*: Mike Stoklasa demonstrates this in the RedLetterMedia video *"Star Trek* ('09)," September 1, 2010.

59 *Vulcans have green blood*: "Vulcan," Memory Alpha, February 26, 2017.

59 *Klingons have reddish-pink blood*: "Klingon," Memory Alpha, March 10, 2017.

61 *"an essential" . . . "storytelling"*: Charlie Jane Anders, "7 Deadly Sins of Worldbuilding," *io9*, August 2, 2013.

61 *"eusocial life-forms"*: "Alien (creature in *Alien* franchise)," Wikipedia: The Free Encyclopedia, March 27, 2014.

61 *"straight drama" [and following]*: "Empire Podcast: Sharlto Copley and Neill Blomkamp *Elysium* Special," *Empire Online*, August 21, 2013. MP3.

62 *"they both had an incredible"*: Biskind, *Easy Riders, Raging Bulls*, 253.

63 *"very, very grounded"*: James Hibberd, *"Daredevil*: 7 Things We Learned About Netflix's New Series," *Entertainment Weekly*, December 29, 2014.

63 *"geared towards" . . . "gritty"*: Daniel Krupa, "Netflix's *Luke*

Cage Is 'Geared Towards an Adult Audience,' " *IGN*, March 3, 2015.

63 *"do the* Godfather II *of the X-Men world"*: "Empire Podcast: Matthew Vaughn, *Kingsman: The Secret Service* Podcast Spoiler Special," *Empire Online*, February 9, 2015.

63 *"guiding star"* . . . *"information"*: Owen Williams and James White, "Future Perfect: *Empire*'s Guide to the Biggest Movies Being Made Right Now," *Empire* #298 (April 2014): 33.

63 *"gritty realism"* . . . *" '70s Westerns"*: Amy Pascale, *Joss Whedon: The Biography* (Chicago Review Press, 2014), 199.

3. GEEK GOES MAINSTREAM

66 *Lucas, upset by what he perceived*: Pollock, *Skywalking*, 197–98.

67 *Starting in 1979, the Klingons . . . spoke an actual language*: Mark Okrand, Michael Adams, Judith Hendriks-Hermans, and Sjaak Kroon, "Wild and Whirling Words: The Invention and Use of Klingon," *From Elvish to Klingon: Exploring Invented Languages*, ed. Michael Adams (Oxford University Press, 2011), 111–34.

76 *"I was born free" [and following]*: Chris Claremont (writer) and Bill Sienkiewicz (penciller), *Uncanny X-Men*, Vol. 1, #159, "Night Screams!," Marvel Comics, July 1982.

76 *the article on cobras (the venomous snakes):* "Cobra," Wikipedia: The Free Encyclopedia, January 25, 2017.

76 *The article on Cobra, the ruthless terrorist organization*: "Cobra (G.I. Joe)," Wikipedia: The Free Encyclopedia, February 4, 2017.

76 *And the article "List of* Teen Wolf *characters"*: "List of *Teen Wolf* characters," Wikipedia: The Free Encyclopedia, March 15, 2017.

77 *"no hugging, no learning"*: Edward Kosner, "No Hugging, No Learning: The *Seinfeld* Credo," *Wall Street Journal*, August 12, 2016.

77   *"in the worst possible spot"*: "The Finale," *Seinfeld*, NBC, May 14, 1998.

77   *the 76.3 million people watching "The Finale"*: Brian Lowry, *"Seinfeld*'s Finale Ends Up in Sixth Place of All Time," *Los Angeles Times*, May 16, 1998.

77   *the series premiere . . . was viewed by only 15.4 million*: @the ryanwallis, "SEINFELD @SeinfeldTV Pilot TV Ratings from July 5, 1989: 15.4m viewers & 10.8/19 rating/share. Ranked #21," Twitter, May 3, 2015, 6:30 p.m., twitter.com/theryan wallis/status/594992510403014657.

78   *Between 1999 and 2008, the convention's attendance tripled*: "San Diego Comic-Con," Wikipedia: The Free Encyclopedia, March 19, 2017.

79   *It cost $176 million to make*: *"Jupiter Ascending* (2015)–Box Office Mojo," *Box Office Mojo*, n.d.

80   *Lucas claims to have initially limited* Star Wars *merchandising*: Pollock, *Skywalking*, 255.

80   *the merchandising revenue for* Star Wars *quickly surpassed*: Pollock, *Skywalking*, 194–95.

81   *In the late 1980s, Warner merged with Time Inc.*: Kathryn Harris, "Steven Ross, Chairman of Time Warner, Dies at 65," *Los Angeles Times*, December 21, 1992.

81   *Today, that massive company owns*: "Company | Time Warner Inc.," Time Warner, n.d., www.timewarner.com/company, April 13, 2017.

81   *Time Warner no longer owns Time Inc.*: David Lieberman, "Time Inc. Shares Slip as Magazine Company Goes Public," *Deadline Hollywood*, June 9, 2014.

81   *It's also currently in the process*: Meg James, "Time Warner Shareholders Vote to Sell Company to AT&T for $85.4 Billion," *Los Angeles Times*, February 15, 2017.

81   *Ted Turner bought in 1991*: Charles Haddad, "Turner Serious About Yogi Bear," *Chicago Tribune*, June 6, 1994.

81 *"today, the franchise is often the star"*: Kristin Thompson, *The Frodo Franchise: The Lord of the Rings and Modern Hollywood* (Berkeley: University of California Press, 2007), 6.

82 *The website Bond Lifestyle*: Remmert van Braam, James Bond Lifestyle, 2017.

4. DO YOU BLEED?

87 *in 1966 the character had sold*: John Jackson Miller, *"Batman* Annual Sales Figures," Comichron, n.d.

88 *before consigning Bats to the dustbin*: Joe Strike, "Frank Miller's *Dark Knight* Brought Batman Back to Life," New York *Daily News*, July 15, 2008.

88 *"Part of Daredevil's appeal"*: Dwight Decker, "Interview One," 1981, *The Comics Journal Library, Volume Two: Frank Miller* (Seattle: Fantagraphics Books, 2003), 21.

88 *This more practical approach*: Decker, "Interview One," 26.

89 *"walking dead, torture, vampires"*: "The Comics Code of 1954," Comic Book Legal Defense Fund, 2017.

89 *In 1971, the Comics Code was softened somewhat*: "Comics Code Revision of 1971," Comic Book Legal Defense Fund, 2017.

90 *"You've got to overcome"*: Kim Thompson, "Interview Two," 1985, *The Comics Journal Library, Volume Two: Frank Miller* (Seattle: Fantagraphics Books, 2003), 39.

90 *"romances"*: Kim Thompson, "Interview Two," 40.

90 *driven by his desire*: Decker, "Interview One," 31.

90 *"prestige format"*: A. D. Jameson, "Reading Frank Miller's *Batman: The Dark Knight Returns*, part 2," *Big Other*, February 8, 2010.

90 *a heftier price tag*: Brian Cronin, "The Fascinating Behind-the-Scenes Story of Frank Miller's *Dark Knight* Saga," Comic Book Resources, November 24, 2015.

91 *The first film in that series*: Joe Strike, "Frank Miller's *Dark*

Knight Brought Batman Back to Life," New York *Daily News*, July 15, 2008.

91 *"attitude" . . . "being lonely"*: Richard Thompson, "Stoked," *Film Comment* 12.4 (July–August 1976): 10–21.

95 *"my hand"*: Frank Miller, *Batman: The Dark Knight Returns*, 1986, DC Comics (2002 edition), 195.

95 *"Kids with a sort of happy"*: Kim Thompson, "Interview Two," 36.

98 *"a Tim Burton movie" [and following]*: David Crow, *"Batman Returns*: The Greatest Anti-Christmas Gift of All!," Den of Geek, December 21, 2016.

99 *"We might have killed the franchise"*: Mac Daniel, "Who Is Batman? Savior or Tortured Soul? After All These Years, We Still Don't Know," *Boston Globe*, June 12, 2005.

102 *"scruffier, grungier"*: Dan Jolin, "Fear Has a Face," *Empire* #223 (January 2008): 87–88.

102 *whose appearance and demeanor*: "Dressing the Joker," *IGN*, February 25, 2008.

104 *the Comics Code Authority, which officially came to an end in 2011*: "Legacy of the Comics Code," Comic Book Legal Defense Fund, 2017.

105 *"Rocket was a punchline"*: Sean T. Collins, "The Rise of *Guardian of the Galaxy*'s Rocket Raccoon," *Rolling Stone*, July 29, 2014.

106 *"Ain't no thing like me, except me"*: *Guardians of the Galaxy*, Marvel Studios, 2013.

106 *"a real, little, somewhat mangled beast" [and following]*: Ben Mortimer, "James Gunn Comes Clean on a Lot of *Guardians of the Galaxy* Rumours," HeyUGuys.com, April 18, 2013.

107 *ALF appeared not only*: Jordan Zakarin, "Greetings from Melmac: ALF Creator Paul Fusco on His Star Alien and Potential Comeback," *Hollywood Reporter*, May 22, 2012.

107 *Kermit has . . . appeared with Pepé the King Prawn*: "Empire

Podcast #16: June 15, 2012—Kermit the Frog and Pepe the King Prawn," *Empire Online*, June 15, 2012.

108 *and later Miss Piggy*: "Empire Podcast #104: Kermit, Miss Piggy, Anthony Mackie, Sebastian Stan—March 28 2014," *Empire Online*, March 28, 2014.

108 *"spoil the illusion"* . . . *"was really upsetting"*: Edward Douglas, "CinemaCon Exclusive: Jason Segel & Amy Adams on *The Muppets!*," *Collider*, March 30, 2011.

108 *"documentary-style"* . . . *"wants and desires"*: James Hibberd, "*Muppets* Scoop: ABC Revival to Explore Their Personal Lives in 'More Adult' Show," *Entertainment Weekly*, April 22, 2015.

108 *George Lucas reportedly annoyed*: Pollock, *Skywalking*, 167.

109 *Later, Lucasfilm made an Artoo mockumentary*: *R2-D2: Beneath the Dome*, 2001, YouTube, uploaded by Star Wars on February 11, 2013, youtube/tmkq-WGWvbk.

5. HISTORICAL DOCUMENTS

112 *"this Jim Henson fellow" [and following]*: "The Muppets Celebrate Jim Henson," November 21, 1990, YouTube, uploaded by the Jim Henson Collection on May 19, 2015, youtube/ubt Qf0df8Ms.

116 *"360 degree" [and following]*: Germain Lussier, "Gareth Edwards Explains Why *Rogue One* Was Shot Differently from Every Other *Star Wars* Film," *io9*, July 15, 2016.

116 *"strange graphics of fantasy"*: "A Young, Enthusiastic Crew Employs Far-Out Technology to Put a Rollicking Intergalactic Fantasy onto the Screen," *American Cinematographer*, American Society of Cinematographers, n.d.

116 *"approach to world-building" [and following]*: Ian Nathan, "Best of Both Worlds," *Empire* magazine (December 2013): 71.

117 *"documentary"*: *Firefly: The Complete Series*, DVD audio commentary, dir. Joss Whedon, 20th Century Fox, 2003.

117 The Star Trek Encyclopedia: Michael Okuda, Denise Okuda,

and Debbie Mirek, *The Star Trek Encyclopedia: A Reference Guide to the Future* (New York: Pocket Books, 1994).

118 *even scans of faux documents*: *Star Trek Blueprints Database*, Cygnus-X1.net, January 12, 2017.

118 *LucasBooks has published its own books of this ilk*: See *The* Millennium Falcon *Owner's Workshop Manual* (2012) and *The Death Star Owner's Technical Manual: Imperial DS-1 Orbital Battle Station* (2013), both by Ryder Windham, Chris Reiff, and Chris Trevas.

119 *Random House has published*: Jonathan Roberts, "The Lands of Ice and Fire—The Maps of *Game of Thrones*," Fantastic Maps, April 24, 2013.

120 *Rowling has used her Pottermore website*: Lauren Davis, "We Can Now Read About Ginny Weasley's Post-Hogwarts Career," *io9*, April 17, 2014.

120 *"which produces much the same effect"*: Sir Arthur Conan Doyle, *The Sign of the Four* (1889; *The Complete Sherlock Holmes*, vol. 1 (New York: Doubleday & Company, 1930), 87–158, 90.

121 *"so wild a story" [and following]*: Bram Stoker, *Dracula* (1897; New York: Penguin Books, 2007), 402.

121 Fantastic Four *#10 (January 1963) [and following]*: Stan Lee (writer), Jack Kirby (penciller), Dick Ayers (inker), "The Return of Doctor Doom!," *Fantastic Four*, vol. 1, #10, Marvel Comics (January 1963): 5–7.

122 *A later issue, #176*: Roy Thomas (writer), George Pérez (penciller), Joe Sinott (inker), "Improbable as It May Seem—The Impossible Man Is Back in Town!" *Fantastic Four*, vol. 1, #176 (Marvel Comics, November 1976). For more on this phenomenon, see Brian Cronin, "Drawing Crazy Patterns—Marvel Characters Visiting the Offices of Marvel Comics," Comic Book Resources, January 3, 2015.

122 *"an X-Men fan" [and following]*: *Logan*, 20th Century Fox, 2017.

123 *At* io9, *Charlie Jane Anders*: Charlie Jane Anders, "Why We Love Spoilers," *io9*, June 25, 2009.

125   *"bring me out of the film"*: "Empire Podcast: Empire's *Dark Knight Rises* Spoiler Special," *Empire Online*, July 24, 2012.

125   *"first as tragedy, then as farce"*: Karl Marx, "The Eighteenth Brumaire of Louis Napoleon," 1852, trans. Saul K. Padover, Marxists Internet Archive, n.d.

125   *According to movie studios*: Joe McGovern, "Why Do Trailers Spoil Their Movies? Because You Want Them To," *Entertainment Weekly*, July 27, 2015.

126   *There's no guarantee that more casual moviegoers*: Scott Beggs, "6 Reasons Why Trailers Have to Spoil Movies," *Film School Rejects*, September 16, 2015.

126   *articles that contain spoilers are heavily signposted as such*: See, for instance, Cheryl Eddy, "This *Alien: Covenant* Rumor Is Just Insane Enough to Make Us Hope It's True," *io9*, June 9, 2016.

126   *The lead designer of the card game* Magic: The Gathering: Mark Rosewater, *Blogatog*, Tumblr, October 22, 2015, markrose water.tumblr.com/post/131727660383/i-know-your-stance -on-trailers-but-are-you-really.

126   *encouraging others to follow his lead*: Mark Rosewater, *Blogatog*, Tumblr, May 14, 2016, markrosewater.tumblr.com/post /144356709553/i-also-started-avoiding-trailers-of-movies -ill.

127   *"real stakes"*: Adam Holmes, "7 Characters That You Don't Have to Worry About Dying in *Captain America: Civil War*," *CinemaBlend*, January 2016.

127   *"the fact that no one of tremendous importance"*: Johnny Brayson, "Only 3 Characters Die in *Captain America: Civil War* & Here's What That Says About Marvel's Greater Plan," *Bustle*, May 12, 2016.

127   *"No one of importance dies in* Captain America: Civil War*"*: Tom Ley, "Someone Should Have Died in *Captain America: Civil War*," *The Concourse*, May 9, 2016.

129   *"behind-the-scenes footage"*: Peter Sciretta, "CinemaCon: Ten

Minutes of *The Hobbit* Underwhelms; Higher Frame Rates Might Not Be the Future of Cinema," */Film*, April 24, 2012.

129 *"soap opera effect"* . . . *"motion smoothing"*: Bryant Frazer, "*The Hobbit*, the 'Soap Opera Effect,' and the 48fps (and Faster) Future of Movies," *Studio Daily*, April 30, 2012.

129 *Katharine Trendacosta's* io9 *article*: Katharine Trendacosta, "The Model Spaceships That Made *Interstellar* Look as Real as Possible," *io9*, December 9, 2014.

129 *"functional, because the desert"*: Damon Lavrinc, "How the Man Behind the Machines of *Mad Max* Put a Hellscape on Wheels," *Jalopnik*, May 13, 2015.

129 *"more ageless"* . . . *"date badly"*: Max Nicholson and Roth Cornet, "*Star Wars: The Force Awakens*: Harrison Ford's Advice to Oscar Isaac," *IGN*, December 4, 2014.

131 *"I remember I had it all worked out" [and following]*: *Galaxy Quest*, DreamWorks Pictures, 1999.

132 *Patrick Stewart, Jonathan Frakes*: "The Questrian-*Galaxy Quest* Databank-Trek Talks," *The Questrian*, n.d.

132 *attendees of the 2013 Creation* Star Trek *convention*: Devin Faraci, "The *Star Trek* Movies, as Ranked by *Star Trek* Con-Goers," *Birth.Movies.Death*, August 11, 2013.

132 *J. J. Abrams went even further*: J. J. Abrams, Blu-ray audio commentary, *Star Trek*, Paramount Pictures, 2009.

6. THE GREAT GEEK GAME

134 *"shaped forcefields"* . . . *"substrate treadmills"*: Rick Sternbach and Michael Okuda, *Star Trek: The Next Generation: Technical Manual* (New York: Pocket Books, November 1, 1991), 156.

136 *"Suddenly Hammer Head was an Ithorian" [and following]*: Jonathan Hicks, "The RPGnet Interview #25: Bill Slavicsek, *Star Wars* d6 RPG," *RPGnet*, 2012.

136 *wound up winning an Origins Award*: Chris Baker, "How a Pen
     and Paper RPG Brought *Star Wars* Back from the Dead,"
     Glixel, December 21, 2016.

137 *Bantam selected Timothy Zahn*: "An Interview with Timothy
     Zahn, Author of *Heir to*," Totse.com, May 21, 2010.

139 *all laid out in* Galaxy Guide 1: A New Hope: "Momaw Nadon,"
     Wookiepedia, the Star Wars Wiki, December 12, 2016.

139 *In 1995, that information appeared*: Dave Wolverton, "The
     Sand Tender: The Hammerhead's Tale," *Tales from Mos Eis-*
     ley Cantina, ed. Kevin J. Anderson (New York: Bantam Spec-
     tra, 1995), 131–53.

140 *Another version followed in 2006*: "Saga 2006 #031 Momaw
     Nadon," Andrew's Toyz, n.d.

140 *Yet another figure followed in 2010*: Newton, "Figure Review:
     Sideshow Star Wars Momaw Nadon," *Infinite Hollywood*,
     March 5, 2011.

140 *"it's almost like he found it"*: "Momaw Nadon-Hammerhead
     12-inch Figure," YouTube, uploaded by Sideshow Collect-
     ibles on July 7, 2010, youtube/8QRsBRtDzXQ.

141 *"the Holocron" . . . "creating this universe"*: "Mark Cotta Vaz,
     The Secrets of Star Wars: Shadows of the Empire (New York:
     Ballantine Books, 1996), 29.

141 *"The world he [Lucas] created" [and following]*: The People vs.
     George Lucas, dir. Alexandre O. Philippe, Wrekin Hill Enter-
     tainment, 2010.

141 *Typical was Noah Berlatsky's* Guardian *article*: Noah Ber-
     latsky, "We Don't Need a *Die Hard* Origin Story," *The Guard-*
     ian, October 24, 2015.

142 *Marvel is currently planning a half-dozen further TV shows*: Zak
     Wojnar, "Every Marvel Cinematic Universe Project Cur-
     rently in Development," *Screen Rant*, April 9, 2017.

143 *"Jezail bullet shattered the bone"*: Sir Arthur Conan Doyle, *A*
     Study in Scarlet (1887; New York: Penguin Books, 2001), 7.

143 *Later on, though, in* The Sign of the Four: Sir Arthur Conan Doyle, *The Sign of the Four* (1893, *The Complete Sherlock Holmes*, vol. 1 (New York: Doubleday & Company, 1930), 87–158, 90.

143 *and even later he says, much more vaguely*: Sir Arthur Conan Doyle, "The Adventure of the Noble Bachelor," 1892, *The Adventures and Memoirs of Sherlock Holmes* (New York: Penguin Books, 2001), 202.

144 *Decades later, in the 1960s, Marvel Comics [and following]*: Brian Cronin, "Knowledge Waits: The History of Marvel's No-Prize," Comic Book Resources, February 11, 2016.

146 *a pair of episodes of the series* Enterprise: "Affliction," *Enterprise*, February 18, 2005, and "Divergence," *Enterprise*, February 25, 2005.

149 *Sony and Marvel announced in early 2015*: Marc Graser and Brent Lang, "Spider-Man: How Sony, Marvel Will Benefit from Unique Deal (Exclusive)," *Variety*, February 10, 2015.

150 Empire *magazine's Chris Hewitt has jokingly suggested*: Chris Hewitt, "The *Gremlins 2* Viewing Guide: In-Jokes, Sight Gags and Easter Eggs Galore," *Empire Online*, July 5, 2014.

150 *Another more popular fan theory posits*: Ria Misra, "Do *Indiana Jones, Star Wars*, and *E.T.* Take Place in a Shared Universe?" *io9*, September 23, 2014.

150 *Other theories attempt to resolve all the Pixar films*: Jon Negroni, "The Pixar Theory," jonnegroni.com, July 11, 2013.

150 *and even the films and TV shows starring Kyle MacLachlan*: Matthew Catania, "New Favorite Theory: All of Kyle Mac-Lachlan's Roles Are the Same Person!" *io9*, March 28, 2015.

151 *they have encountered other comics characters, including Batman*: James Tynion IV (writer), Freddie Williams II (penciller), *Batman/Teenage Mutant Ninja Turtles,* DC & IDW, December 2015–May 2016.

154 *the 2003 short* Batman: Dead End: "*Batman Dead End* HD (720p)," YouTube, uploaded by Agent47Chris Official on April 2, 2010, youtube/3j7d3lIAkes.

154 *Collora's next fan film*: "*Superman and Batman—World's Finest* Trailer," YouTube, uploaded by Damage, Inc. on January 8, 2011, youtube/t3oN3EJcfwE.

154 *In one short film on YouTube, Captain Picard*: "Star Wars Vs. Star Trek," YouTube, uploaded by TheGreatLink on November 21, 2008, youtube/vFCBwob65Nw.

155 *In another, the* Next Generation *crew stumbles upon the Death Star*: "Star-Trek vs. Star-Wars," YouTube, uploaded by scifibattles on December 21, 2009, youtube/035Dhsxr4sw.

155 *Yet another video imagines what would happen*: "Star Wars vs Startrek; Borg Attack the Death Star [Re-edited version]," YouTube, uploaded by 1978Prime on December 22, 2013, youtube/nK3y7UMDrtI.

155 *The Web series* How It Should Have Ended: "Super Cafe Compilation-Volume One," YouTube, uploaded by How It Should Have Ended on March 22, 2017, youtube/wAkbC GNbvw8.

155 *The director claimed as his inspiration* Mad Magazine: Dan Snierson, "*The Simpsons*: Guillermo del Toro on Creating the Epic Opening to *Treehouse of Horror XXIV*," *Entertainment Weekly*, October 3, 2013.

155 *Geeks gave the same attention to del Toro*: See for instance Prestigeww (Stefan Tieß), "Alle Filmreferenzen in Guillermo del Toros Simpsons—Intro," *Movie Pilot*, October 4, 2013.

7. GEEKING OUT

157 *"one of the great hang-out movies"* . . . *"and Feathers"*: "Rare: Quentin Tarantino loves *Rio Bravo*—Cannes 2007," YouTube, uploaded by Waterbucket on May 25, 2007, youtube/KjX 010pdIro.

158 *"a wandering explorer"* . . . *"for the overbold"*: Tolkien, "On Fairy-Stories."

159 *"creating a world for people to go to"*: "Empire Podcast: Sharlto Copley and Neill Blomkamp *Elysium* Special."

159 *One comic book artist, George Pérez*: Michael Offut, "The Incredible George Pérez," *Michael Offut*, July 27, 2012.

160 *"the strongest emotion which the mind"*: Edmund Burke, *On the Sublime and Beautiful,* Vol. XXIV, Part 2, The Harvard Classics (New York: P. F. Collier & Son, 1909–14), accessed through Bartleby.com, 2001.

160 *"every single image"* . . . *"so many things going on"*: "Rick McCallum-it's so dense," YouTube, uploaded by Derobetan on September 29, 2012, youtube/qvc9_GDoWI4.

161 *"36,000 years"* . . . *"294 planets"*: George Dvorsky, "Computer Analysis Reveals the Stunning Complexity of the *Star Wars Expanded Universe*," *Gizmodo*, February 10, 2016.

161 *"a realm"* . . . *"stars uncounted"*: Tolkien, "On Fairy-Stories."

161 *the writer-director James Gunn teased fans*: Germain Lussier, "James Gunn and Kevin Feige Tease *Guardians of the Galaxy* Easter Eggs," */Film*, July 29, 2014.

162 *"Easter eggs"* . . . *"three or four times"*: "Empire Podcast: *Man of Steel* Spoiler Special—Zack Snyder, David S. Goyer," *Empire Online*, June 17, 2013.

164 *"In this current age of* Star Wars*"*: "About," *Making Star Wars*, n.d.

164 *"walk the entire length"* . . . *"every room"*: "About," *Enterprise-D Construction Project*, 2016.

165 *thanks to the person who posted a twenty-four-hour-long loop*: "*Star Trek TNG* Ambient Engine Noise (Idling for 24 hrs)," YouTube, uploaded by crysknife007 on October 10, 2011, youtube/ZPoqNeR3_UA.

165 *"ambient geek sleep aids"*: crysknife007, "crysknife007—YouTube," YouTube, n.d.

165 *Industrial Light & Magic's* Star Wars *program*: Charlie Jane Anders, "A Brand New *Star Wars* VR Experience Put Me on Tatooine and It Was Incredible," *io9*, March 15, 2016.

165 "Star Trek *megafan*": Cheryl Eddy, "Step into the *Enterprise* by Touring This Incredible *Star Trek* Set Recreation," *io9*, July 14, 2016.

166 *Since its creation in 2005 at Vermont's Middlebury College*: "About," International Quidditch Association, n.d.

167 *WhatIsTheMatrix.com*: "WhatIsTheMatrix.com," Matrix Wiki, March 13, 2017.

167 *"not minding it hurts"* . . . *"to change the world"*: "Prometheus Viral-Peter Weyland at TED 2023-Guy Pierce, Ridley Scott, Alien Movie (2012) HD," YouTube, uploaded by Movieclips Coming Soon on February 28, 2012, youtube/GRO rp3XBRrE.

168 *"I can assist . . . distressing or unethical"*: "Prometheus—Viral Video—Meet David (2012) Ridley Scott Movie HD," YouTube, uploaded by Movieclips Coming Soon on April 17, 2012, youtube/RJ7E7Qp-s-8.

168 *"preserving humanity"* . . . *"the genetic threat"*: *Trask Industries*, 20th Century Fox, 2014.

168 *includes its own fake industrial videos*: "Trask Industries: Your Future," YouTube, uploaded by X-Men Movies on July 30, 2013, youtube/92YBR9gEyYI.

169 *"Do you think Magneto"*: "The Bent Bullet: JFK and the Mutant Conspiracy | X-Men," YouTube, uploaded by X-Men Movies on November 25, 2013, youtube/ByCY2UYLHG8.

169 *the company making the cookies, Primary Colors*: "Licensed Brand Cookies | Primary Colors," Primary Colors, n.d.

170 *In 2014, Hasbro even tried to purchase DreamWorks Animation*: Michael J. de la Merced and Brooks Barnes, "Hasbro Said to End Talks to Take Over DreamWorks Animation," *New York Times*, November 14, 2014.

170 *"'immersive' strategy" . . . "any format they wanted"*: Lawrence C. Strauss, "The Playful Transformer," *Barron's*, August 27, 2011.

171 *Said Butterbeer, which is vanilla soda*: "Price of Butterbeer Gets a Boost at Universal Studios," CBS Miami, January 19, 2017.

171 *The cheapest wands, meanwhile*: "Ollivander's | Universal's Islands of Adventure," *TouringPlans*, 2017.

171 *A second section of the attraction opened in 2014*: "The Wizarding World of Harry Potter™—Diagon Alley™ | Universal Studios Florida™," *Universal Orlando Resort*, 2017.

172 *Those attractions, scheduled to open in 2019*: Joseph Pimentel, Mark Eades, and Peter Larsen, "Video: It's Official: *Star Wars* Theme Land Coming to Disneyland," *Orange County Register*, August 15, 2015.

172 *visitors will be able to pledge their allegiance*: Germain Lussier, "Your Decisions at the New *Star Wars* Theme Parks Will Have Consequences," *io9*, April 16, 2017.

172 *James Cameron has built his own*: Ethan Anderton, "Disney's *Avatar* Theme Park Officially Opening Summer 2017, New Rides & Photos Revealed," */Film*, November 19, 2016.

172 *"greet you" . . . "a documentary"*: Germain Lussier, "You May Not Care About *Avatar*, but Its New Theme Park Is a Glimpse into Disney's Future," *io9*, May 26, 2017.

173 *"1500 pages of notes . . . and so on"*: Germain Lussier, "How James Cameron Wrote Three *Avatar* Sequels Simultaneously," */Film*, June 1, 2014.

173 *"bible" . . . "worth their time"*: Geoff Boucher, "James Cameron: I Want to Compete with *Star Wars* and Tolkien," *Hero Complex*, August 25, 2010.

173 *"20 years or more"*: Michael Cieply, "For Fox, Much Is Riding on 3 Sequels to *Avatar*," *New York Times*, June 15, 2014.

174 *Red Bull routinely sponsors*: "World Record Jump," RedBull Stratos.com, n.d.

8. I'VE GOT A BAD FEELING ABOUT THIS: THE IMPORTANCE OF BEING GEEKY

178 *"The Ancient Secret of the Massassi"*: "The Ancient Secret of the Massassi Temples on Yavin 4," YouTube, uploaded by Star Wars Explained on February 16, 2017, youtube/o2ZCMUWEojo.

178 *"The Tragic Story of Mas Amedda"*: "The Tragic Story of Mas Amedda After the Battle of Endor and the End of the Galactic Civil War," YouTube, uploaded by Star Wars Explained on March 9, 2017, youtube/tHPSI6pit_g.

179 *"serious Tolkien fans" [and following]*: Frank Ahrens, *"Rings* Has Two Targets," *Washington Post*, December 19, 2001.

183 *One fan even made a video*: Zachary Antell, *"A New Awakening— Star Wars Episode IV* and *VII* Shot Comparison," Vimeo, March 25, 2016.

184 *"Are audiences ready" . . . "merely an illusion"*: Rob Bricken, "Why *Rogue One* Is as Important to *Star Wars* as *Episode VII*," *io9*, February 24, 2016.

185 *they wondered why Rey and Finn*: Cheryl Wassenaar, "Disney Might Have a *Rogue One* Problem on Its Hands," FanSided, September 19, 2016.

185 *Those additions apparently expanded Darth Vader's presence*: Marcus Errico, "How Darth Vader Got His Groove Back in *Rogue One* Thanks to Last-Minute Tweak," Yahoo Movies, January 12, 2017.

185 *the Mouse House was right to worry*: "*Star Wars: The Force Awakens*," Box Office Mojo, n.d., and "*Rogue One: A Star Wars Story*," Box Office Mojo, n.d.

187 *"understand subtle allusions"*: Roger Ebert, "*X-Men* (review)," rogerebert.com, July 14, 2000.

187 *"should only be reviewed by" . . . "innocent of* Hitchhiker *knowledge"*: Roger Ebert, "*The Hitchhiker's Guide to the Galaxy* (review)," rogerebert.com, April 28, 2005.

189 *the 1986 feature-length animated*: "*Transformers: The Movie*," Box Office Mojo, n.d.

189 *"a robot clone"*: "*Teenage Mutant Ninja Turtles* Theme Song (Michael Bay Parody)," YouTube, uploaded by The Warp Zone on March 27, 2012, youtube/onHtoKkGaoE.

190 *Sir Arthur Conan Doyle tried to kill Sherlock Holmes*: Sir Arthur Conan Doyle, "The Final Problem," 1893, *The Complete Sherlock Holmes*, vol. 1 (New York: Doubleday & Company, 1930), 469–80.

190 *"baritsu"*: Sir Arthur Conan Doyle. "The Adventure of the Empty House," 1903, *The Complete Sherlock Holmes*, vol. 2 (New York: Doubleday & Company, 1930), 483–95.

190 *Frank Miller learned a similar lesson*: Frank Miller, *Daredevil*, vol. 1, #181, "Last Hand," Marvel Comics, April 1982.

191 *"He must never know"*: Frank Miller, *Daredevil*, vol. 1, #190, "Resurrection," Marvel Comics, January 1983.

192 "Star Wars Legends": "The Legendary *Star Wars Expanded Universe* Turns a New Page," StarWars.com, April 25, 2014.

193 *"too philosophical"* . . . *"people like you"*: *The Daily Show with Jon Stewart*, May 14, 2013.

194 *"The publicity for* Into Darkness*"*: Gavia Baker Whitelaw, "*Star Trek Into Darkness*: Too Many D*cks on the *Enterprise*," *The Daily Dot*, May 17, 2013.

194 *"Too Many Dicks on the Dance Floor"*: ". . . on the dance floor," YouTube, uploaded by sloanesomething on June 8, 2009, youtube/deQuFc3BP74.

194 *"was met with boos"*: Faraci, "The *Star Trek* Movies."

195 *Abrams later apologized*: Kevin P. Sullivan and Josh Horowitz, "J. J. Abrams Shares One *Star Trek Into Darkness* Regret that Might Surprise You," MTV, December 2, 2013.

195 *But this apology still annoyed fans*: Rob Bricken, "J. J. Abrams Admits Lying About *Star Trek 2*'s Khan Was a Mistake," *io9*, December 12, 2013.

195 *"more inclusive"* . . . *"a heist movie"*: Fullerton, "Simon Pegg Criticises Science-Fiction and Genre Films."

196 Furious 7 . . . *grossed $1.5 billion worldwide*: "*Furious 7* (2015)—Box Office Mojo," *Box Office Mojo*, n.d.

197 *According to geeks, when Lucas changed the length of the crawl*: Drew Stewart, "*Star Wars Special Edition* Changes HD," Google Plus, slide 10, November 8, 2010.

197 *Geeks were further incensed when Lucas was photographed wearing*: Jay Garmon, "Lucas Admits It: Han Shot First!" *TechRepublic*, July 26, 2007.

197 *a 2002 episode of* South Park: *South Park*, "Free Hat," dir. Trey Parker and Matt Stone, July 10, 2002.

198 *Lucas did release those cuts on DVD in 2006*: "List of Changes in *Star Wars* Re-releases," Wookiepedia, the Star Wars Wiki, January 26, 2016.

198 *Despecialized*: Harmy, "Harmy's *Star Wars* Despecialized Edition HD-V2.5 MKV Is Out Now," Original Trilogy, April 5, 2011.

198 *Other fans have restored*: James Whitbrook, "An Original Film Print of *Star Wars* Has Been Restored and Released Online," *io9*, February 18, 2016.

199 "*My heart sank when [Jar Jar]*": *The People vs. George Lucas*.

201 *In the British sitcom* Spaced: "Back," *Spaced: The Complete Series*, February 23, 2001.

201 "*jumped-up firework display*" . . . "*It still hurts!*": "Change," *Spaced: The Complete Series*, March 2, 2001.

201 "*totally beyond repair*" . . . "*can never be undone*": Mike Stoklasa, "Red Letter Media Star Wars: Episode 1—The Phantom Menace," RedLetterMedia, December 10, 2009.

202 "*In my* Star Wars *universe*" . . . "The Last Crusade": *The People vs. George Lucas*.

9. WHY SO SERIOUS?

204 "*walking out of the cinema*" . . . "*amoral art movies*": Fullerton, "Simon Pegg Criticises Science-Fiction and Genre Films."

204 *Pegg later walked back his comments*: "Empire Podcast #163: Simon Pegg-May 29," *Empire Online*, May 29, 2015.

206 *"a new chance for superheroes"* . . . *"beyond a set point"*: Helen O'Hara, "Why *Fantastic Four*'s Failure Doesn't Signal the End of Superhero Films," *GQ*, August 19, 2015.

207 *"giggly pastiche"* . . . *"Romero's underlying moral seriousness"*: Dave Kehr, "*Raiders of the Lost Ark* (review)," *Chicago Reader*, 1981.

207 *The seams may show more in* Dawn: According to the IMDb box office / business pages for the respective films, *Dawn of the Dead* was shot for an estimated $650,000, *Raiders* for an estimated $18 million.

208 *"dignify the gaping-idiot spectacle"* . . . *"serious drama"*: J. R. Jones, "*Avengers: Age of Ultron* (review)," *Chicago Reader*, April 29, 2015.

208 *"clearly jabbing his light saber"* . . . *"bring them back"*: A. O. Scott, "Some Surprises in That Galaxy Far, Far Away," *New York Times*, May 16, 2005.

212 *"emotionally still a teenager"* . . . *"uncomfortable around them"*: Biskind, *Easy Riders, Raging Bulls*, 259–60.

212 *"a $2000 gun" [and following]*: Thomas H. Green, "John Milius: The Craziest Man in Hollywood?" *The Telegraph*, November 1, 2013.

212 *"Good night, good luck"*: *Mean Streets*, Warner Bros., 1973.

213 *"a very small town" [and following]*: *WTF with Marc Maron*, "Episode 445: Edgar Wright," November 21, 2013.

213 *"I grew up as a comic-book junkie"*: Decker, "Interview One," 15.

213 *He also admitted that his desire*: Decker, "Interview One," 24–25.

213 *"the one time where I actually"*: Decker, "Interview One," 31.

216 *"2000 songs"* . . . *"difficult days"*: Jann S. Wenner, "Obama in Command: The Rolling Stone Interview," *Rolling Stone*, October 14, 2010.

217 *"that maybe only exists in your imagination"*: *The Limey*, Artisan Entertainment, 1999.

217 *"no more than a skit"* . . . *"old* Batman *shows"*: Anthony Lane, "The Current Cinema: Tough Guys."

217 *"an exemplary portrait"* . . . *"any teen comedy I've seen"*: Richard Brody, "The Kids Really Are All Right," *New Yorker*, August 11, 2010.

219 *"retire from geekdom"* . . . *"some serious acting"*: Fullerton, "Simon Pegg Criticises Science-Fiction and Genre Films."

221 *"They thought we were fabulous!" [and following]*: theroaring girlcosplay, "They thought we were fabulous! . . ." *The Roaring Girl Cosplay*, June 4, 2016, theroaringgirlcosplay.tumblr .com/post/145417604606/they-thought-we-were-fabulous.

10. BACK OUT IN SPACE AGAIN:
THE BEAUTY OF *STAR WARS*

225 *"Grimm fairy tale"* . . . *"how it is about it"*: Roger Ebert, "Review of *Freeway*," rogerebert.com, January 24, 1997.

227 *Biskind has so little regard*: Biskind, *Easy Riders, Raging Bulls*, 410–12.

228 *"Metropolis is NYC by day" [and following]*: Kenton Campbell, "Gotham City/Metropolis/etc," rec.arts.comics, March 14, 1990.

232 *"It was the classic triangle plot"*: Pollock, *Skywalking*, 209–10.

232 *"fit [his] plan to duplicate"*: Pollock, *Skywalking*, 212.

233 *"whenever he looked at her . . . a conference room"*: Alan Dean Foster, *Splinter of the Mind's Eye* (New York: Ballantine Books, 1978), 3.

233 *"Who is Luke Skywalker?"*: Anthony Breznican, "*Star Wars: The Force Awakens*: J. J. Abrams explores 'Who Is Luke Skywalker . . . ?'" *Entertainment Weekly*, August 12, 2015.

241 *From Fritz Lang, Lucas borrowed*: Pollock, *Skywalking*, 246.

241 *Some geeks have decried*: John Wenz, "Could the Planets in *Star Wars* Actually Support Life?" *Wired*, April 23, 2015.

242 *Lucas read Carlos Castaneda's 1974 book* Tales of Power: Pollock, *Skywalking*, 140.

242 *Han Solo was modeled on Francis Ford Coppola*: See, for instance, Biskind, *Easy Riders, Raging Bulls*, 324–25.

243 *Lucas refused to speak to . . . Ted Ashley*: Pollock, *Skywalking*, 97.

243 *He was similarly outraged when Universal cut four minutes*: Pollock, *Skywalking*, 120–21.

243 *"The studio system is dead"*: Pollock, *Skywalking*, 246.

244 *Ben Burtt created the sound*: Benn Burtt, *Star Wars Trilogy: The Definitive Collection*, Lucasfilm, 1993.

ACKNOWLEDGMENTS

Many people helped me with the writing of this book, and as such I'm indebted to Jennifer Ashton, David Bordwell, Nicholas Brown, Blake Butler and everyone at *HTML Giant*, Chiya Chai Café, Tim Feeney, Sarah French, Aloysius T. Furball, Elisa Gabbert and John Cotter, Gaslight Coffee, Elvira Godek-Kiryluk, Christopher Grimes, Lily Hoang, Joel

Janiurek, the Kraken Podcast, John Madera and everyone at *Big Other*, Cris Mazza, Tanner McSwain and Uncharted Books, Walter Benn Michaels, Mary Anne Mohanraj, Sally O'Brien, Tom L. Rodebaugh III, Mazin Saleem, Brooks Sterritt, Justin Stillmaker and Yajaira Marie, the UIC English department and Program for Writers, and Colin Winnette. Special thanks are due to my sister and brother-in-law, and to my mother and father, who despite not being geeks have always supported and encouraged me. I'm especially grateful to my editor, Jeremy M. Davies, as well as James Curley, Philip Durkin, Melissa McEwen, Curtis White, and, finally, Justin Roman, to whom these pages are dedicated.

INDEX

35–37, 45, 46, 52–53, 60–61,
118, 241
Scorsese, Martin, 24, 26, 29,
32–33, 40, 88, 209, 212, 214,
227, 228
Scott, A. O., 208–209
Scott Pilgrim vs. the World, 15,
18, 217–18
Secret History of Star Wars, The,
34
Segel, Jason, 108, 159
Shelley, Mary, 218
Seinfeld, 7, 77
Serkis, Andy, 13
Serpico, 96
Shatner, William, 44, 65, 132,
212
Sideshow Collectibles, 140
Silmarillion, The (Tolkien), 55
Simpsons, The, 155–56, 162
Sin City, 96
Singer, Bryan, 7, 8, 100, 192
Skyfall, 125
Skywalker Ranch, 197,
243–46
Skywalking (Pollock), 232
Slavicsek, Bill, 136, 138
Snyder, Zack, 14, 162, 234, 235
Soderbergh, Steven, 216
Song of Ice and Fire, A (Martin),
119
Sony, 149
Sorcerer, 30, 39, 227
South Park, 197

Space, Time and Gravitation
(Eddington), 53
Spaced, 201
Spider-Man, 8, 130–31, 147,
149
Spielberg, Steven, 12–13, 26,
30, 38, 40, 202, 207–208,
212, 227, 228
spoilers, 125–26
stakes, 127
Stan, Sebastian, 221
Star Trek, 5, 7, 11, 14, 16, 35,
49, 58–59, 66–67, 69, 71, 75,
81–82, 117–18, 124, 137, 165,
193–96, 213, 125, 221;
Beyond, 31–32, 195–96;
convention, 132, 194;
crossovers and mash-ups,
153–55; *Deep Space Nine*, 7,
67, 145–46; *Enterprise*,
123–24, 146; *The Final
Frontier*, 158; *Galaxy Quest*
and, 115, 131–32; Holodeck
in, 133–34; *Into Darkness*,
125, 193–95; Klingons in, 59,
67, 74, 83, 145–46; moral
values and vision of future
in, 214–15, 221; *The Motion
Picture*, 145; *The Next
Generation*, 4, 67, 74, 75,
133–34, 137, 155, 158, 164,
181, 213–15; novels, 137; *The
Original Series*, 4, 66, 74, 146;
The Search for Spock, 158;

Printed in the USA
CPSIA information can be obtained
at www.ICGtesting.com
LVHW091130150724
785511LV00001B/64